A·FORCE

RAGE AGAINST THE DYING OF THE LIGHT

WRITER
KELLY THOMPSON

ARTISTS
BEN CALDWELL (#5-7),
PAULO SIQUEIRA (#8-10)
& JOE BENNETT (#10)

INKS/FINISHES, #6-7
SCOTT HANNA

COLORISTS
IAN HERRING (#5-7) **&**
RACHELLE ROSENBERG (#8-10)

LETTERER
VC's CORY PETIT

COVER ART
BEN CALDWELL (#5-7), **PAULO SIQUEIRA & RACHELLE ROSENBERG** (#8-9)
AND STEPHANIE HANS (#10)

ASSISTANT EDITOR
ALANNA SMITH

EDITOR
KATIE KUBERT

EXECUTIVE EDITOR
TOM BREVOORT

COLLECTION EDITOR
JENNIFER GRÜNWALD

VP PRODUCTION & SPECIAL PROJECTS
JEFF YOUNGQUIST

EDITOR IN CHIEF
AXEL ALONSO

ASSOCIATE MANAGING EDITOR
KATERI WOODY

SVP PRINT, SALES & MARKETING
DAVID GABRIEL

CHIEF CREATIVE OFFICER
JOE QUESADA

ASSOCIATE EDITOR
SARAH BRUNSTAD

BOOK DESIGNER
JAY BOWEN

PUBLISHER
DAN BUCKLEY

EDITOR, SPECIAL PROJECTS
MARK D. BEAZLEY

EXECUTIVE PRODUCER
ALAN FINE

A-FORCE VOL. 2: RAGE AGAINST THE DYING OF THE LIGHT. Contains material originally published in magazine form as A-FORCE #5-10. First printing 2017. ISBN# 978-0-7851-9606-8. Published by MARVEL WORLDWIDE, INC., a subsidiary of MARVEL ENTERTAINMENT, LLC. OFFICE OF PUBLICATION: 135 West 50th Street, New York, NY 10020. Copyright © 2017 MARVEL No similarity between any of the names, characters, persons, and/or institutions in this magazine with those of any living or dead person or institution is intended, and any such similarity which may exist is purely coincidental. **Printed in Canada.** ALAN FINE, President, Marvel Entertainment; DAN BUCKLEY, President, TV, Publishing & Brand Management; JOE QUESADA, Chief Creative Officer; TOM BREVOORT, SVP of Publishing; DAVID BOGART, SVP of Business Affairs & Operations, Publishing & Partnership; C.B. CEBULSKI, VP of Brand Management & Development, Asia; DAVID GABRIEL, SVP of Sales & Marketing, Publishing; JEFF YOUNGQUIST, VP of Production & Special Projects; DAN CARR, Executive Director of Publishing Technology; ALEX MORALES, Director of Publishing Operations; SUSAN CRESPI, Production Manager; STAN LEE, Chairman Emeritus. For information regarding advertising in Marvel Comics or on Marvel.com, please contact Vit DeBellis, Integrated Sales Manager, at vdebellis@marvel

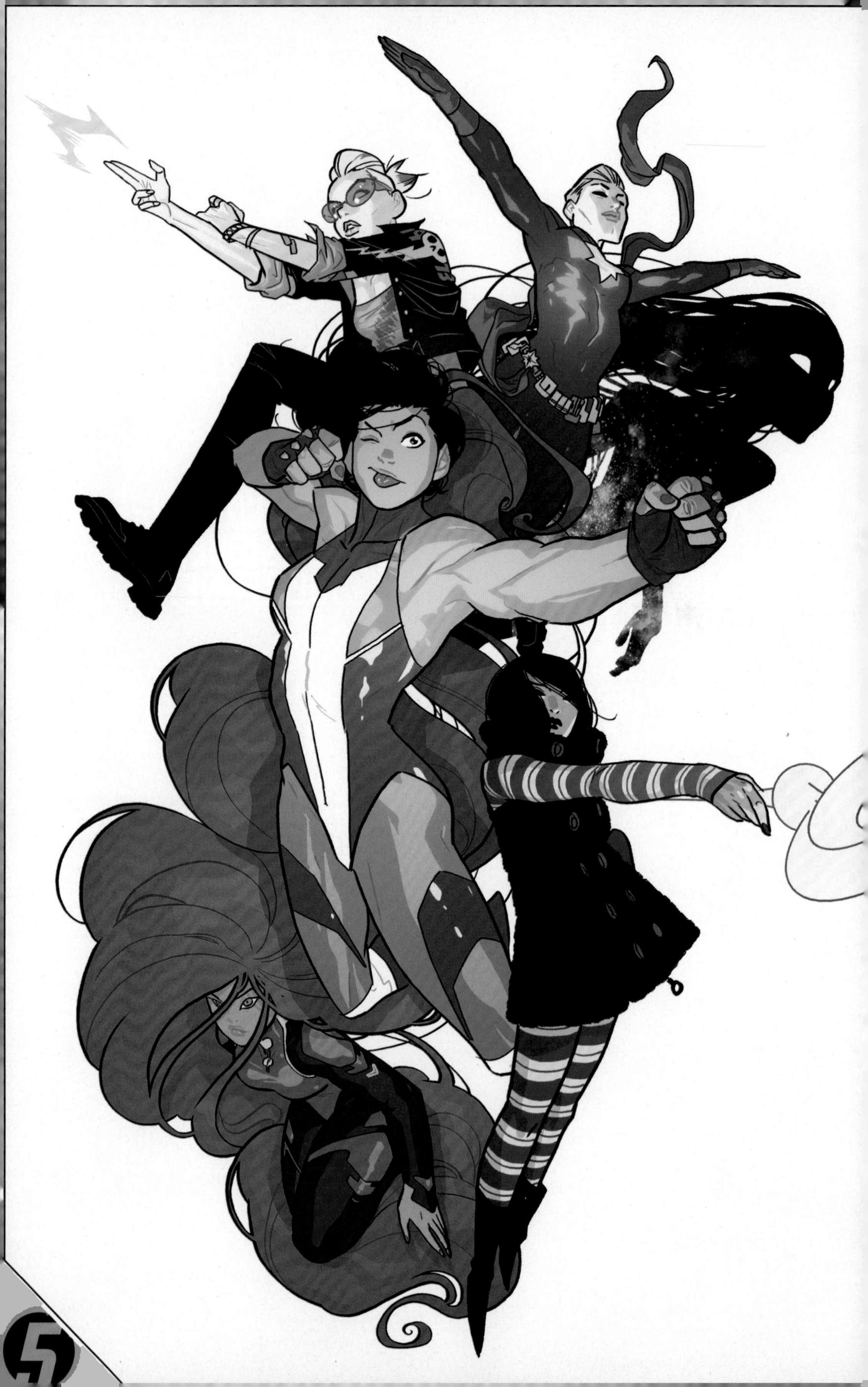

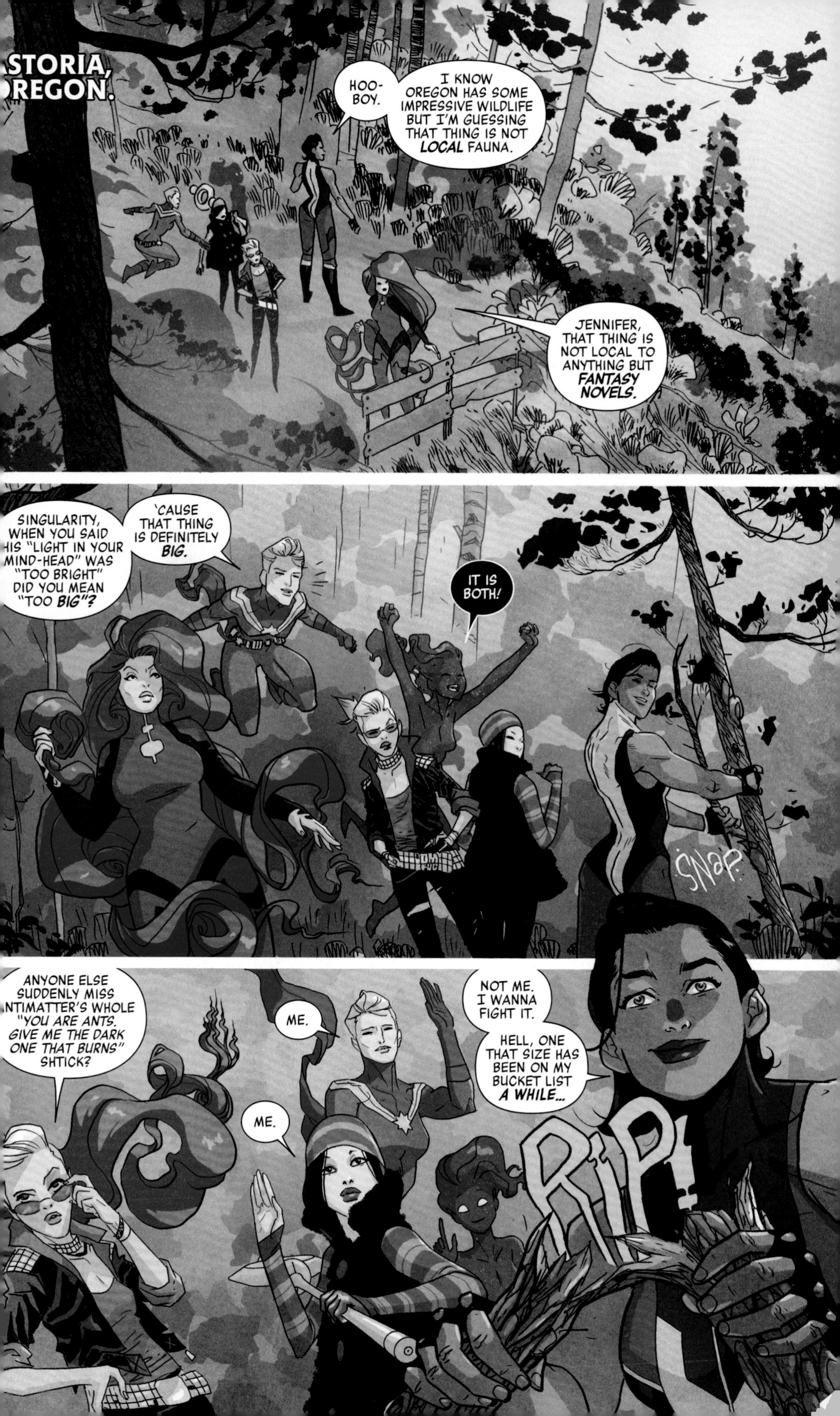
STORIA,
REGON.
HOO-BOY.
I KNOW OREGON HAS SOME IMPRESSIVE WILDLIFE BUT I'M GUESSING THAT THING IS NOT LOCAL FAUNA.
JENNIFER, THAT THING IS NOT LOCAL TO ANYTHING BUT FANTASY NOVELS.
SINGULARITY, WHEN YOU SAID HIS "LIGHT IN YOUR MIND-HEAD" WAS "TOO BRIGHT" DID YOU MEAN "TOO BIG"?
'CAUSE THAT THING IS DEFINITELY BIG.
IT IS BOTH!
SNAP!
ANYONE ELSE SUDDENLY MISS NTIMATTER'S WHOLE "YOU ARE ANTS. GIVE ME THE DARK ONE THAT BURNS" SHTICK?
ME.
ME.
NOT ME. I WANNA FIGHT IT.
HELL, ONE THAT SIZE HAS BEEN ON MY BUCKET LIST A WHILE...
RIP!

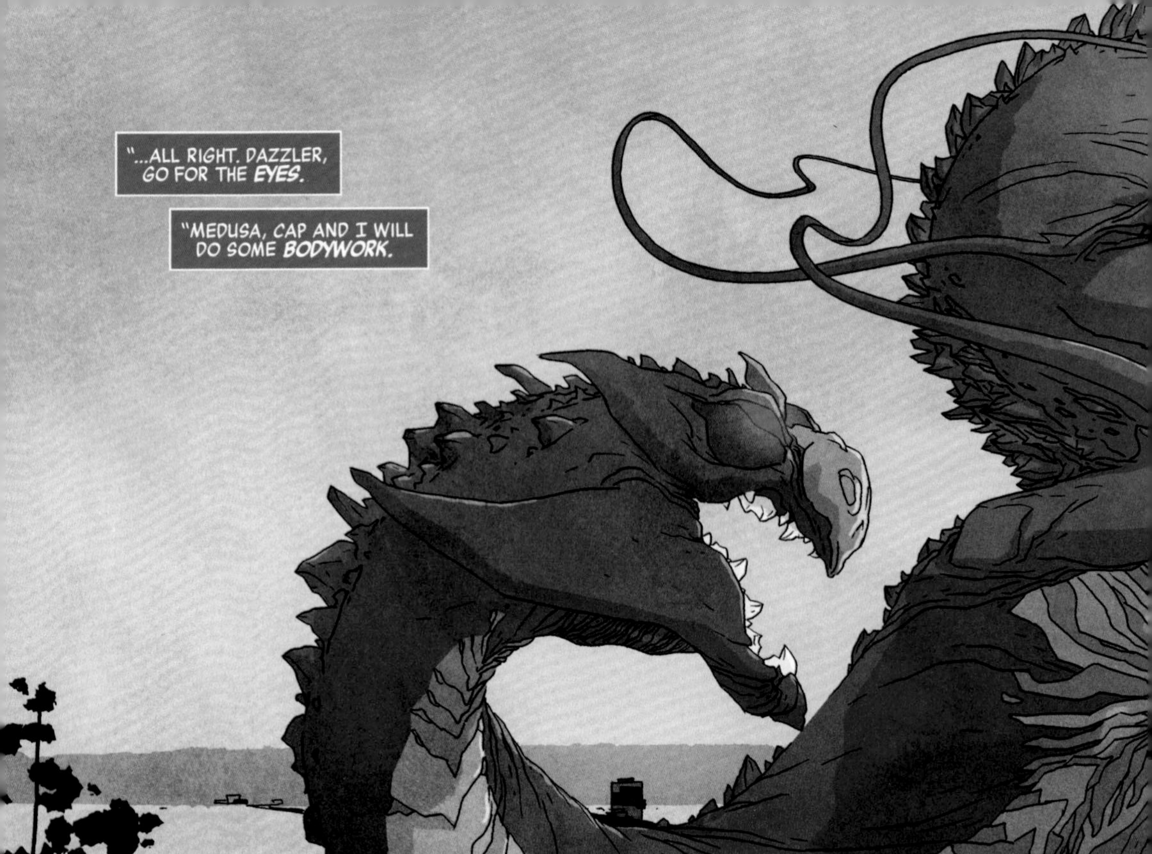
"...ALL RIGHT. DAZZLER, GO FOR THE EYES.
"MEDUSA, CAP AND I WILL DO SOME BODYWORK.

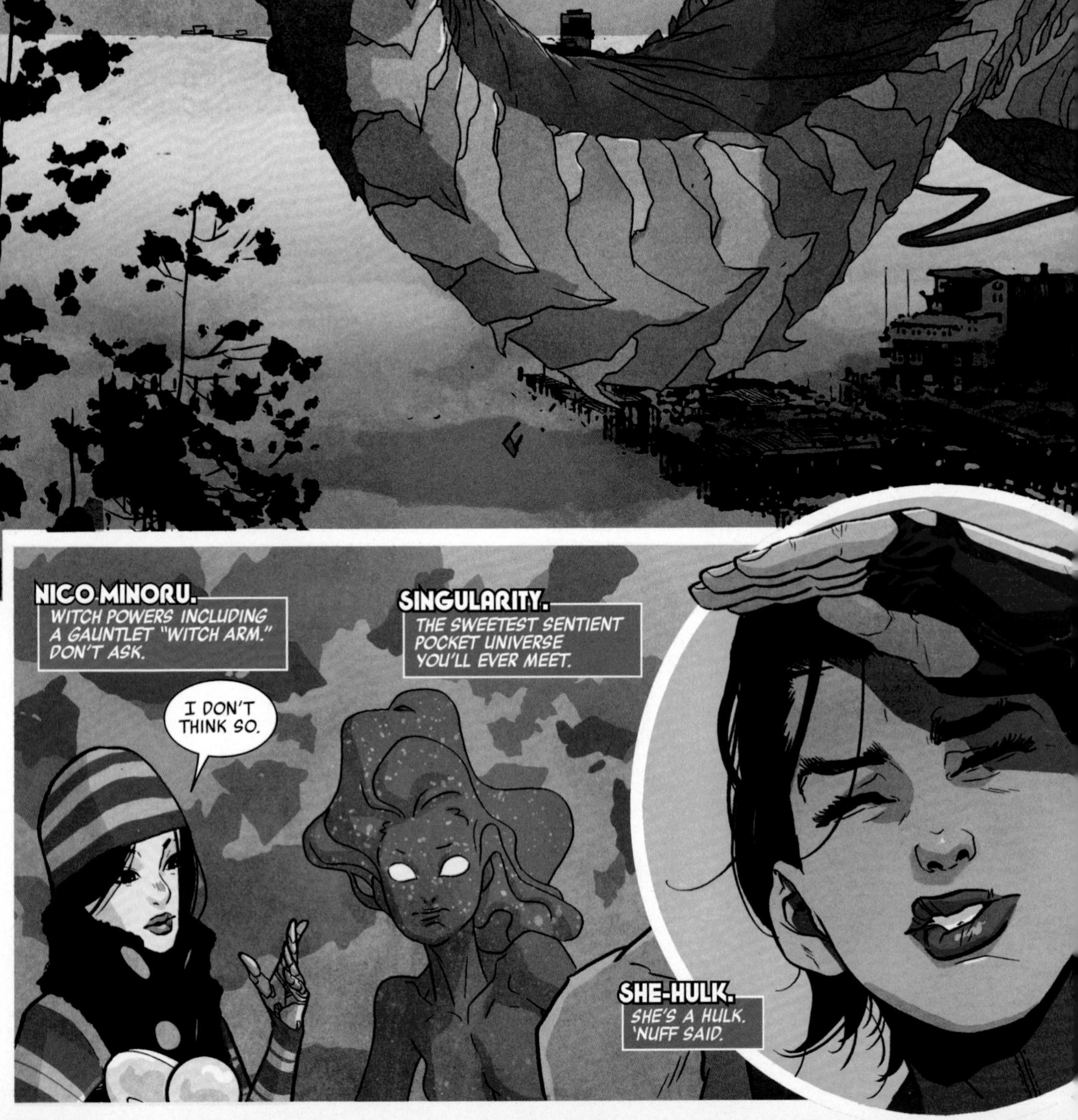
NICO MINORU.
WITCH POWERS INCLUDING A GAUNTLET "WITCH ARM." DON'T ASK.
SINGULARITY.
THE SWEETEST SENTIENT POCKET UNIVERSE YOU'LL EVER MEET.
I DON'T THINK SO.
SHE-HULK.
SHE'S A HULK. 'NUFF SAID.

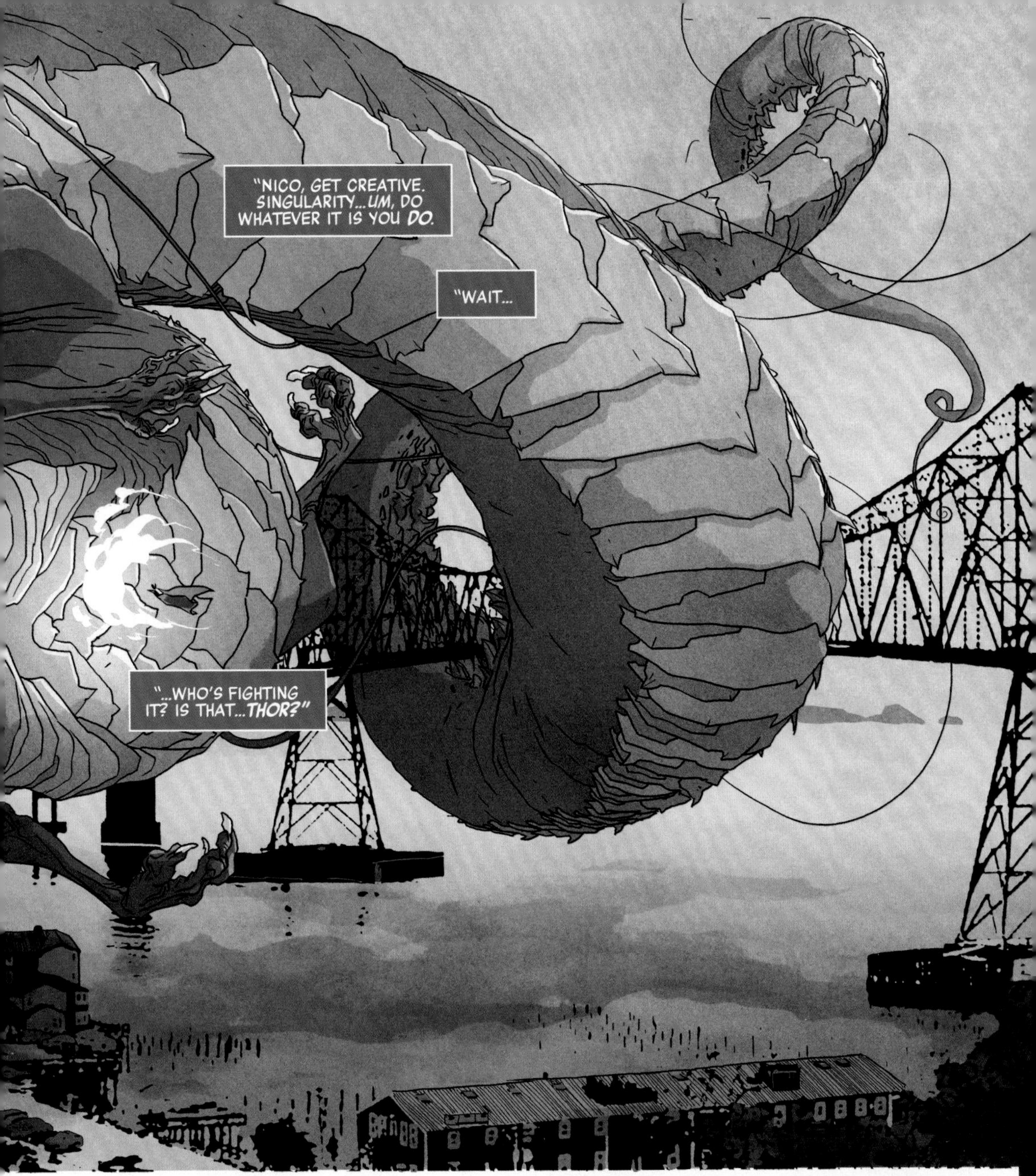
"NICO, GET CREATIVE. SINGULARITY...UM, DO WHATEVER IT IS YOU DO.
"WAIT...
"...WHO'S FIGHTING IT? IS THAT...THOR?"

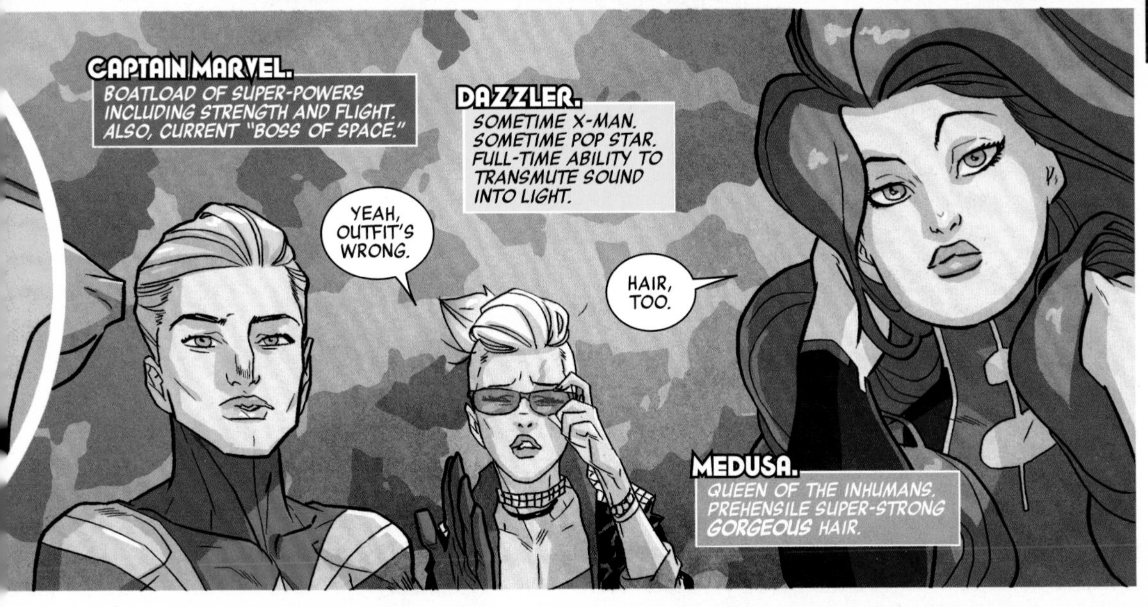
CAPTAIN MARVEL.
BOATLOAD OF SUPER-POWERS INCLUDING STRENGTH AND FLIGHT. ALSO, CURRENT "BOSS OF SPACE."
DAZZLER.
SOMETIME X-MAN. SOMETIME POP STAR. FULL-TIME ABILITY TO TRANSMUTE SOUND INTO LIGHT.
YEAH, OUTFIT'S WRONG.
HAIR, TOO.
MEDUSA.
QUEEN OF THE INHUMANS. PREHENSILE SUPER-STRONG GORGEOUS HAIR.

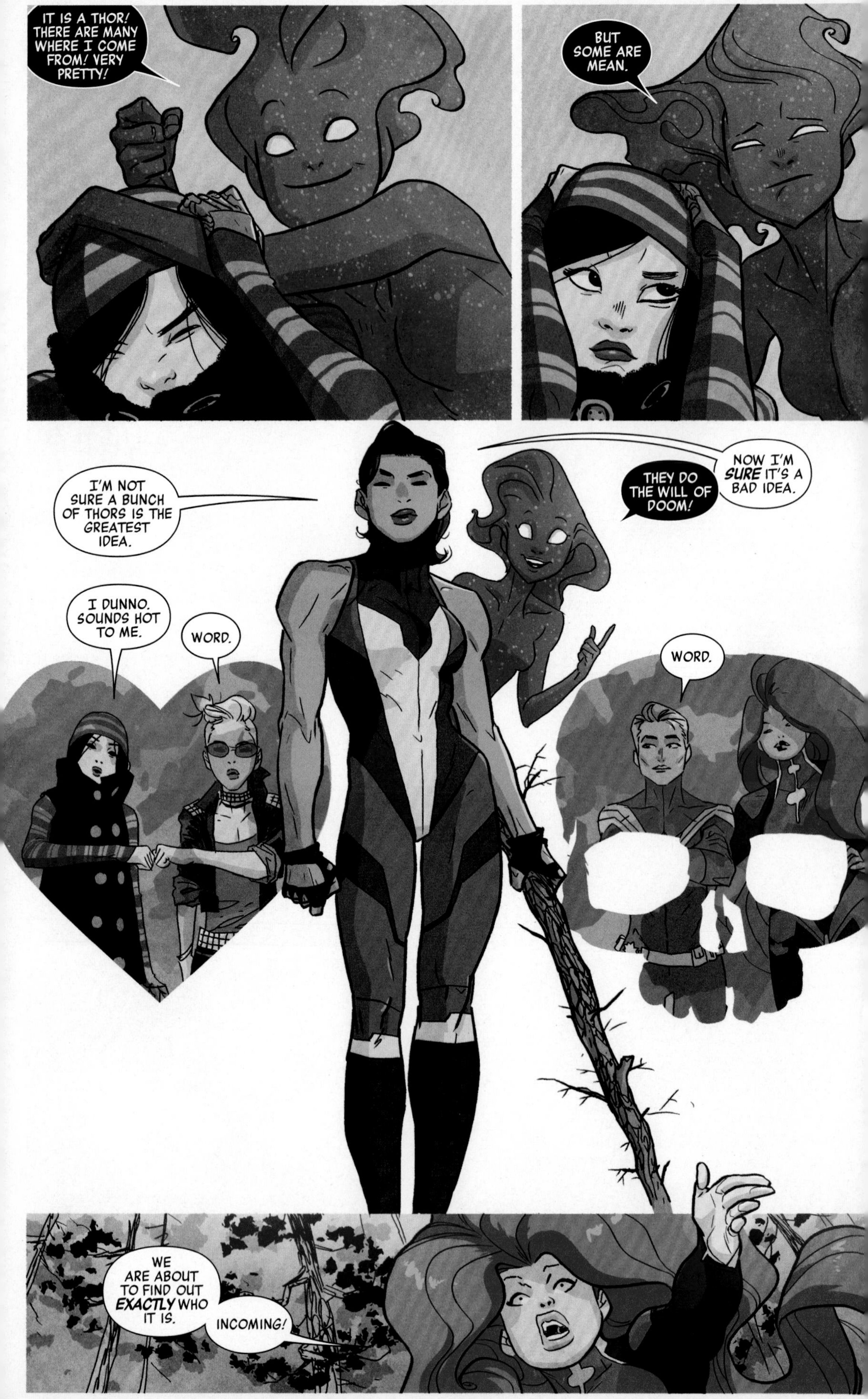
IT IS A THOR! THERE ARE MANY WHERE I COME FROM! VERY PRETTY!
BUT SOME ARE MEAN.
I'M NOT SURE A BUNCH OF THORS IS THE GREATEST IDEA.
THEY DO THE WILL OF DOOM!
NOW I'M SURE IT'S A BAD IDEA.
I DUNNO. SOUNDS HOT TO ME.
WORD.
WORD.
WE ARE ABOUT TO FIND OUT EXACTLY WHO IT IS.
INCOMING!

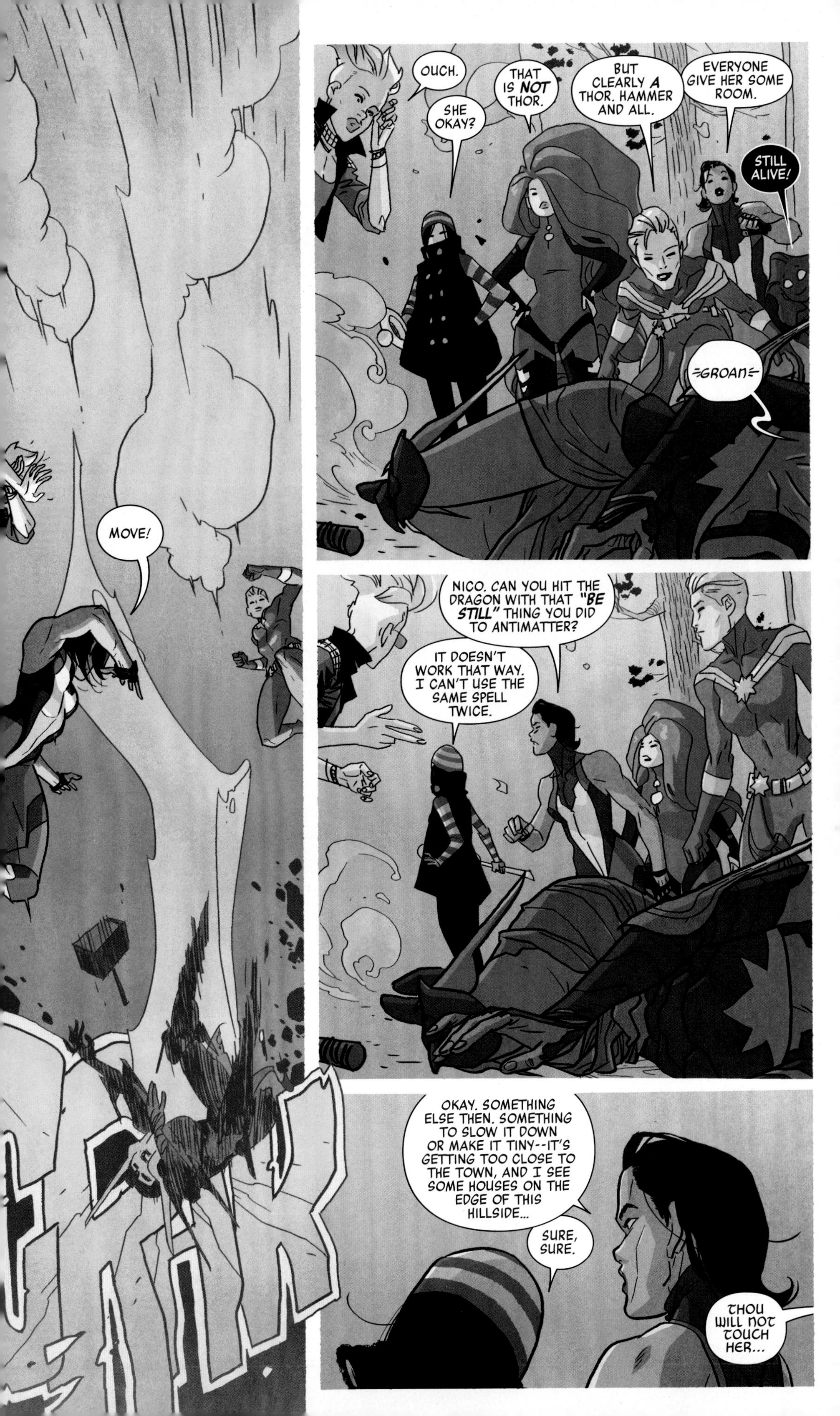
MOVE!
OUCH.
SHE OKAY?
THAT IS **NOT** THOR.
BUT CLEARLY **A** THOR. HAMMER AND ALL.
EVERYONE GIVE HER SOME ROOM.
STILL ALIVE!
=GROAN=
NICO. CAN YOU HIT THE DRAGON WITH THAT **"BE STILL"** THING YOU DID TO ANTIMATTER?
IT DOESN'T WORK THAT WAY. I CAN'T USE THE SAME SPELL TWICE.
OKAY. SOMETHING ELSE THEN. SOMETHING TO SLOW IT DOWN OR MAKE IT TINY--IT'S GETTING TOO CLOSE TO THE TOWN, AND I SEE SOME HOUSES ON THE EDGE OF THIS HILLSIDE...
SURE, SURE.
THOU WILL NOT TOUCH HER...

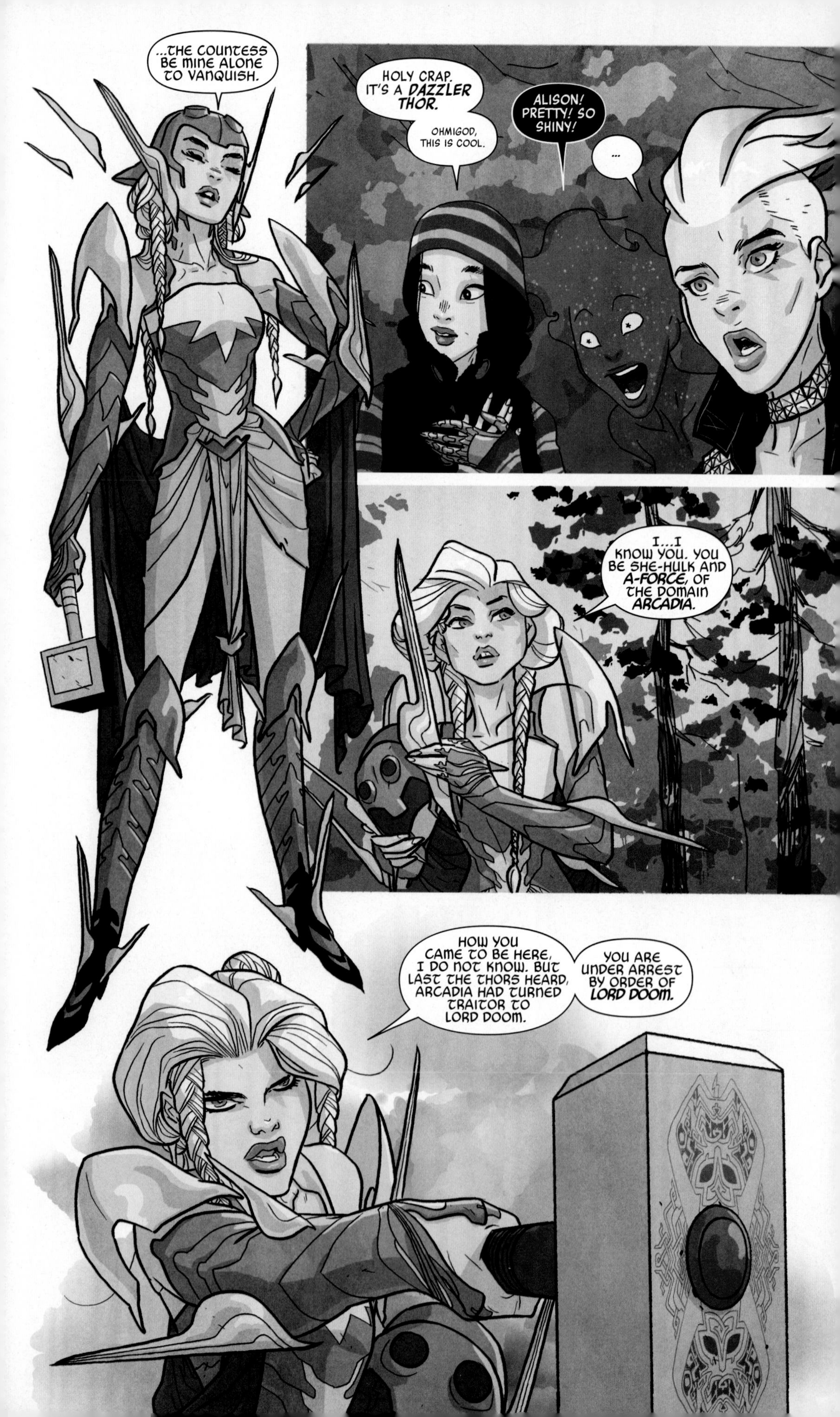
...THE COUNTESS BE MINE ALONE TO VANQUISH.
HOLY CRAP. IT'S A DAZZLER THOR.
OHMIGOD, THIS IS COOL.
ALISON! PRETTY! SO SHINY!
...
I...I KNOW YOU. YOU BE SHE-HULK AND A-FORCE, OF THE DOMAIN ARCADIA.
HOW YOU CAME TO BE HERE, I DO NOT KNOW. BUT LAST THE THORS HEARD, ARCADIA HAD TURNED TRAITOR TO LORD DOOM.
YOU ARE UNDER ARREST BY ORDER OF LORD DOOM.

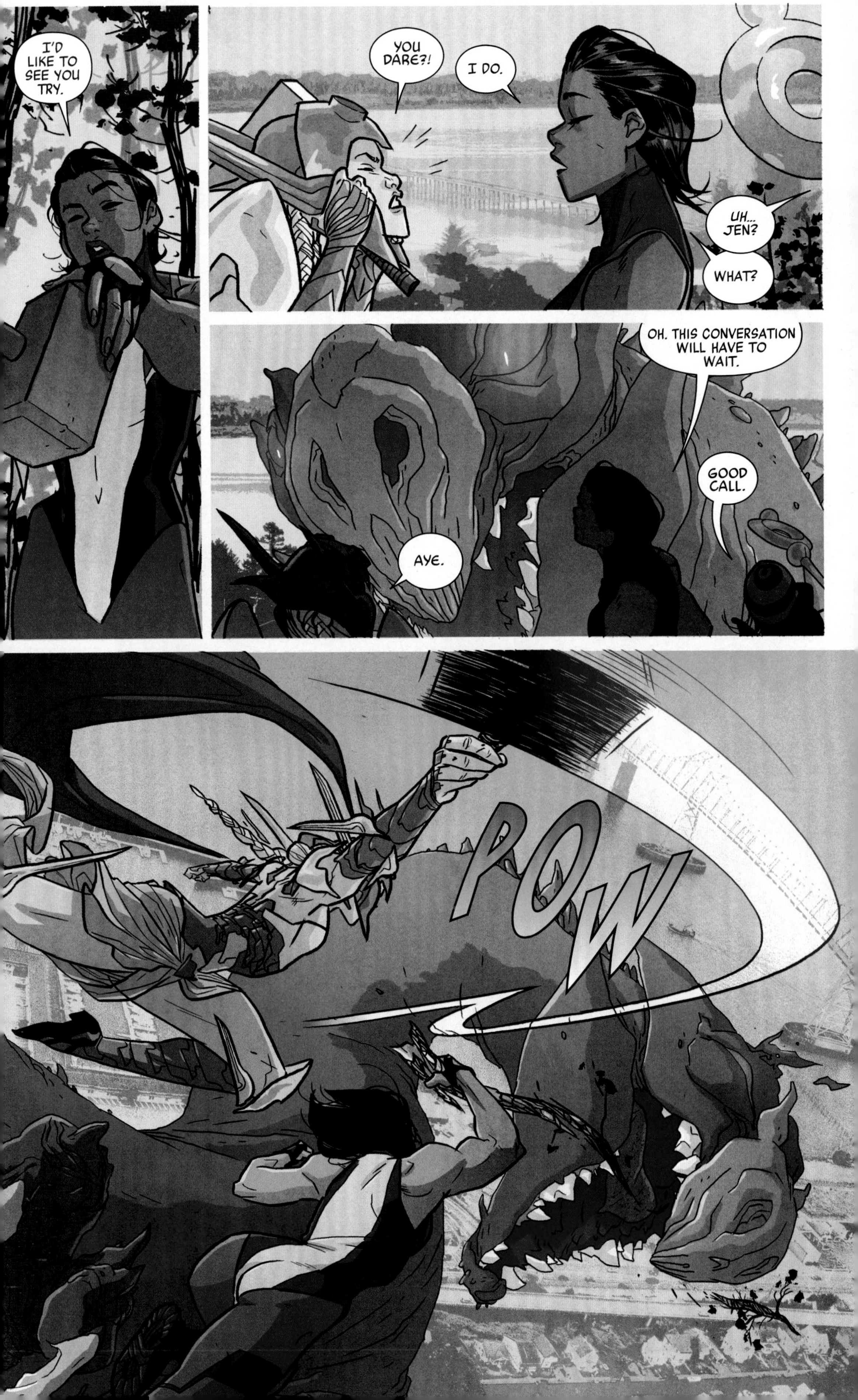

I'D LIKE TO SEE YOU TRY.
YOU DARE?!
I DO.
UH... JEN?
WHAT?
OH. THIS CONVERSATION WILL HAVE TO WAIT.
GOOD CALL.
AYE.
POW

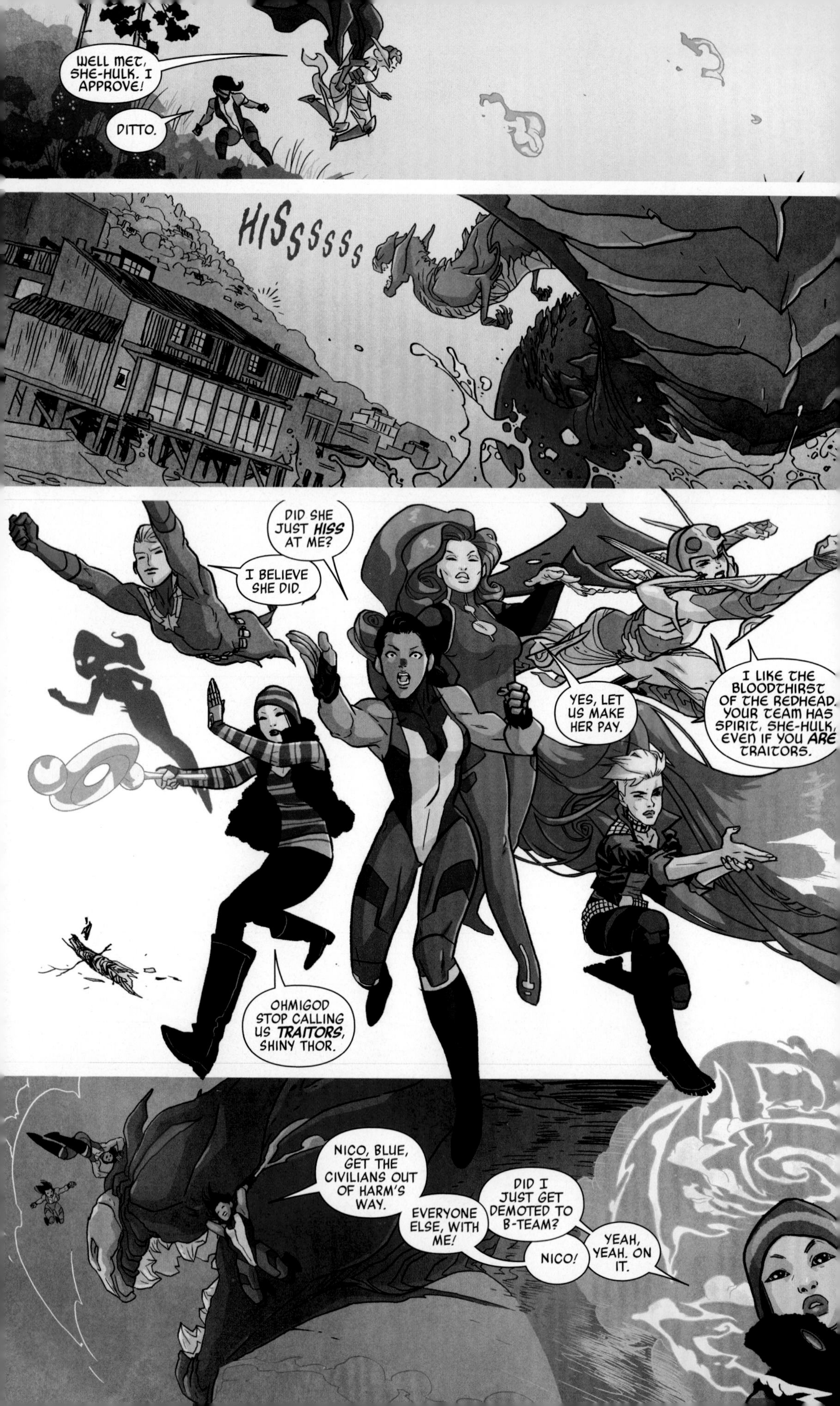

WELL MET, SHE-HULK. I APPROVE!
DITTO.
HISSSSSS
DID SHE JUST HISS AT ME?
I BELIEVE SHE DID.
YES, LET US MAKE HER PAY.
I LIKE THE BLOODTHIRST OF THE REDHEAD. YOUR TEAM HAS SPIRIT, SHE-HULK, EVEN IF YOU ARE TRAITORS.
OHMIGOD STOP CALLING US TRAITORS, SHINY THOR.
NICO, BLUE, GET THE CIVILIANS OUT OF HARM'S WAY.
EVERYONE ELSE, WITH ME!
DID I JUST GET DEMOTED TO B-TEAM?
NICO!
YEAH, YEAH. ON IT.

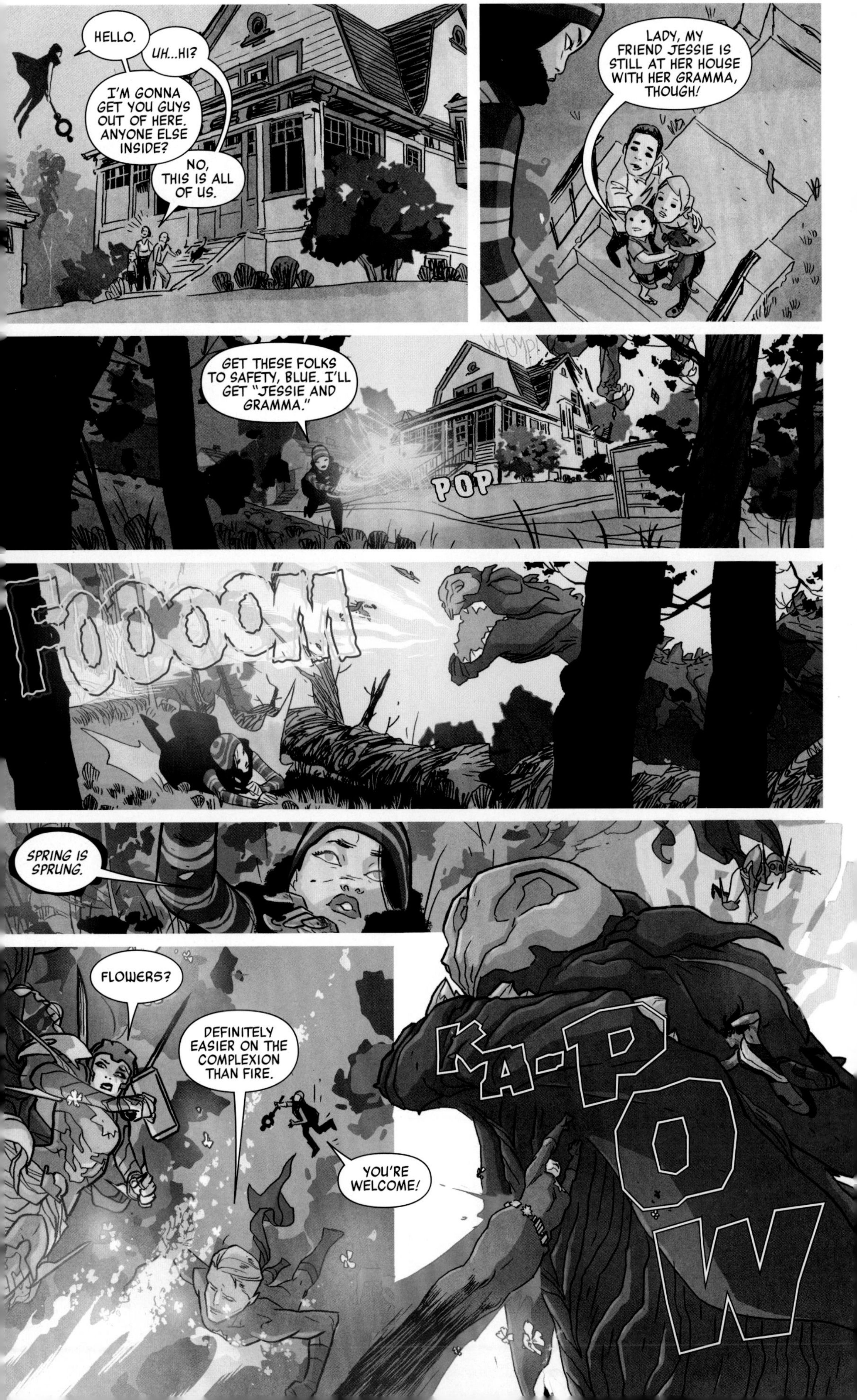
HELLO.
UH...HI?
I'M GONNA GET YOU GUYS OUT OF HERE. ANYONE ELSE INSIDE?
NO, THIS IS ALL OF US.
LADY, MY FRIEND JESSIE IS STILL AT HER HOUSE WITH HER GRAMMA, THOUGH!
GET THESE FOLKS TO SAFETY, BLUE. I'LL GET "JESSIE AND GRAMMA."
WHOMP!
POP
FOOOOM
SPRING IS SPRUNG.
FLOWERS?
DEFINITELY EASIER ON THE COMPLEXION THAN FIRE.
YOU'RE WELCOME!
KA-POW

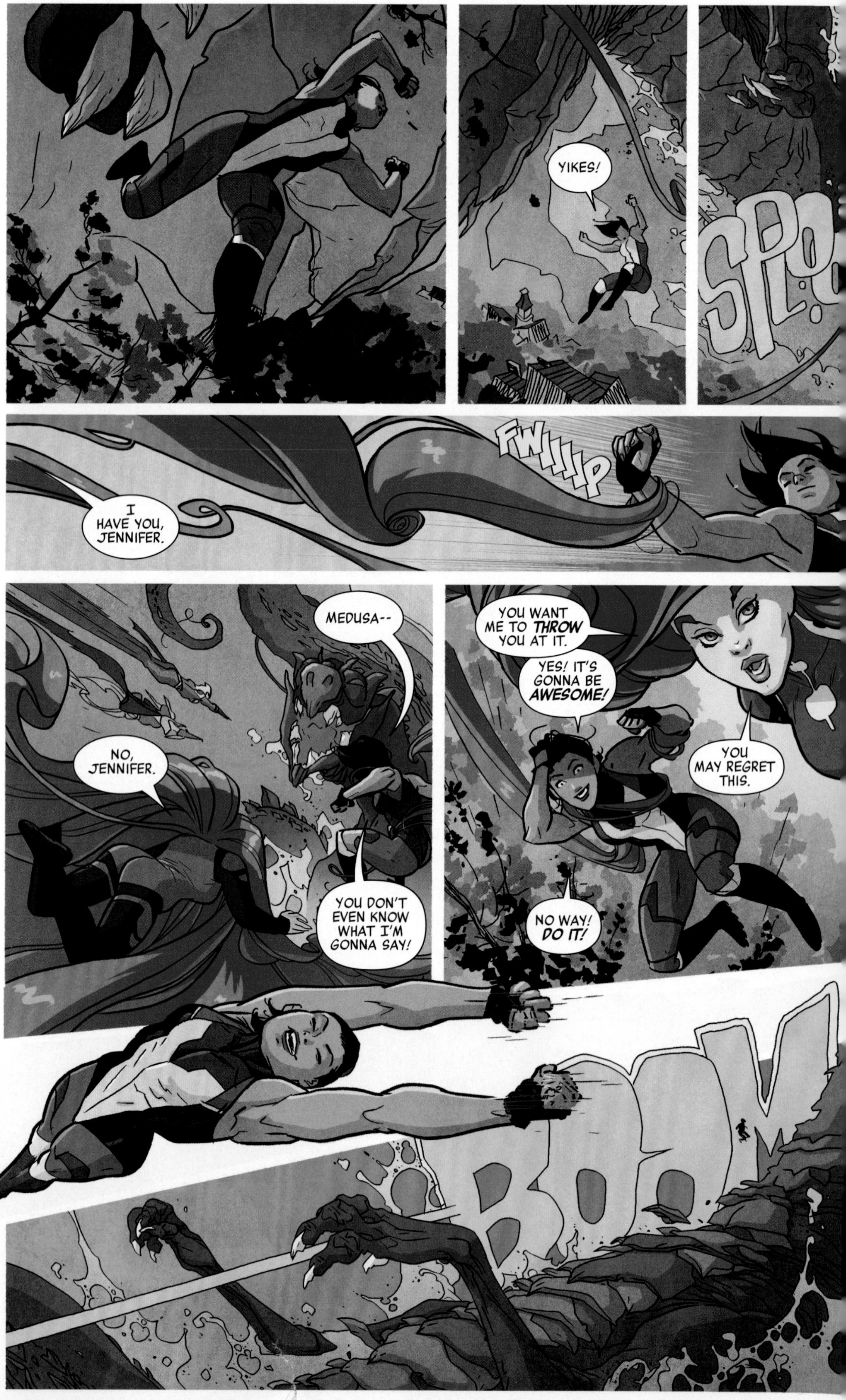
YIKES!
SPLOOSH
FWIIIIP
I HAVE YOU, JENNIFER.
MEDUSA--
NO, JENNIFER.
YOU DON'T EVEN KNOW WHAT I'M GONNA SAY!
YOU WANT ME TO THROW YOU AT IT.
YES! IT'S GONNA BE AWESOME!
YOU MAY REGRET THIS.
NO WAY! DO IT!
BOOM

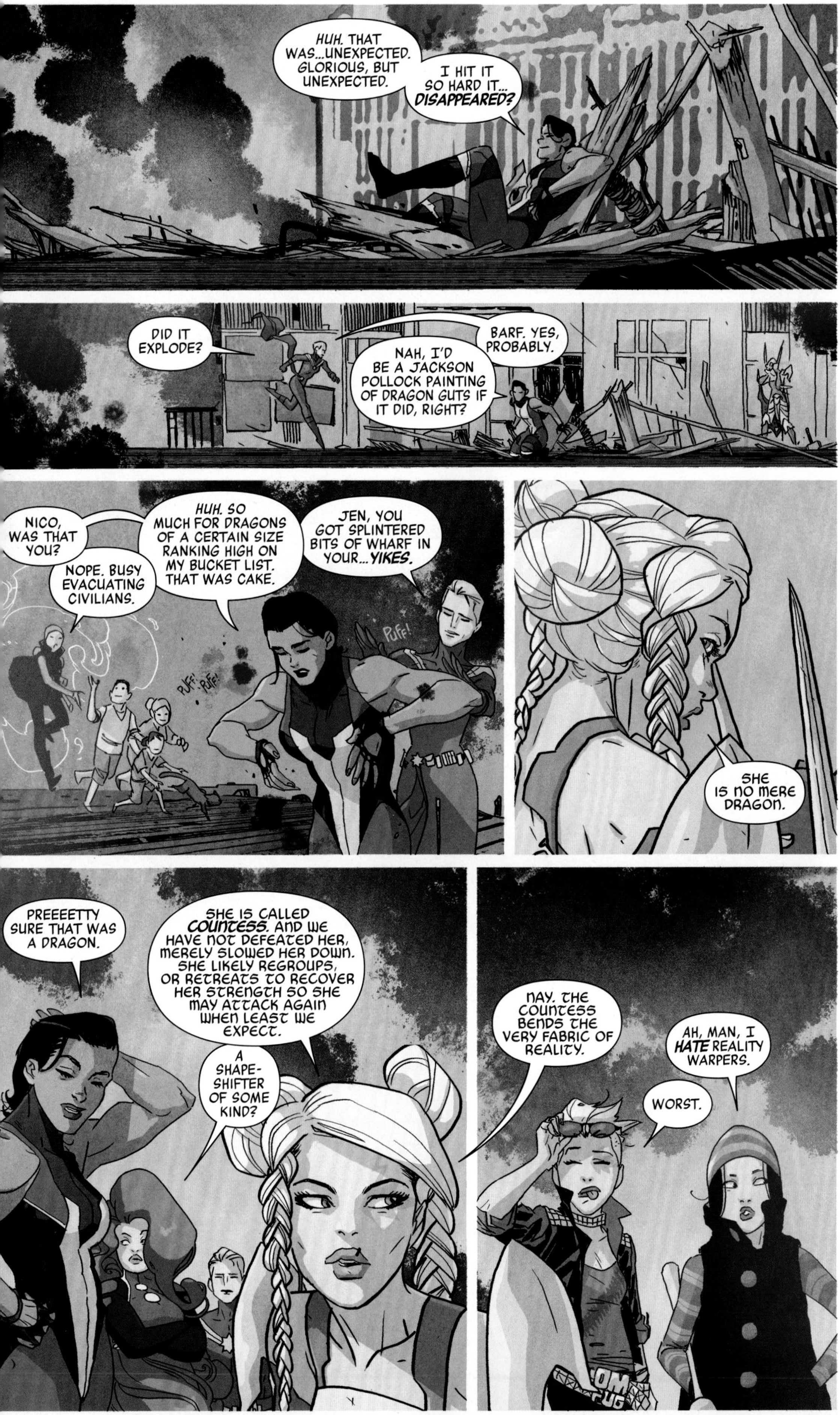
HUH. THAT WAS...UNEXPECTED. GLORIOUS, BUT UNEXPECTED.
I HIT IT SO HARD IT... DISAPPEARED?
DID IT EXPLODE?
BARF. YES, PROBABLY.
NAH, I'D BE A JACKSON POLLOCK PAINTING OF DRAGON GUTS IF IT DID, RIGHT?
NICO, WAS THAT YOU?
NOPE. BUSY EVACUATING CIVILIANS.
HUH. SO MUCH FOR DRAGONS OF A CERTAIN SIZE RANKING HIGH ON MY BUCKET LIST. THAT WAS CAKE.
JEN, YOU GOT SPLINTERED BITS OF WHARF IN YOUR...YIKES.
PUFF!
PUFF! PUFF!
SHE IS NO MERE DRAGON.
PREEEETTY SURE THAT WAS A DRAGON.
SHE IS CALLED COUNTESS. AND WE HAVE NOT DEFEATED HER, MERELY SLOWED HER DOWN. SHE LIKELY REGROUPS, OR RETREATS TO RECOVER HER STRENGTH SO SHE MAY ATTACK AGAIN WHEN LEAST WE EXPECT.
A SHAPE-SHIFTER OF SOME KIND?
NAY. THE COUNTESS BENDS THE VERY FABRIC OF REALITY.
AH, MAN, I HATE REALITY WARPERS.
WORST.

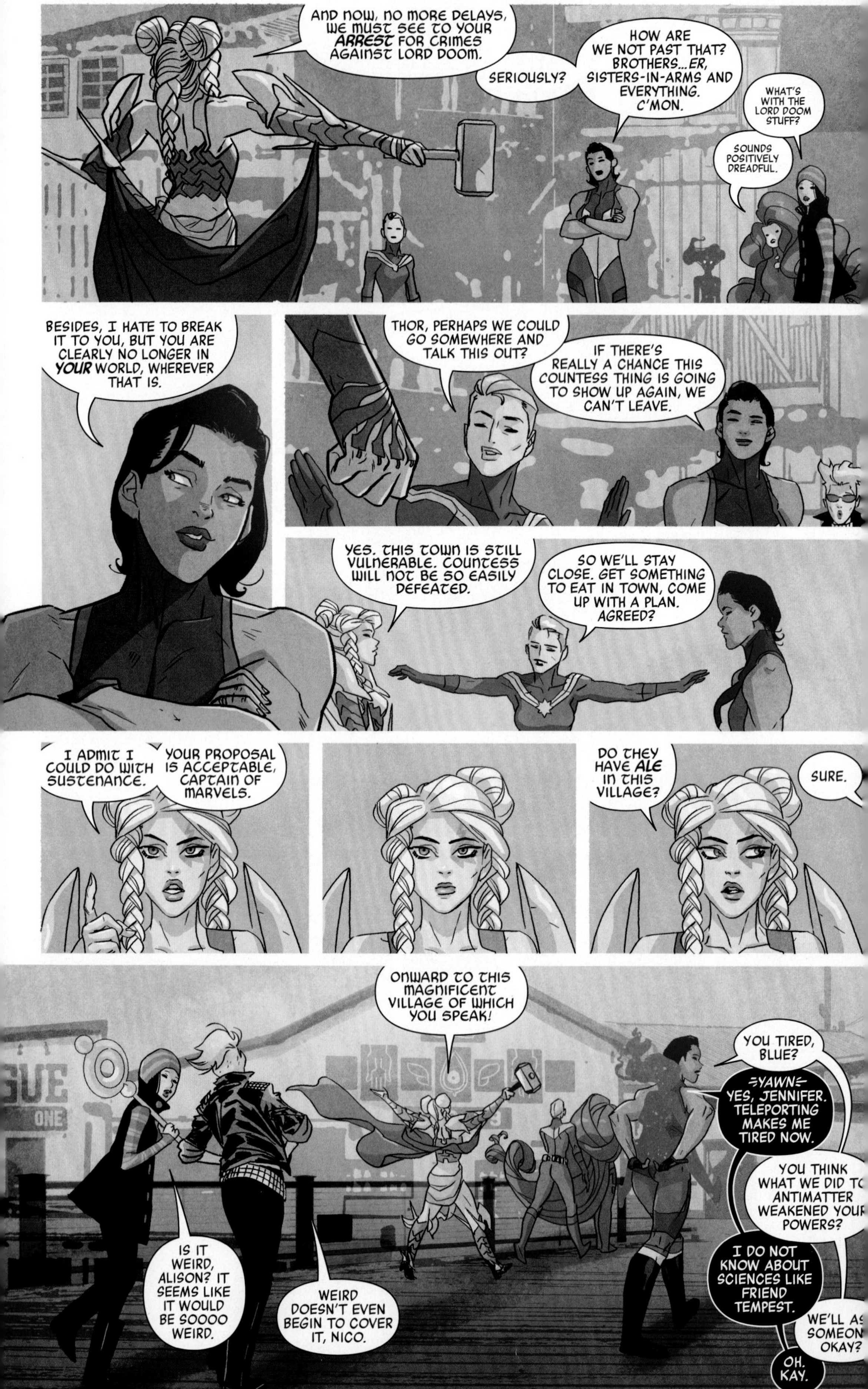
AND NOW, NO MORE DELAYS, WE MUST SEE TO YOUR ARREST FOR CRIMES AGAINST LORD DOOM.
SERIOUSLY?
HOW ARE WE NOT PAST THAT? BROTHERS...ER, SISTERS-IN-ARMS AND EVERYTHING. C'MON.
WHAT'S WITH THE LORD DOOM STUFF?
SOUNDS POSITIVELY DREADFUL.
BESIDES, I HATE TO BREAK IT TO YOU, BUT YOU ARE CLEARLY NO LONGER IN YOUR WORLD, WHEREVER THAT IS.
THOR, PERHAPS WE COULD GO SOMEWHERE AND TALK THIS OUT?
IF THERE'S REALLY A CHANCE THIS COUNTESS THING IS GOING TO SHOW UP AGAIN, WE CAN'T LEAVE.
YES. THIS TOWN IS STILL VULNERABLE. COUNTESS WILL NOT BE SO EASILY DEFEATED.
SO WE'LL STAY CLOSE. GET SOMETHING TO EAT IN TOWN, COME UP WITH A PLAN. AGREED?
I ADMIT I COULD DO WITH SUSTENANCE.
YOUR PROPOSAL IS ACCEPTABLE, CAPTAIN OF MARVELS.
DO THEY HAVE ALE IN THIS VILLAGE?
SURE.
ONWARD TO THIS MAGNIFICENT VILLAGE OF WHICH YOU SPEAK!
IS IT WEIRD, ALISON? IT SEEMS LIKE IT WOULD BE SOOOO WEIRD.
WEIRD DOESN'T EVEN BEGIN TO COVER IT, NICO.
YOU TIRED, BLUE?
=YAWN= YES, JENNIFER. TELEPORTING MAKES ME TIRED NOW.
YOU THINK WHAT WE DID TO ANTIMATTER WEAKENED YOUR POWERS?
I DO NOT KNOW ABOUT SCIENCES LIKE FRIEND TEMPEST.
WE'LL AS SOMEON OKAY?
OH. KAY.

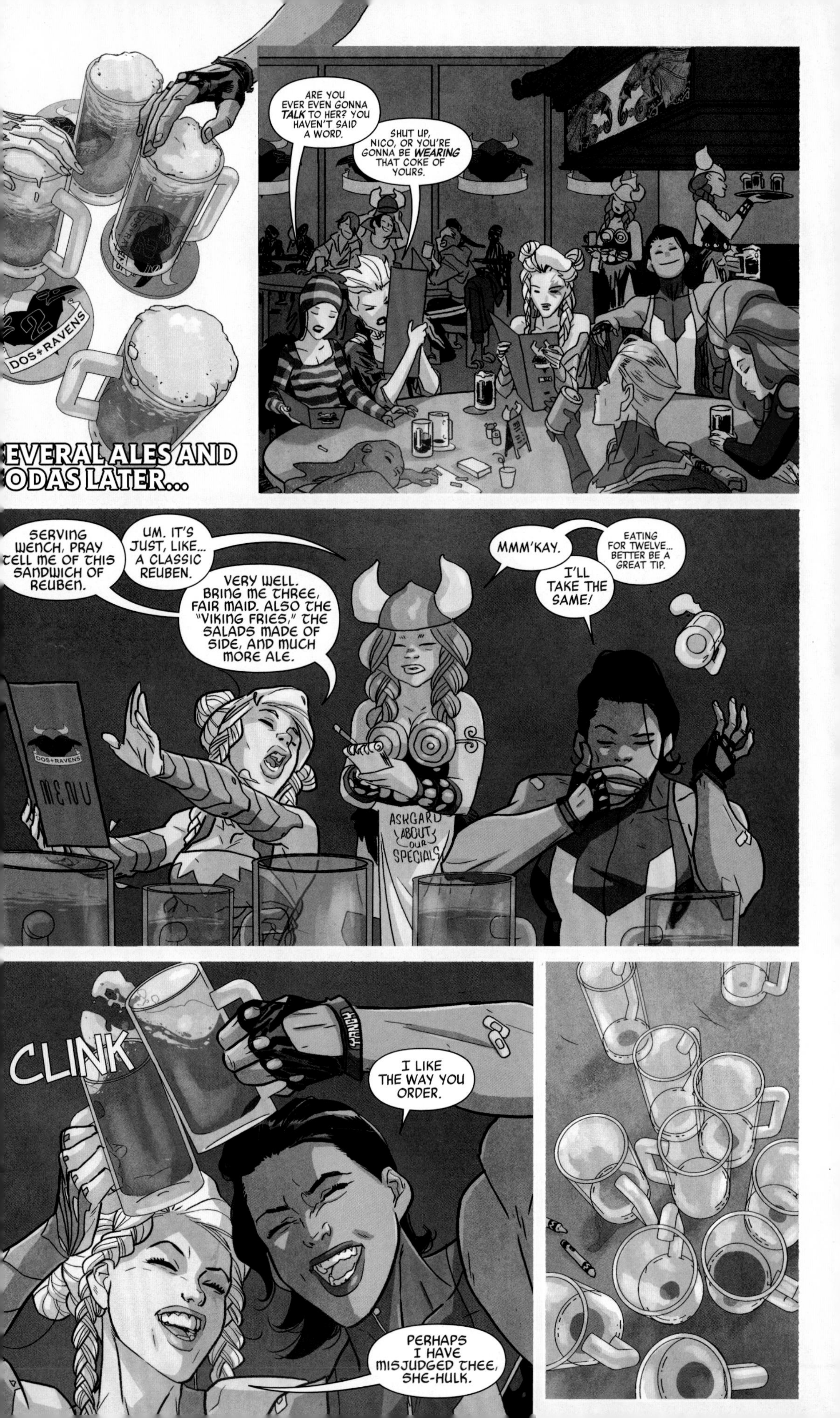
DOS RAVENS
EVERAL ALES AND
ODAS LATER...
ARE YOU EVER EVEN GONNA TALK TO HER? YOU HAVEN'T SAID A WORD.
SHUT UP, NICO, OR YOU'RE GONNA BE WEARING THAT COKE OF YOURS.
SERVING WENCH, PRAY TELL ME OF THIS SANDWICH OF REUBEN.
UM. IT'S JUST, LIKE... A CLASSIC REUBEN.
VERY WELL. BRING ME THREE, FAIR MAID. ALSO THE "VIKING FRIES," THE SALADS MADE OF SIDE, AND MUCH MORE ALE.
MMM'KAY.
EATING FOR TWELVE... BETTER BE A GREAT TIP.
I'LL TAKE THE SAME!
DOS RAVENS
MENU
ASKGARD ABOUT OUR SPECIALS
CLINK
I LIKE THE WAY YOU ORDER.
PERHAPS I HAVE MISJUDGED THEE, SHE-HULK.

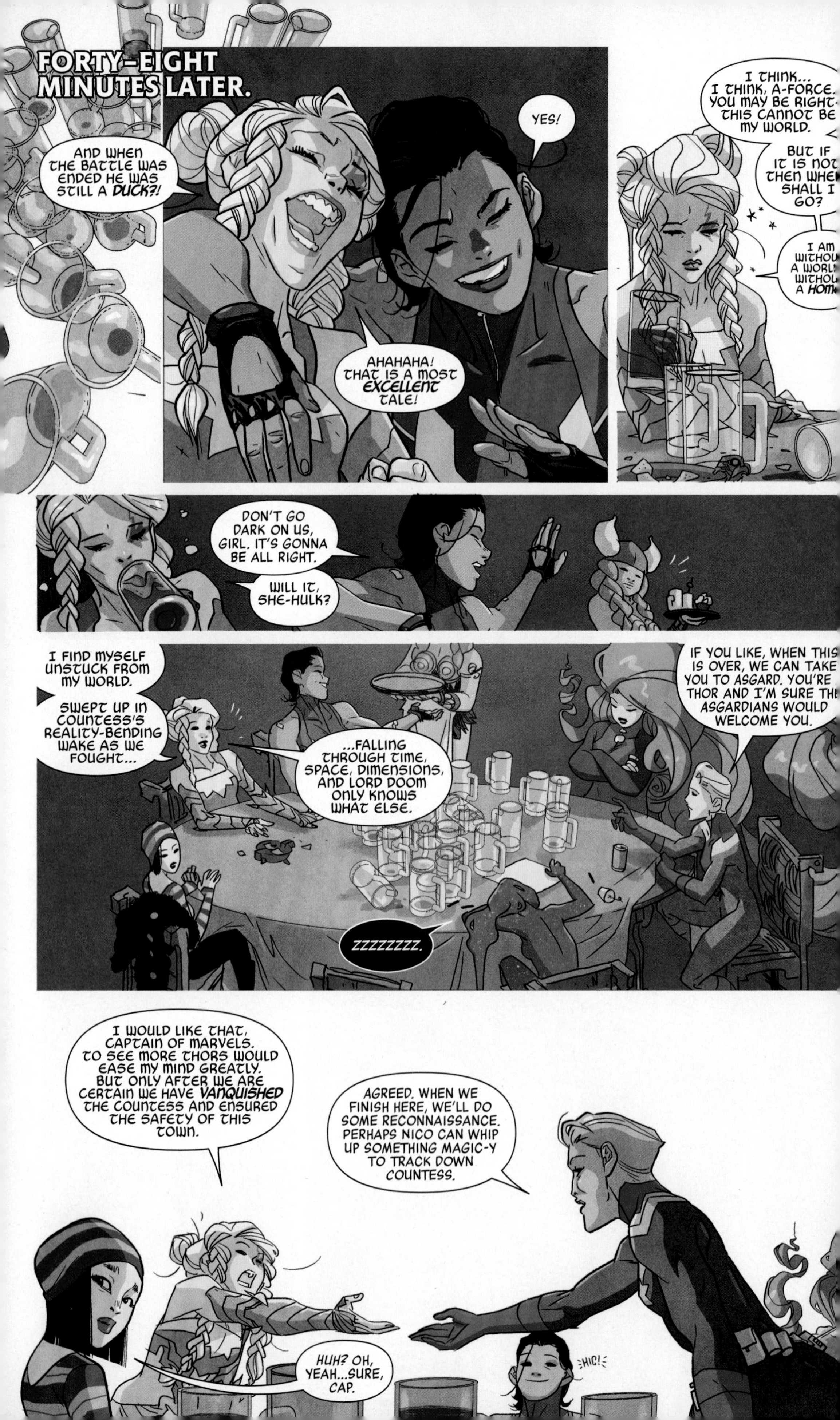
FORTY-EIGHT MINUTES LATER.
AND WHEN THE BATTLE WAS ENDED HE WAS STILL A DUCK?!
YES!
AHAHAHA! THAT IS A MOST EXCELLENT TALE!
I THINK... I THINK, A-FORCE. YOU MAY BE RIGHT. THIS CANNOT BE MY WORLD.
BUT IF IT IS NOT THEN WHE SHALL I GO?
I AM WITHOU A WORL WITHOU A HOM
DON'T GO DARK ON US, GIRL. IT'S GONNA BE ALL RIGHT.
WILL IT, SHE-HULK?
I FIND MYSELF UNSTUCK FROM MY WORLD.
SWEPT UP IN COUNTESS'S REALITY-BENDING WAKE AS WE FOUGHT...
...FALLING THROUGH TIME, SPACE, DIMENSIONS, AND LORD DOOM ONLY KNOWS WHAT ELSE.
IF YOU LIKE, WHEN THIS IS OVER, WE CAN TAKE YOU TO ASGARD. YOU'RE THOR AND I'M SURE TH ASGARDIANS WOULD WELCOME YOU.
ZZZZZZZZ.
I WOULD LIKE THAT, CAPTAIN OF MARVELS. TO SEE MORE THORS WOULD EASE MY MIND GREATLY. BUT ONLY AFTER WE ARE CERTAIN WE HAVE VANQUISHED THE COUNTESS AND ENSURED THE SAFETY OF THIS TOWN.
AGREED. WHEN WE FINISH HERE, WE'LL DO SOME RECONNAISSANCE. PERHAPS NICO CAN WHIP UP SOMETHING MAGIC-Y TO TRACK DOWN COUNTESS.
HUH? OH, YEAH...SURE, CAP.
HIC!

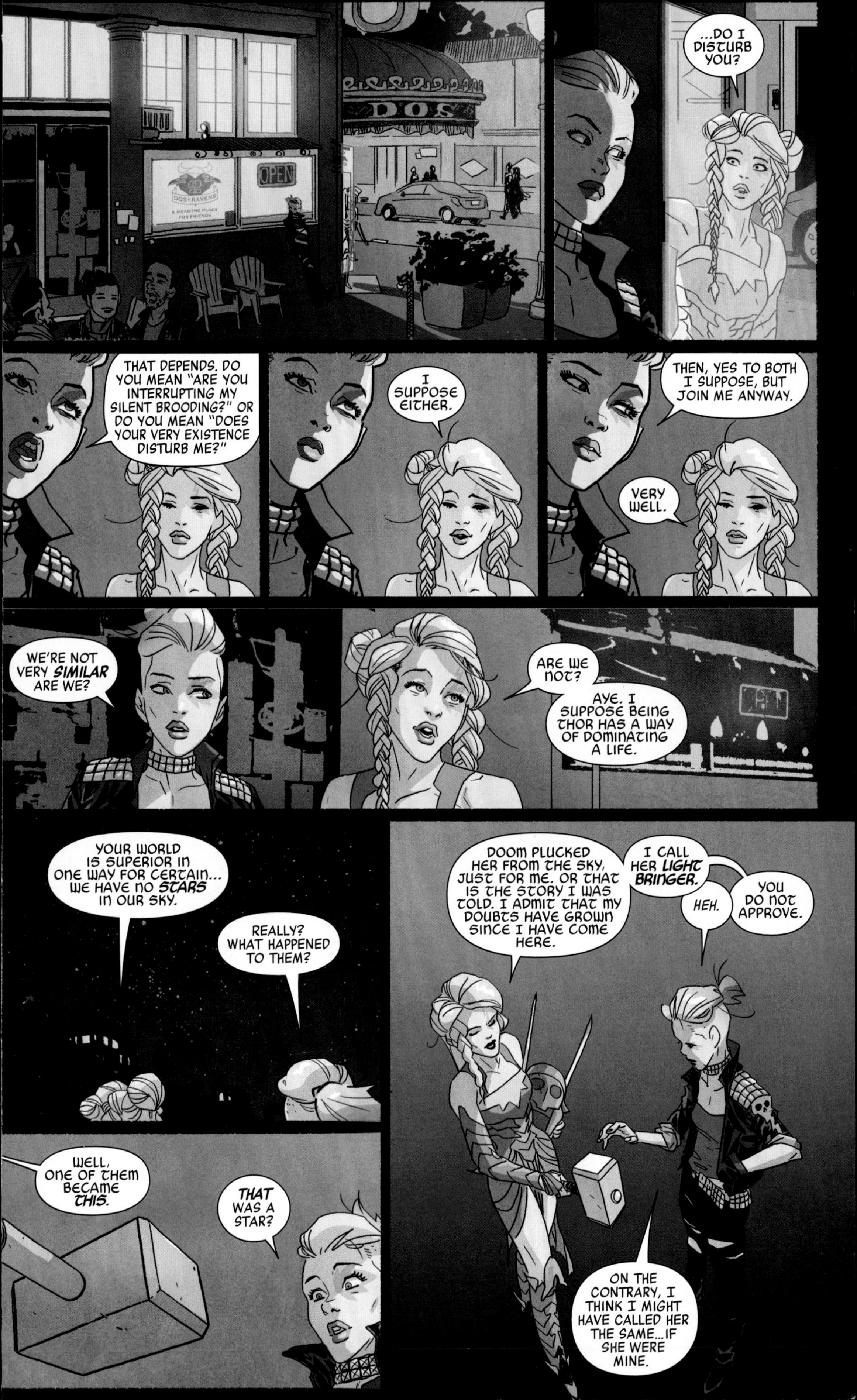
DOS + RAVENS
A MEADING PLACE FOR FRIENDS
OPEN
DOS
...DO I DISTURB YOU?
THAT DEPENDS. DO YOU MEAN "ARE YOU INTERRUPTING MY SILENT BROODING?" OR DO YOU MEAN "DOES YOUR VERY EXISTENCE DISTURB ME?"
I SUPPOSE EITHER.
THEN, YES TO BOTH I SUPPOSE, BUT JOIN ME ANYWAY.
VERY WELL.
WE'RE NOT VERY SIMILAR ARE WE?
ARE WE NOT?
AYE. I SUPPOSE BEING THOR HAS A WAY OF DOMINATING A LIFE.
YOUR WORLD IS SUPERIOR IN ONE WAY FOR CERTAIN... WE HAVE NO STARS IN OUR SKY.
REALLY? WHAT HAPPENED TO THEM?
WELL, ONE OF THEM BECAME THIS.
THAT WAS A STAR?
DOOM PLUCKED HER FROM THE SKY, JUST FOR ME. OR THAT IS THE STORY I WAS TOLD. I ADMIT THAT MY DOUBTS HAVE GROWN SINCE I HAVE COME HERE.
I CALL HER LIGHT BRINGER.
HEH.
YOU DO NOT APPROVE.
ON THE CONTRARY, I THINK I MIGHT HAVE CALLED HER THE SAME...IF SHE WERE MINE.

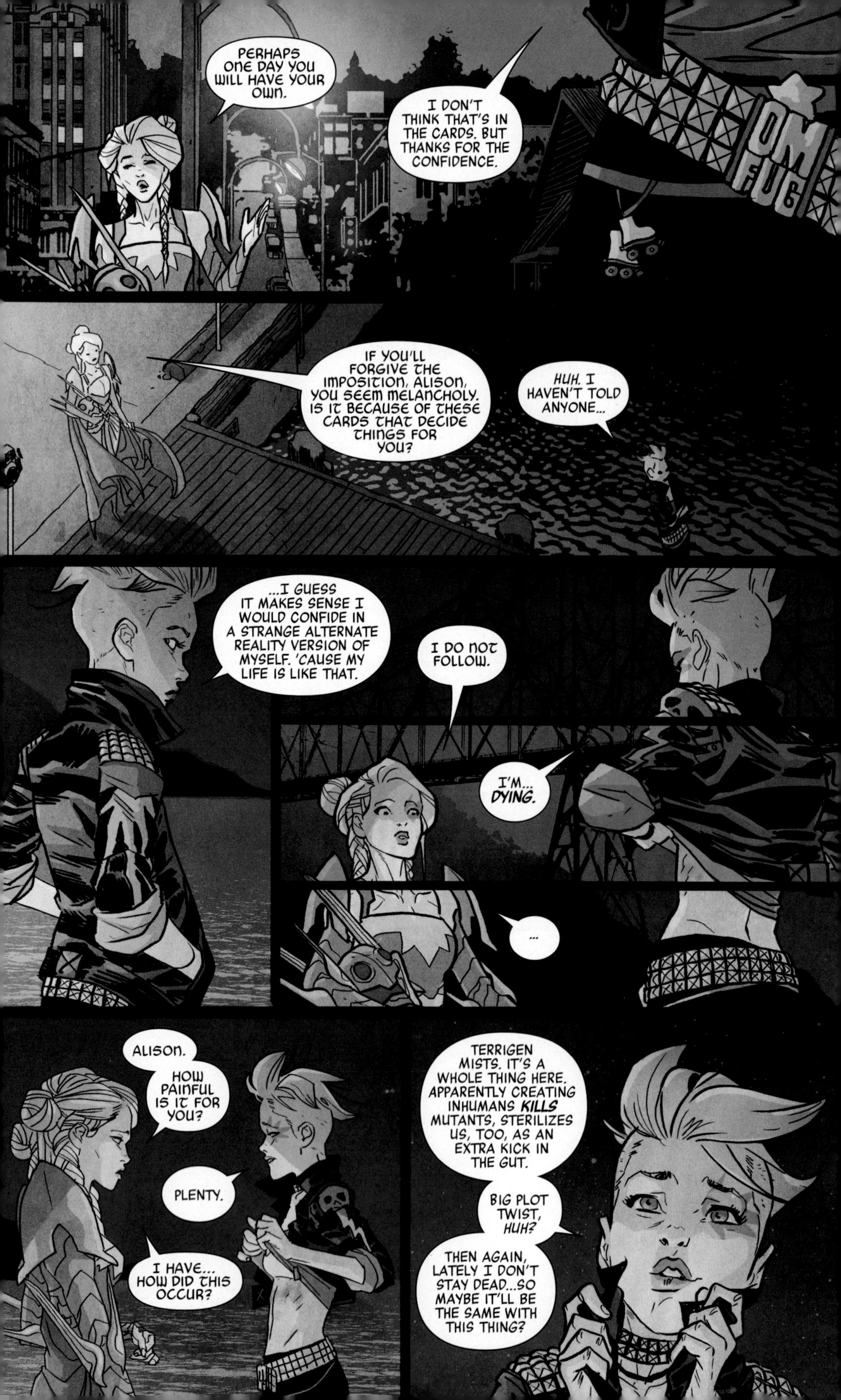
PERHAPS ONE DAY YOU WILL HAVE YOUR OWN.
I DON'T THINK THAT'S IN THE CARDS. BUT THANKS FOR THE CONFIDENCE.
OM
FUG
IF YOU'LL FORGIVE THE IMPOSITION, ALISON, YOU SEEM MELANCHOLY. IS IT BECAUSE OF THESE CARDS THAT DECIDE THINGS FOR YOU?
HUH. I HAVEN'T TOLD ANYONE...
...I GUESS IT MAKES SENSE I WOULD CONFIDE IN A STRANGE ALTERNATE REALITY VERSION OF MYSELF. 'CAUSE MY LIFE IS LIKE THAT.
I DO NOT FOLLOW.
I'M... DYING.
...
ALISON.
HOW PAINFUL IS IT FOR YOU?
PLENTY.
I HAVE... HOW DID THIS OCCUR?
TERRIGEN MISTS. IT'S A WHOLE THING HERE. APPARENTLY CREATING INHUMANS KILLS MUTANTS, STERILIZES US, TOO, AS AN EXTRA KICK IN THE GUT.
BIG PLOT TWIST, HUH?
THEN AGAIN, LATELY I DON'T STAY DEAD...SO MAYBE IT'LL BE THE SAME WITH THIS THING?

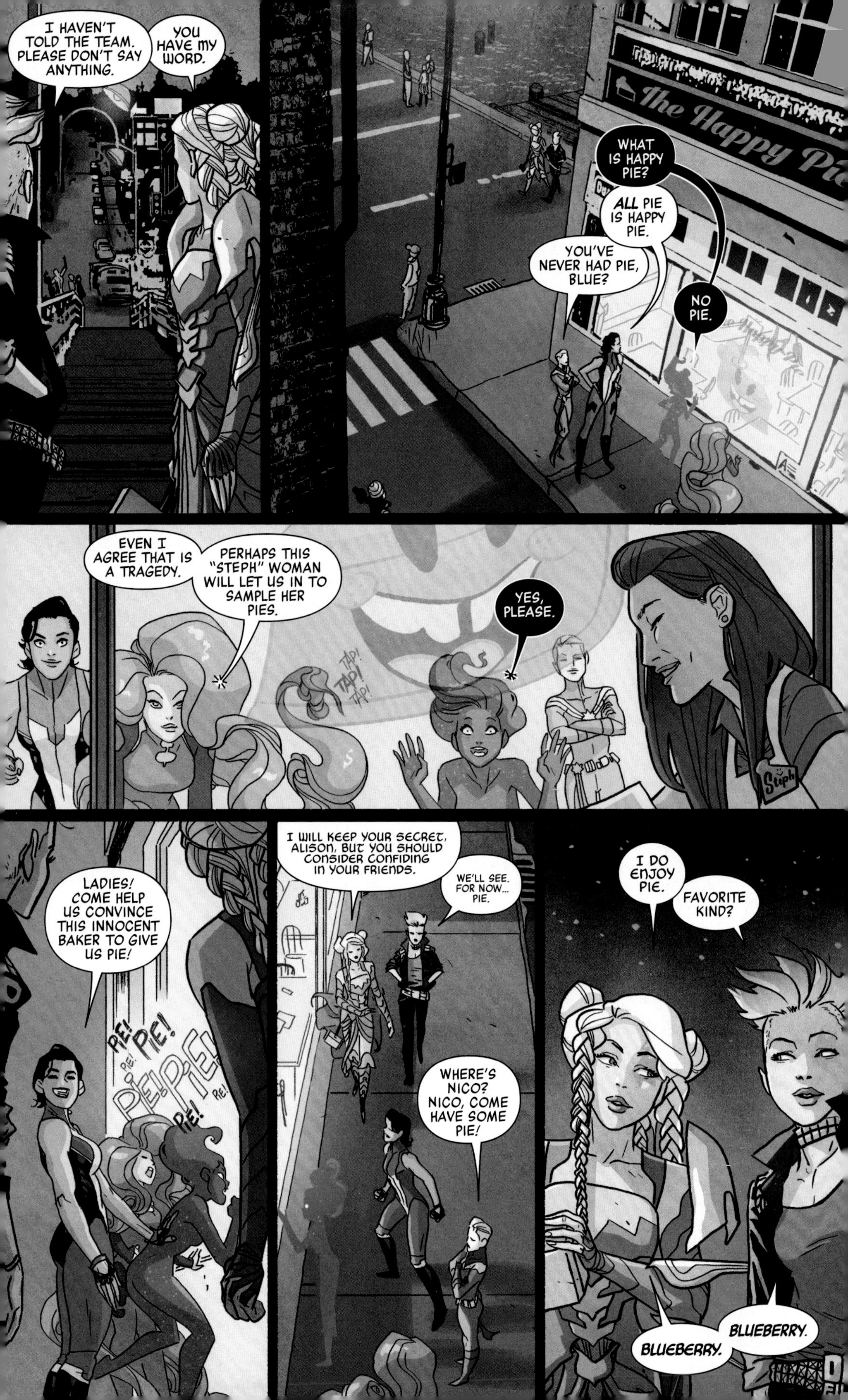
I HAVEN'T TOLD THE TEAM. PLEASE DON'T SAY ANYTHING.
YOU HAVE MY WORD.
The Happy Pie
WHAT IS HAPPY PIE?
ALL PIE IS HAPPY PIE.
YOU'VE NEVER HAD PIE, BLUE?
NO PIE.
EVEN I AGREE THAT IS A TRAGEDY.
PERHAPS THIS "STEPH" WOMAN WILL LET US IN TO SAMPLE HER PIES.
TAP! TAP! TAP!
YES, PLEASE.
Steph
LADIES! COME HELP US CONVINCE THIS INNOCENT BAKER TO GIVE US PIE!
PIE! PIE! PIE! PIE! PIE! PIE! PIE!
I WILL KEEP YOUR SECRET, ALISON, BUT YOU SHOULD CONSIDER CONFIDING IN YOUR FRIENDS.
WE'LL SEE. FOR NOW... PIE.
WHERE'S NICO? NICO, COME HAVE SOME PIE!
I DO ENJOY PIE.
FAVORITE KIND?
BLUEBERRY.
BLUEBERRY.

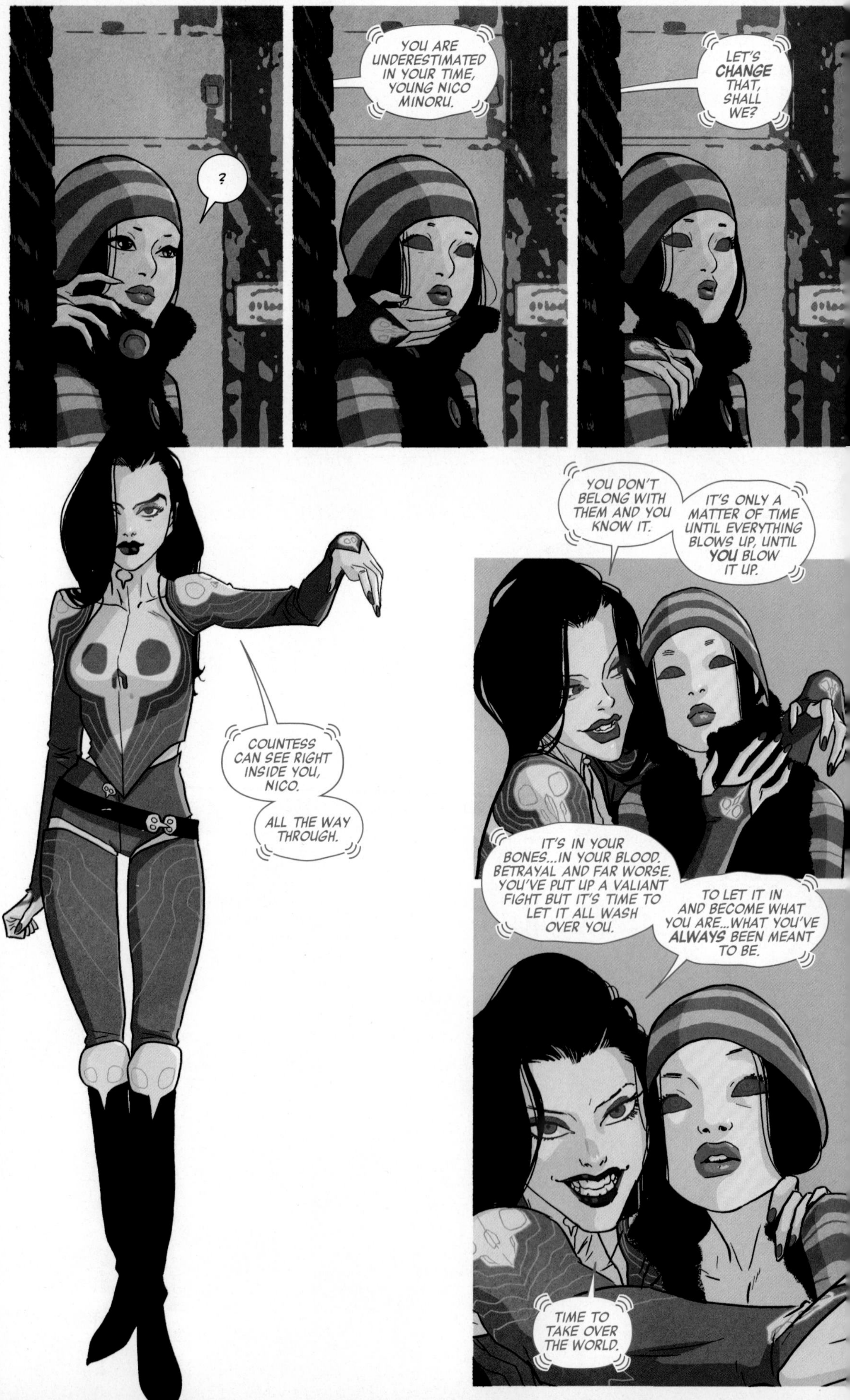
?
YOU ARE UNDERESTIMATED IN YOUR TIME, YOUNG NICO MINORU.
LET'S CHANGE THAT, SHALL WE?
COUNTESS CAN SEE RIGHT INSIDE YOU, NICO.
ALL THE WAY THROUGH.
YOU DON'T BELONG WITH THEM AND YOU KNOW IT.
IT'S ONLY A MATTER OF TIME UNTIL EVERYTHING BLOWS UP, UNTIL YOU BLOW IT UP.
IT'S IN YOUR BONES...IN YOUR BLOOD. BETRAYAL AND FAR WORSE. YOU'VE PUT UP A VALIANT FIGHT BUT IT'S TIME TO LET IT ALL WASH OVER YOU.
TO LET IT IN AND BECOME WHAT YOU ARE...WHAT YOU'VE ALWAYS BEEN MEANT TO BE.
TIME TO TAKE OVER THE WORLD.

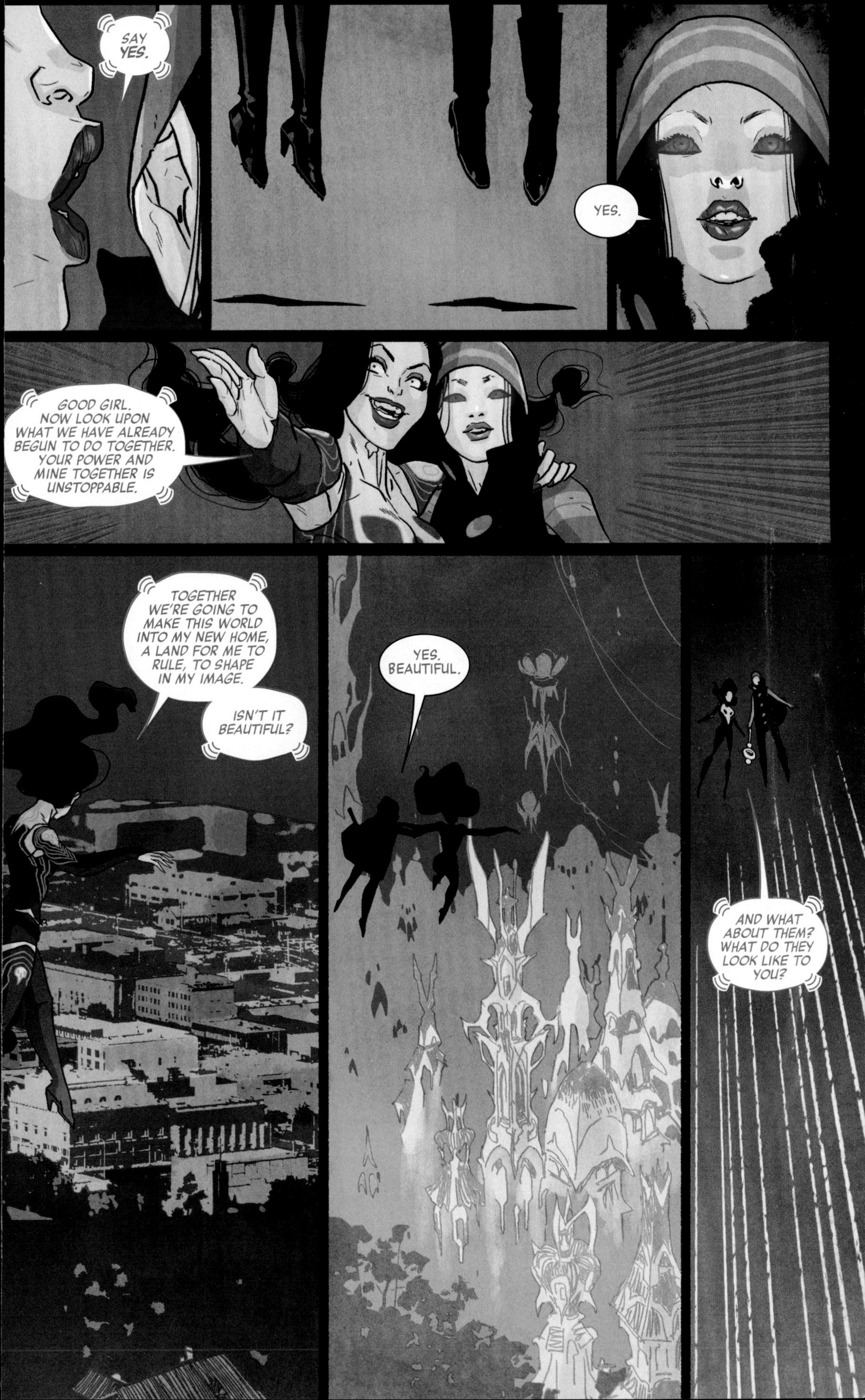
SAY YES.
YES.
GOOD GIRL. NOW LOOK UPON WHAT WE HAVE ALREADY BEGUN TO DO TOGETHER. YOUR POWER AND MINE TOGETHER IS UNSTOPPABLE.
TOGETHER WE'RE GOING TO MAKE THIS WORLD INTO MY NEW HOME, A LAND FOR ME TO RULE, TO SHAPE IN MY IMAGE.
ISN'T IT BEAUTIFUL?
YES. BEAUTIFUL.
AND WHAT ABOUT THEM? WHAT DO THEY LOOK LIKE TO YOU?

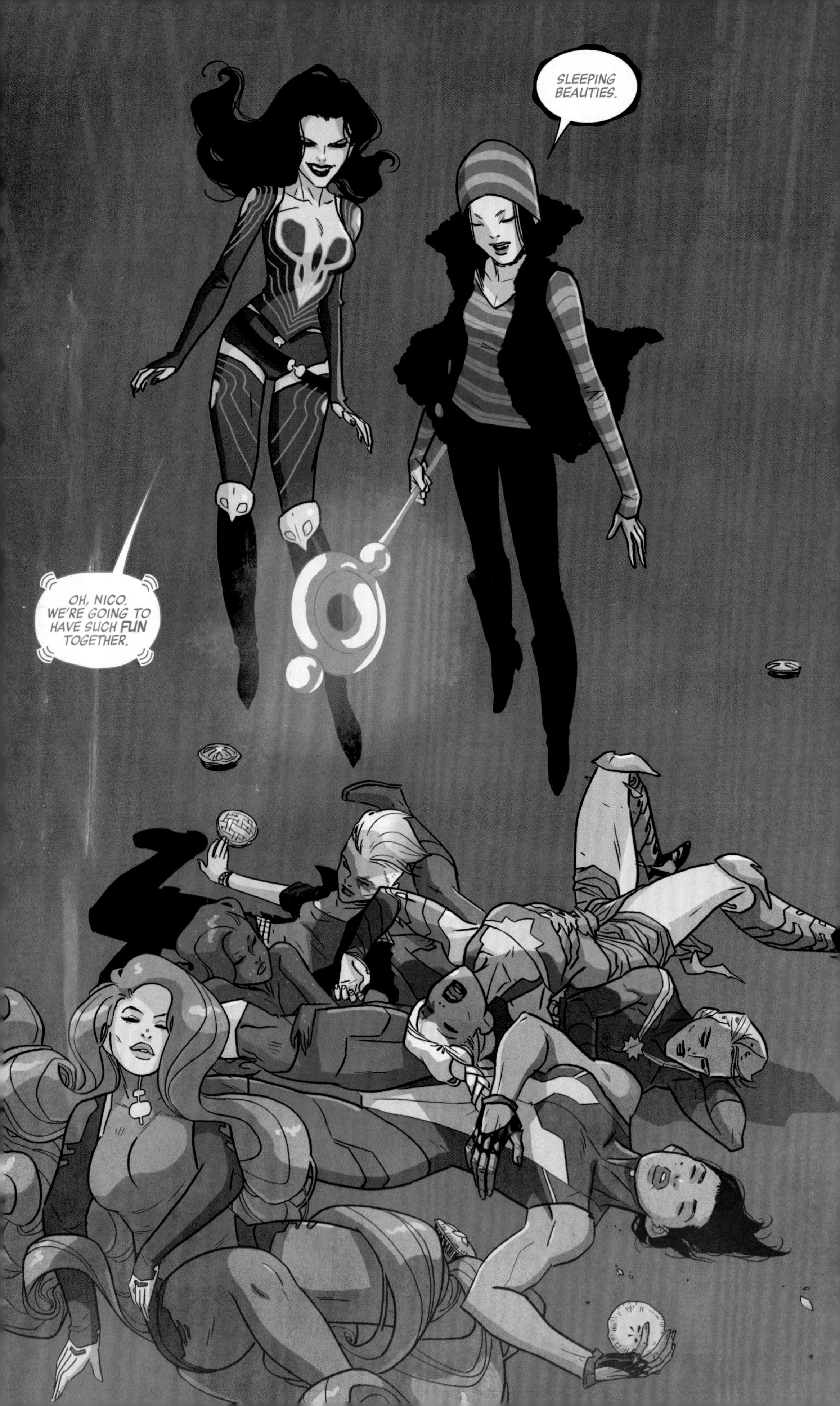
SLEEPING BEAUTIES.
OH, NICO. WE'RE GOING TO HAVE SUCH FUN TOGETHER.

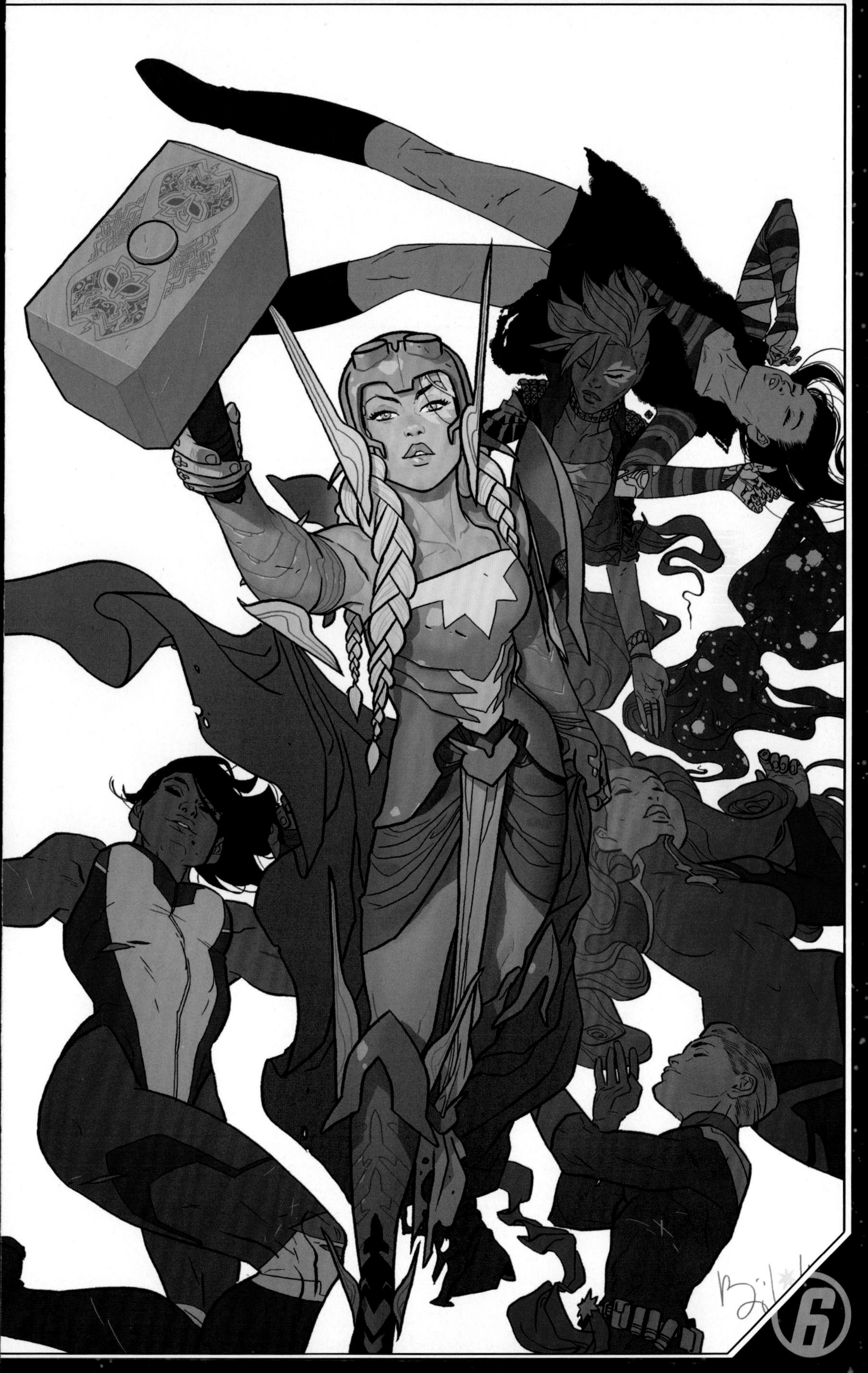
6

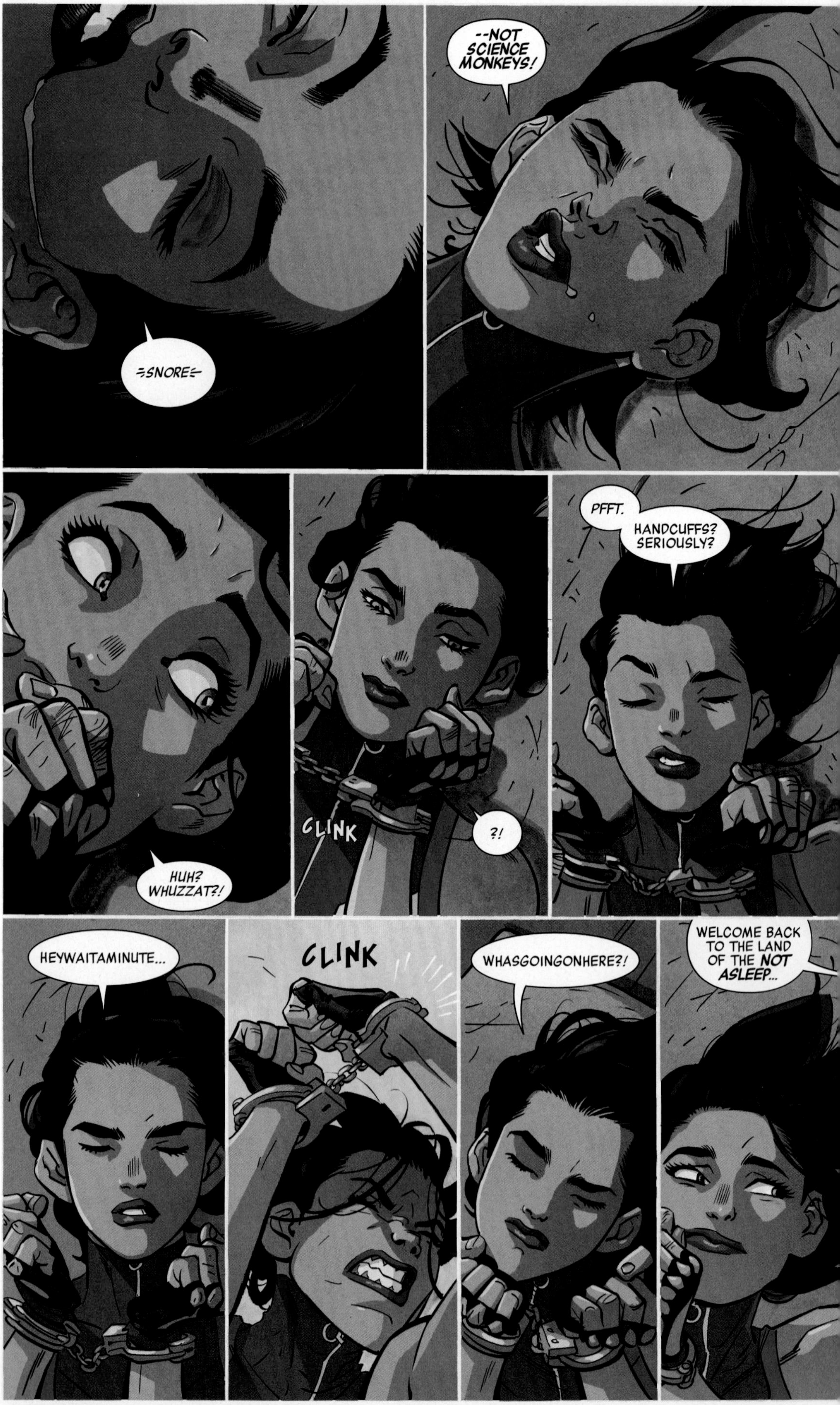

=SNORE=
--NOT SCIENCE MONKEYS!
HUH? WHUZZAT?!
CLINK
?!
PFFT.
HANDCUFFS? SERIOUSLY?
HEYWAITAMINUTE...
CLINK
WHASGOINGONHERE?!
WELCOME BACK TO THE LAND OF THE NOT ASLEEP...

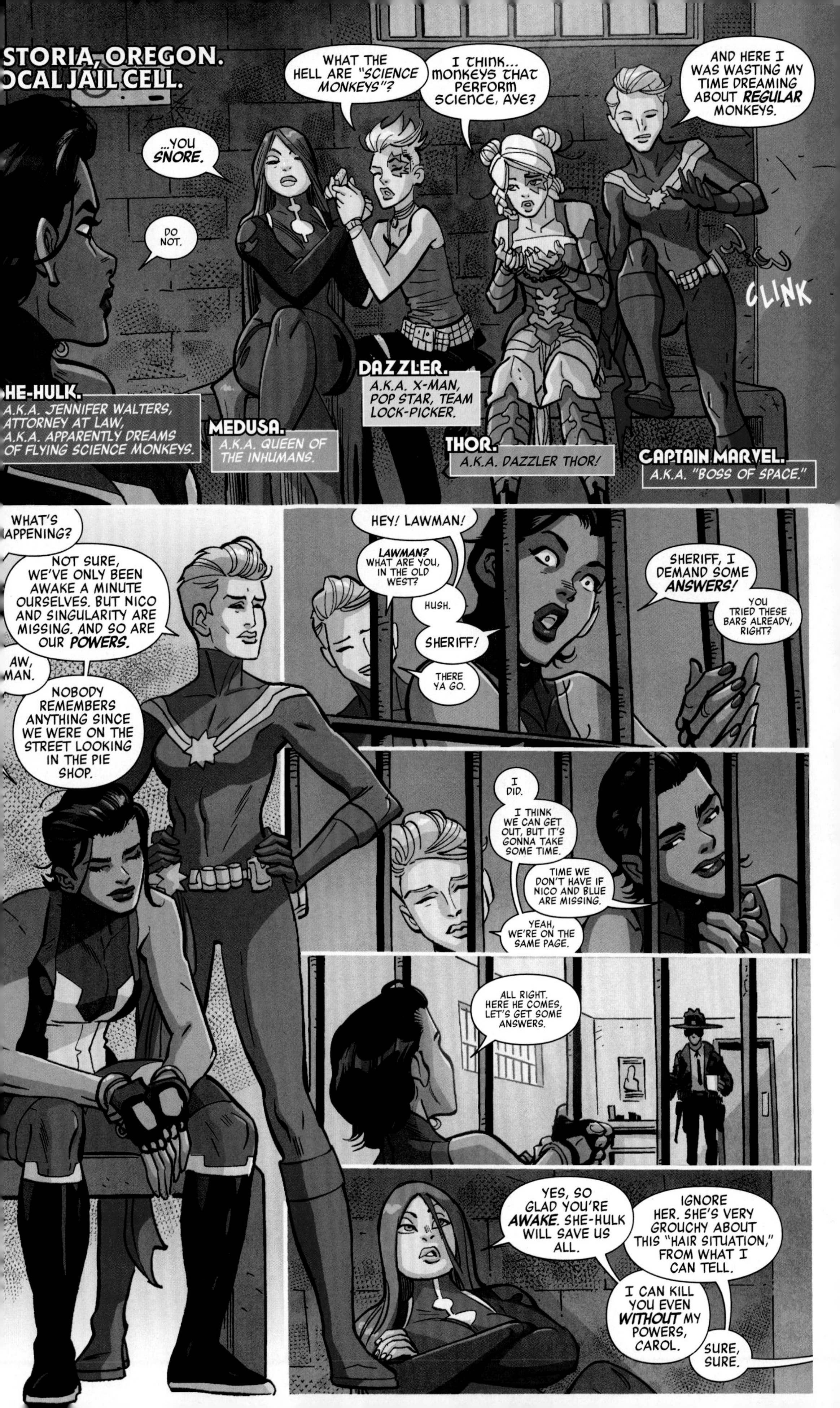

STORIA, OREGON.
OCAL JAIL CELL.
...YOU SNORE.
DO NOT.
WHAT THE HELL ARE "SCIENCE MONKEYS"?
I THINK... MONKEYS THAT PERFORM SCIENCE, AYE?
AND HERE I WAS WASTING MY TIME DREAMING ABOUT REGULAR MONKEYS.
CLINK
HE-HULK.
A.K.A. JENNIFER WALTERS, ATTORNEY AT LAW, A.K.A. APPARENTLY DREAMS OF FLYING SCIENCE MONKEYS.
MEDUSA.
A.K.A. QUEEN OF THE INHUMANS.
DAZZLER.
A.K.A. X-MAN, POP STAR, TEAM LOCK-PICKER.
THOR.
A.K.A. DAZZLER THOR!
CAPTAIN MARVEL.
A.K.A. "BOSS OF SPACE."
WHAT'S APPENING?
NOT SURE, WE'VE ONLY BEEN AWAKE A MINUTE OURSELVES. BUT NICO AND SINGULARITY ARE MISSING. AND SO ARE OUR POWERS.
AW, MAN.
NOBODY REMEMBERS ANYTHING SINCE WE WERE ON THE STREET LOOKING IN THE PIE SHOP.
HEY! LAWMAN!
LAWMAN? WHAT ARE YOU, IN THE OLD WEST?
HUSH.
SHERIFF!
THERE YA GO.
SHERIFF, I DEMAND SOME ANSWERS!
YOU TRIED THESE BARS ALREADY, RIGHT?
I DID.
I THINK WE CAN GET OUT, BUT IT'S GONNA TAKE SOME TIME.
TIME WE DON'T HAVE IF NICO AND BLUE ARE MISSING.
YEAH, WE'RE ON THE SAME PAGE.
ALL RIGHT. HERE HE COMES, LET'S GET SOME ANSWERS.
YES, SO GLAD YOU'RE AWAKE. SHE-HULK WILL SAVE US ALL.
IGNORE HER. SHE'S VERY GROUCHY ABOUT THIS "HAIR SITUATION," FROM WHAT I CAN TELL.
I CAN KILL YOU EVEN WITHOUT MY POWERS, CAROL.
SURE, SURE.

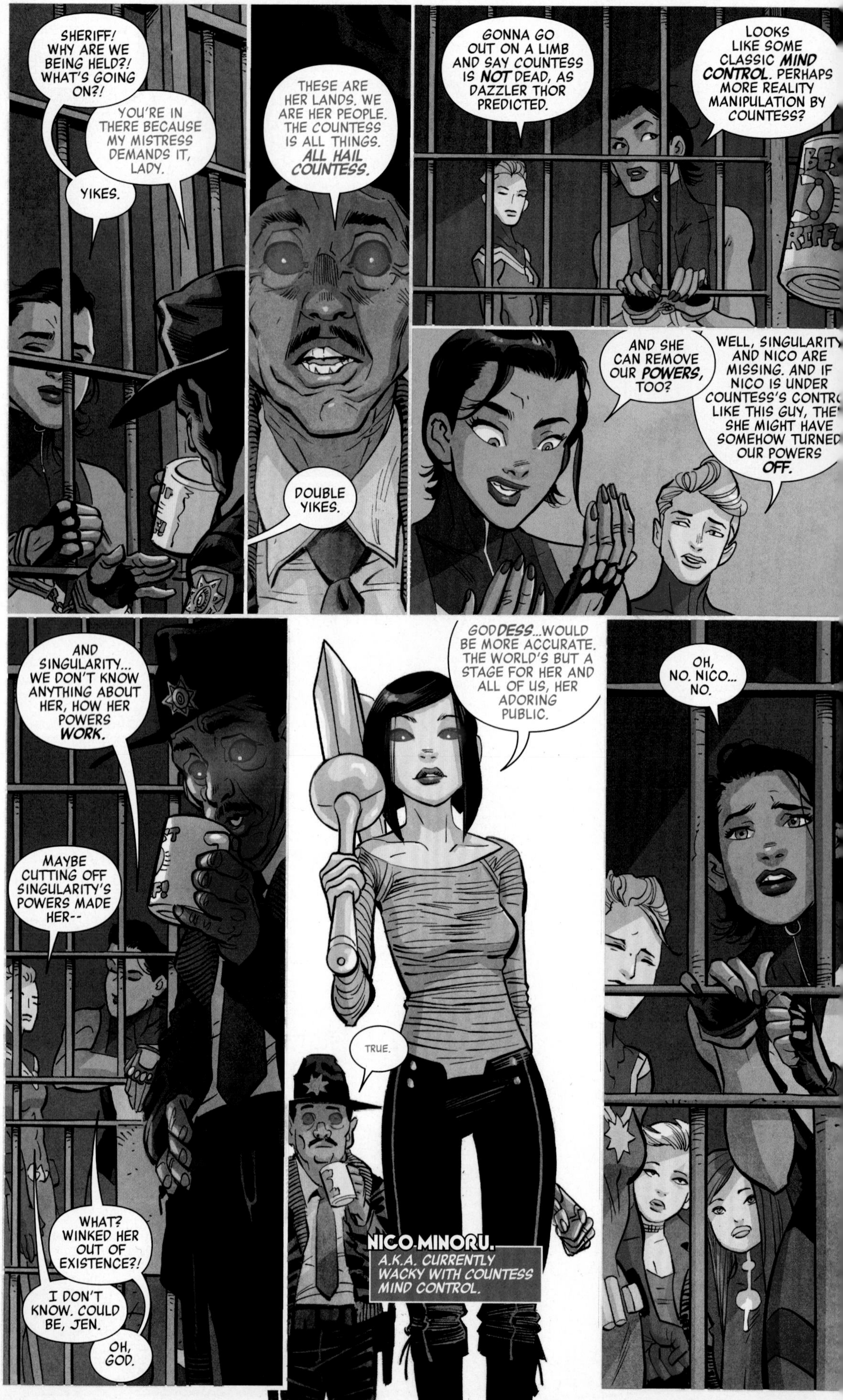

SHERIFF! WHY ARE WE BEING HELD?! WHAT'S GOING ON?!
YOU'RE IN THERE BECAUSE MY MISTRESS DEMANDS IT, LADY.
YIKES.
THESE ARE HER LANDS. WE ARE HER PEOPLE. THE COUNTESS IS ALL THINGS. ALL HAIL COUNTESS.
DOUBLE YIKES.
GONNA GO OUT ON A LIMB AND SAY COUNTESS IS NOT DEAD, AS DAZZLER THOR PREDICTED.
LOOKS LIKE SOME CLASSIC MIND CONTROL. PERHAPS MORE REALITY MANIPULATION BY COUNTESS?
AND SHE CAN REMOVE OUR POWERS, TOO?
WELL, SINGULARITY AND NICO ARE MISSING. AND IF NICO IS UNDER COUNTESS'S CONTRO LIKE THIS GUY, THE SHE MIGHT HAVE SOMEHOW TURNED OUR POWERS OFF.
AND SINGULARITY... WE DON'T KNOW ANYTHING ABOUT HER, HOW HER POWERS WORK.
MAYBE CUTTING OFF SINGULARITY'S POWERS MADE HER--
WHAT? WINKED HER OUT OF EXISTENCE?!
I DON'T KNOW. COULD BE, JEN.
OH, GOD.
GODDESS...WOULD BE MORE ACCURATE. THE WORLD'S BUT A STAGE FOR HER AND ALL OF US, HER ADORING PUBLIC.
TRUE.
NICO MINORU.
A.K.A. CURRENTLY WACKY WITH COUNTESS MIND CONTROL.
OH, NO. NICO... NO.

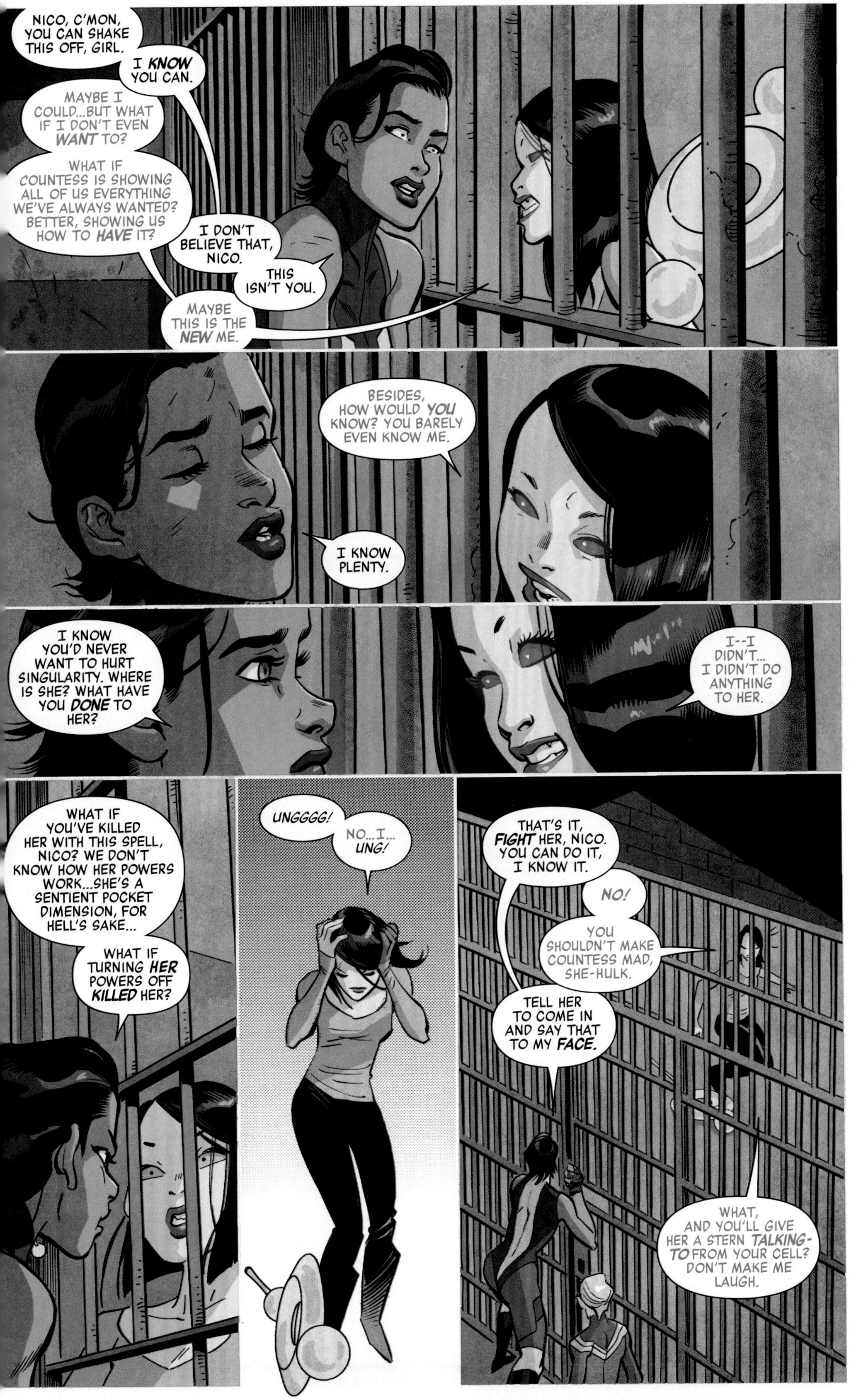
NICO, C'MON, YOU CAN SHAKE THIS OFF, GIRL.
I KNOW YOU CAN.
MAYBE I COULD...BUT WHAT IF I DON'T EVEN WANT TO?
WHAT IF COUNTESS IS SHOWING ALL OF US EVERYTHING WE'VE ALWAYS WANTED? BETTER, SHOWING US HOW TO HAVE IT?
I DON'T BELIEVE THAT, NICO.
THIS ISN'T YOU.
MAYBE THIS IS THE NEW ME.
BESIDES, HOW WOULD YOU KNOW? YOU BARELY EVEN KNOW ME.
I KNOW PLENTY.
I KNOW YOU'D NEVER WANT TO HURT SINGULARITY. WHERE IS SHE? WHAT HAVE YOU DONE TO HER?
I--I DIDN'T... I DIDN'T DO ANYTHING TO HER.
WHAT IF YOU'VE KILLED HER WITH THIS SPELL, NICO? WE DON'T KNOW HOW HER POWERS WORK...SHE'S A SENTIENT POCKET DIMENSION, FOR HELL'S SAKE...
WHAT IF TURNING HER POWERS OFF KILLED HER?
UNGGGG!
NO...I... UNG!
THAT'S IT, FIGHT HER, NICO. YOU CAN DO IT, I KNOW IT.
NO!
YOU SHOULDN'T MAKE COUNTESS MAD, SHE-HULK.
TELL HER TO COME IN AND SAY THAT TO MY FACE.
WHAT, AND YOU'LL GIVE HER A STERN TALKING-TO FROM YOUR CELL? DON'T MAKE ME LAUGH.

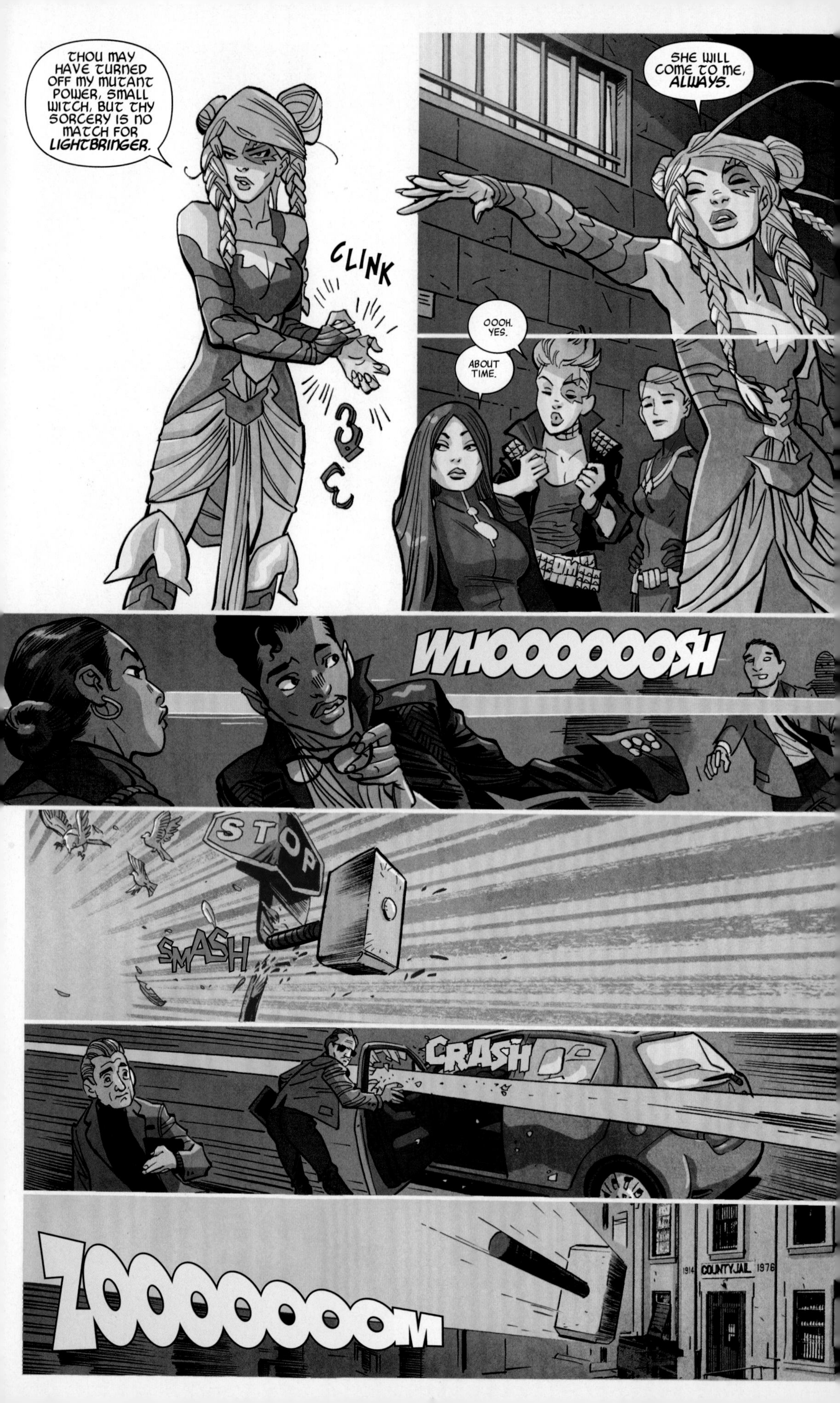
THOU MAY HAVE TURNED OFF MY MUTANT POWER, SMALL WITCH, BUT THY SORCERY IS NO MATCH FOR LIGHTBRINGER.
CLINK
SHE WILL COME TO ME, ALWAYS.
OOOH. YES.
ABOUT TIME.
WHOOOOOOOSH
STOP
SMASH
CRASH
1914 COUNTY JAIL 1976
ZOOOOOOOM

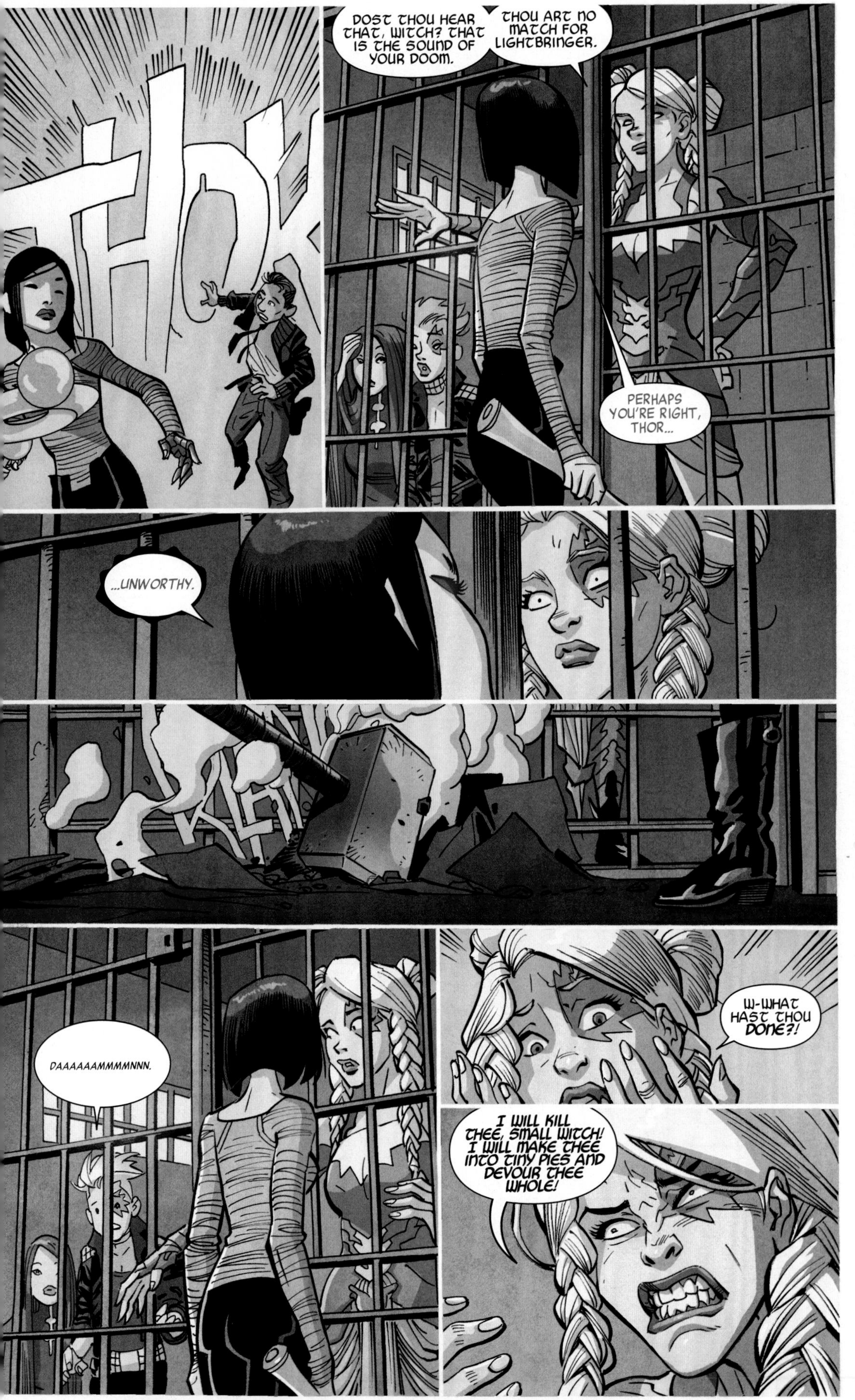
THOK
DOST THOU HEAR THAT, WITCH? THAT IS THE SOUND OF YOUR DOOM.
THOU ART NO MATCH FOR LIGHTBRINGER.
PERHAPS YOU'RE RIGHT, THOR...
...UNWORTHY.
DAAAAAAMMMMNNN.
W-WHAT HAST THOU DONE?!
I WILL KILL THEE, SMALL WITCH! I WILL MAKE THEE INTO TINY PIES AND DEVOUR THEE WHOLE!

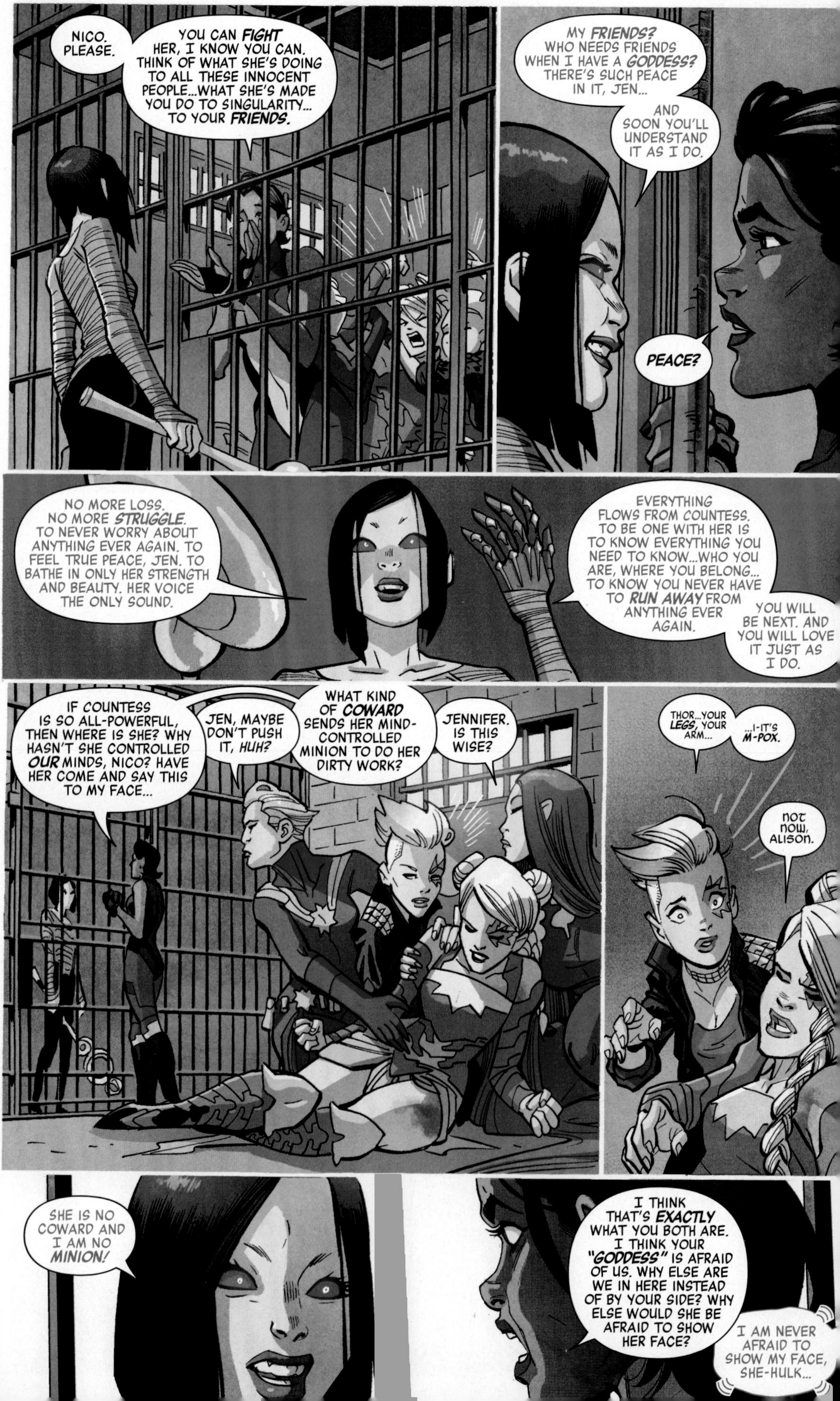
NICO. PLEASE.
YOU CAN FIGHT HER, I KNOW YOU CAN. THINK OF WHAT SHE'S DOING TO ALL THESE INNOCENT PEOPLE...WHAT SHE'S MADE YOU DO TO SINGULARITY... TO YOUR FRIENDS.
MY FRIENDS? WHO NEEDS FRIENDS WHEN I HAVE A GODDESS? THERE'S SUCH PEACE IN IT, JEN...
AND SOON YOU'LL UNDERSTAND IT AS I DO.
PEACE?
NO MORE LOSS. NO MORE STRUGGLE. TO NEVER WORRY ABOUT ANYTHING EVER AGAIN. TO FEEL TRUE PEACE, JEN. TO BATHE IN ONLY HER STRENGTH AND BEAUTY. HER VOICE THE ONLY SOUND.
EVERYTHING FLOWS FROM COUNTESS. TO BE ONE WITH HER IS TO KNOW EVERYTHING YOU NEED TO KNOW...WHO YOU ARE, WHERE YOU BELONG... TO KNOW YOU NEVER HAVE TO RUN AWAY FROM ANYTHING EVER AGAIN.
YOU WILL BE NEXT. AND YOU WILL LOVE IT JUST AS I DO.
IF COUNTESS IS SO ALL-POWERFUL, THEN WHERE IS SHE? WHY HASN'T SHE CONTROLLED OUR MINDS, NICO? HAVE HER COME AND SAY THIS TO MY FACE...
JEN, MAYBE DON'T PUSH IT, HUH?
WHAT KIND OF COWARD SENDS HER MIND-CONTROLLED MINION TO DO HER DIRTY WORK?
JENNIFER. IS THIS WISE?
THOR...YOUR LEGS, YOUR ARM...
...I-IT'S M-POX.
NOT NOW, ALISON.
SHE IS NO COWARD AND I AM NO MINION!
I THINK THAT'S EXACTLY WHAT YOU BOTH ARE. I THINK YOUR "GODDESS" IS AFRAID OF US. WHY ELSE ARE WE IN HERE INSTEAD OF BY YOUR SIDE? WHY ELSE WOULD SHE BE AFRAID TO SHOW HER FACE?
I AM NEVER AFRAID TO SHOW MY FACE, SHE-HULK...

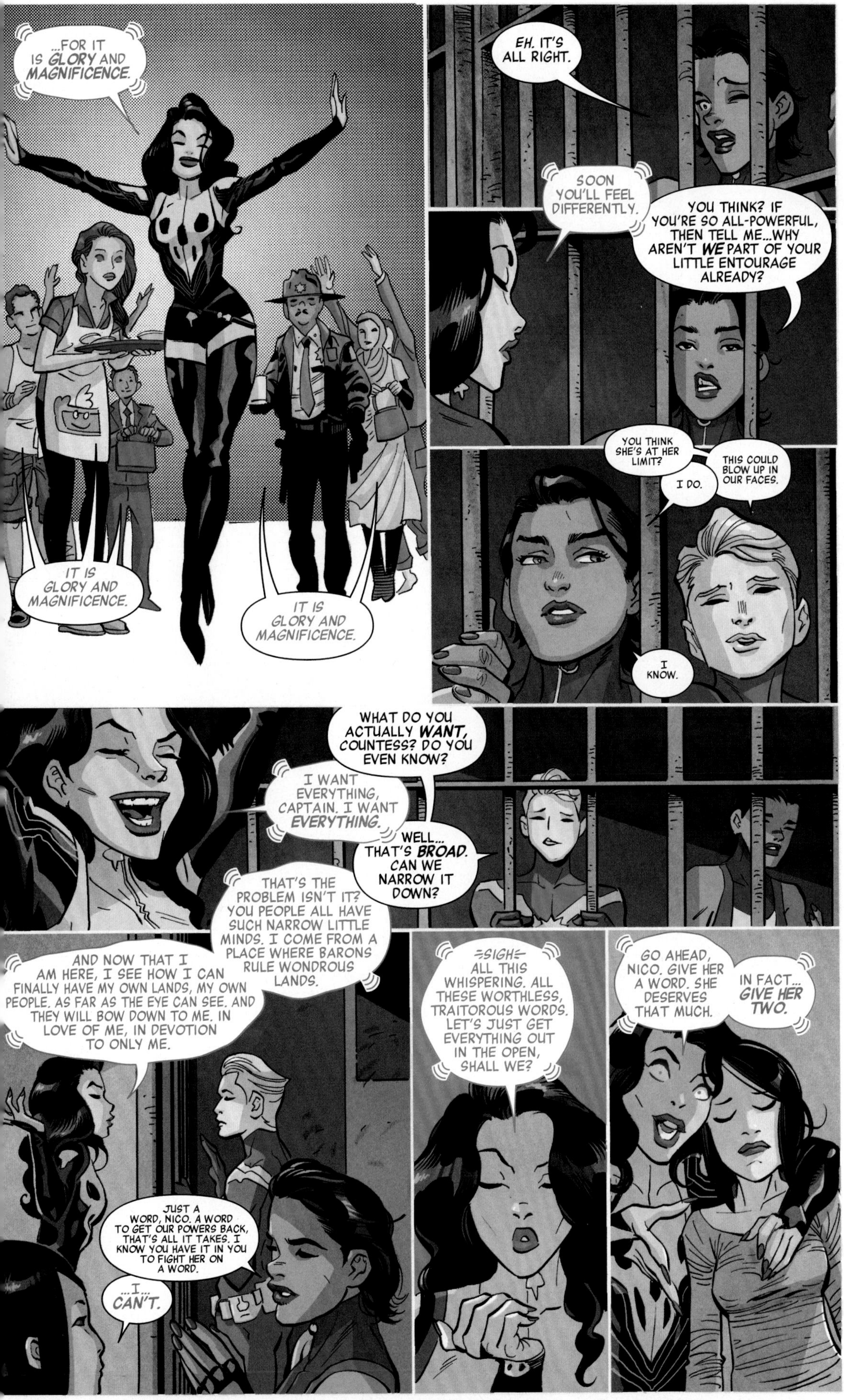
...FOR IT IS GLORY AND MAGNIFICENCE.
IT IS GLORY AND MAGNIFICENCE.
IT IS GLORY AND MAGNIFICENCE.
EH. IT'S ALL RIGHT.
SOON YOU'LL FEEL DIFFERENTLY.
YOU THINK? IF YOU'RE SO ALL-POWERFUL, THEN TELL ME...WHY AREN'T WE PART OF YOUR LITTLE ENTOURAGE ALREADY?
YOU THINK SHE'S AT HER LIMIT?
I DO.
THIS COULD BLOW UP IN OUR FACES.
I KNOW.
WHAT DO YOU ACTUALLY WANT, COUNTESS? DO YOU EVEN KNOW?
I WANT EVERYTHING, CAPTAIN. I WANT EVERYTHING.
WELL... THAT'S BROAD. CAN WE NARROW IT DOWN?
THAT'S THE PROBLEM ISN'T IT? YOU PEOPLE ALL HAVE SUCH NARROW LITTLE MINDS. I COME FROM A PLACE WHERE BARONS RULE WONDROUS LANDS.
AND NOW THAT I AM HERE, I SEE HOW I CAN FINALLY HAVE MY OWN LANDS, MY OWN PEOPLE. AS FAR AS THE EYE CAN SEE. AND THEY WILL BOW DOWN TO ME. IN LOVE OF ME, IN DEVOTION TO ONLY ME.
JUST A WORD, NICO. A WORD TO GET OUR POWERS BACK, THAT'S ALL IT TAKES. I KNOW YOU HAVE IT IN YOU TO FIGHT HER ON A WORD.
...I... CAN'T.
=SIGH= ALL THIS WHISPERING. ALL THESE WORTHLESS, TRAITOROUS WORDS. LET'S JUST GET EVERYTHING OUT IN THE OPEN, SHALL WE?
GO AHEAD, NICO. GIVE HER A WORD. SHE DESERVES THAT MUCH.
IN FACT... GIVE HER TWO.

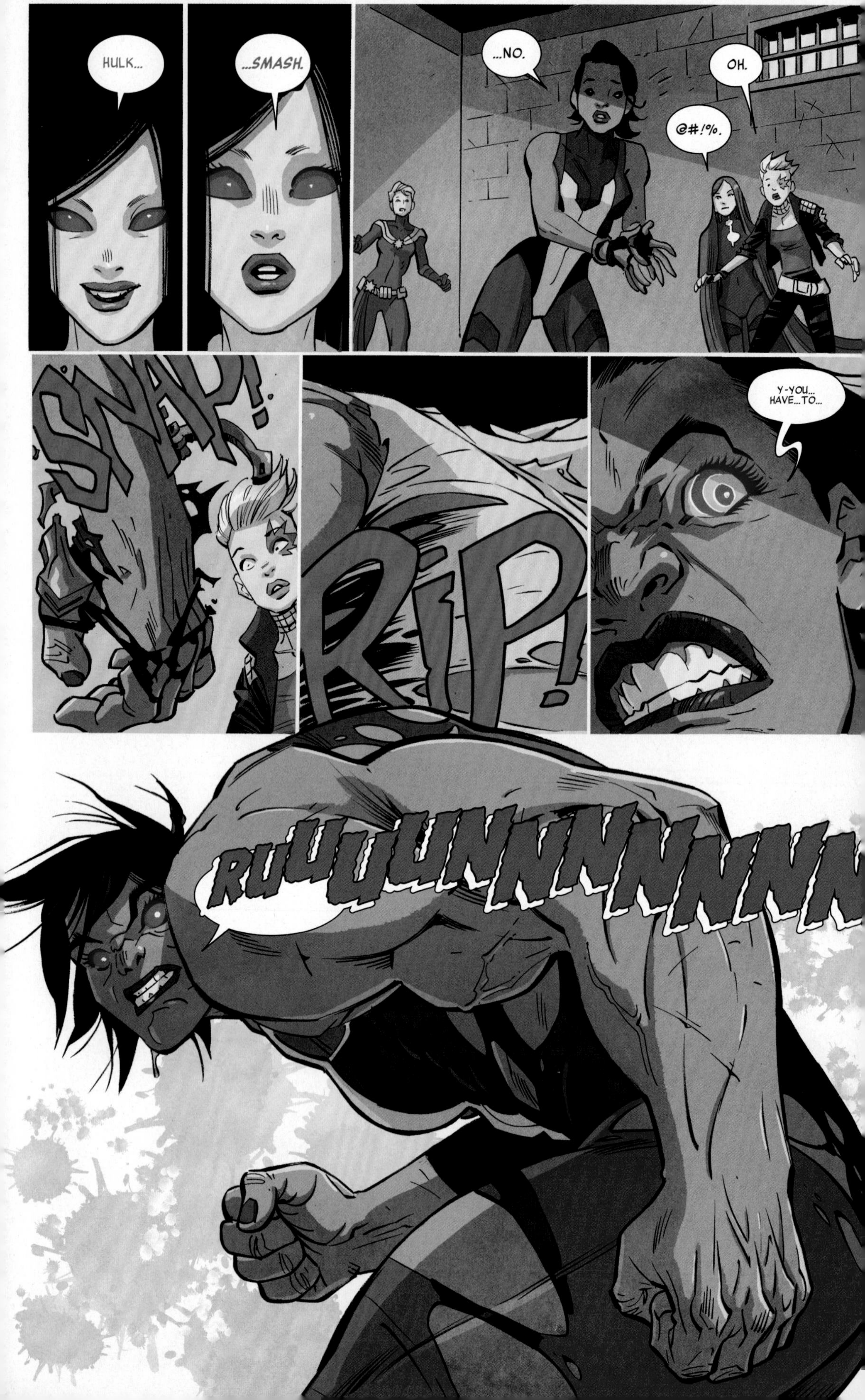
HULK...
...SMASH.
...NO.
OH.
@#!%.
SNAP!
RIP!
Y-YOU... HAVE... TO...
RUUUUNNNNNNNNN

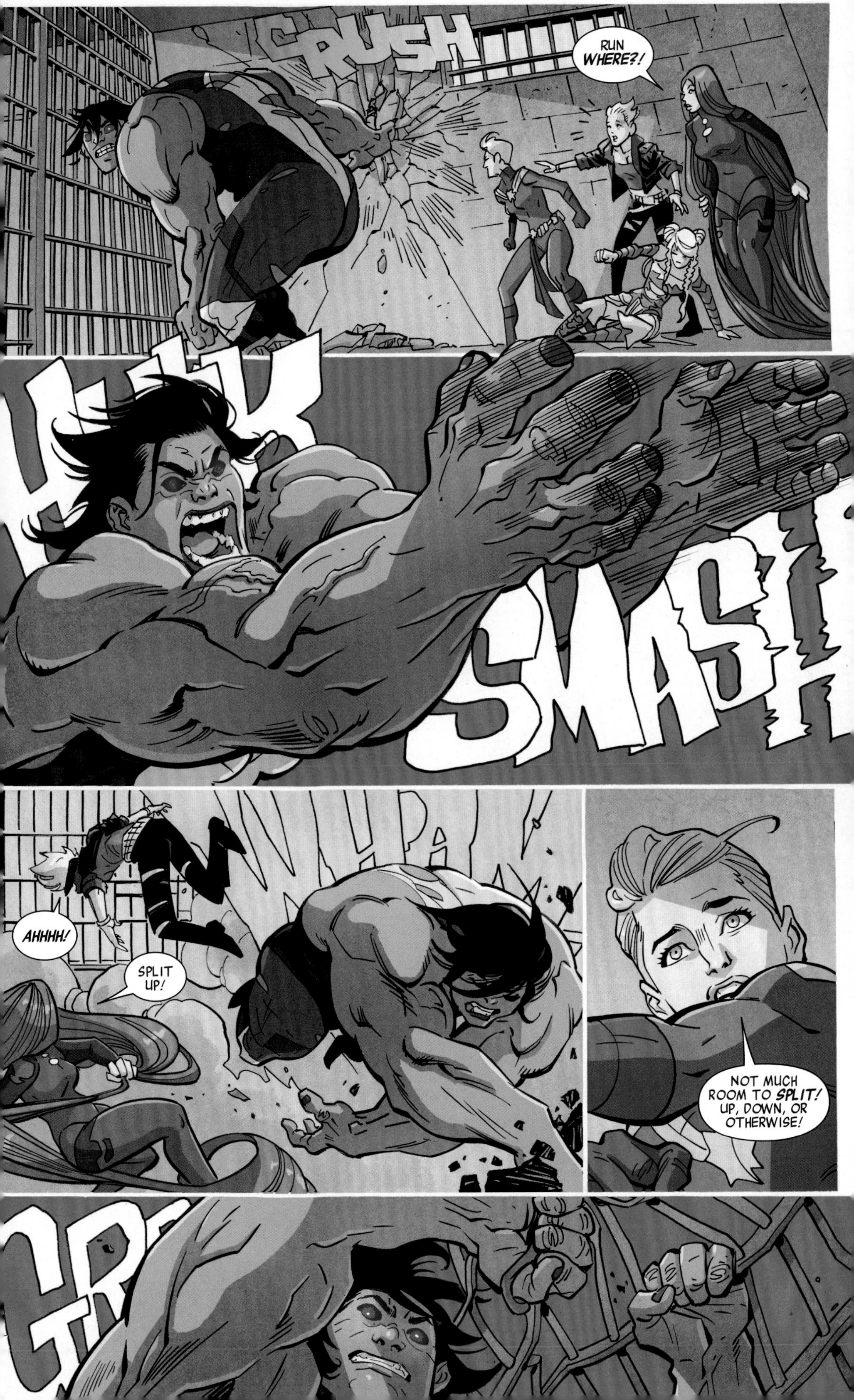
CRUSH
RUN WHERE?!
SMASH
AHHHH!
SPLIT UP!
NOT MUCH ROOM TO SPLIT! UP, DOWN, OR OTHERWISE!

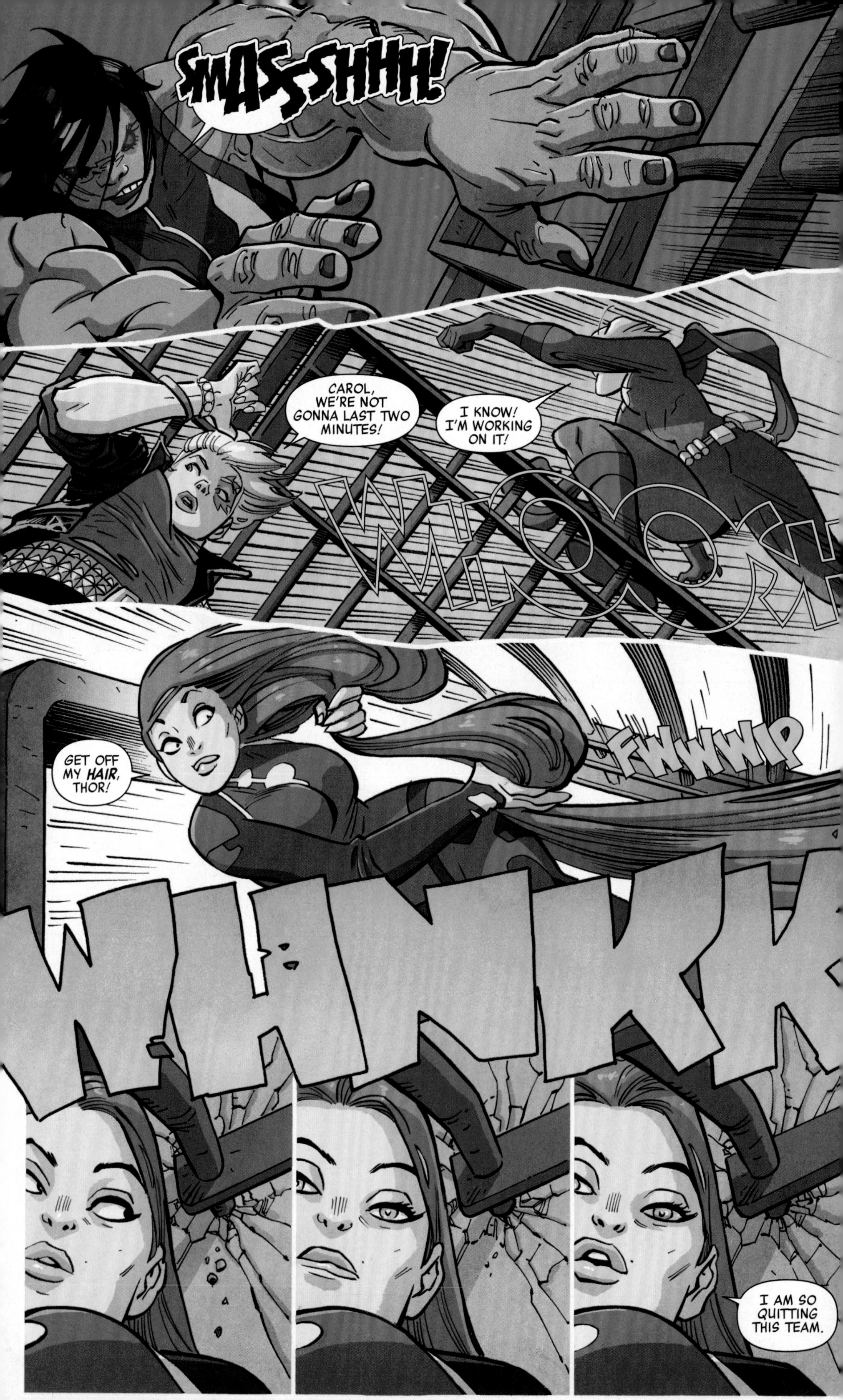
SMASSSHHH!
CAROL, WE'RE NOT GONNA LAST TWO MINUTES!
I KNOW! I'M WORKING ON IT!
GET OFF MY HAIR, THOR!
FWWWIP
WHNKK
I AM SO QUITTING THIS TEAM.

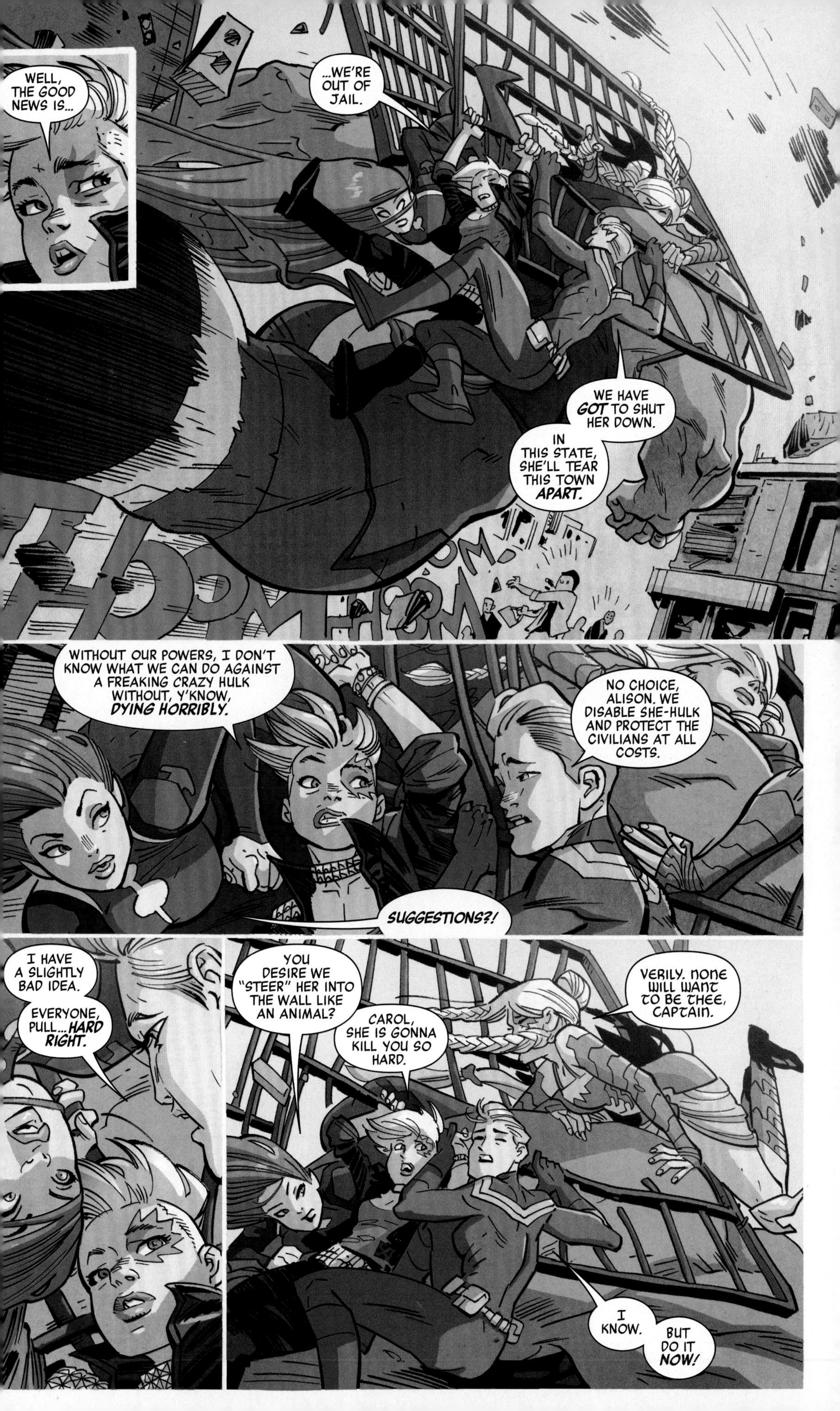

WELL, THE GOOD NEWS IS...
...WE'RE OUT OF JAIL.
WE HAVE GOT TO SHUT HER DOWN.
IN THIS STATE, SHE'LL TEAR THIS TOWN APART.
THOOM
THOOM
WITHOUT OUR POWERS, I DON'T KNOW WHAT WE CAN DO AGAINST A FREAKING CRAZY HULK WITHOUT, Y'KNOW, DYING HORRIBLY.
NO CHOICE, ALISON. WE DISABLE SHE-HULK AND PROTECT THE CIVILIANS AT ALL COSTS.
SUGGESTIONS?!
I HAVE A SLIGHTLY BAD IDEA.
EVERYONE, PULL... HARD RIGHT.
YOU DESIRE WE "STEER" HER INTO THE WALL LIKE AN ANIMAL?
CAROL, SHE IS GONNA KILL YOU SO HARD.
VERILY. NONE WILL WANT TO BE THEE, CAPTAIN.
I KNOW.
BUT DO IT NOW!

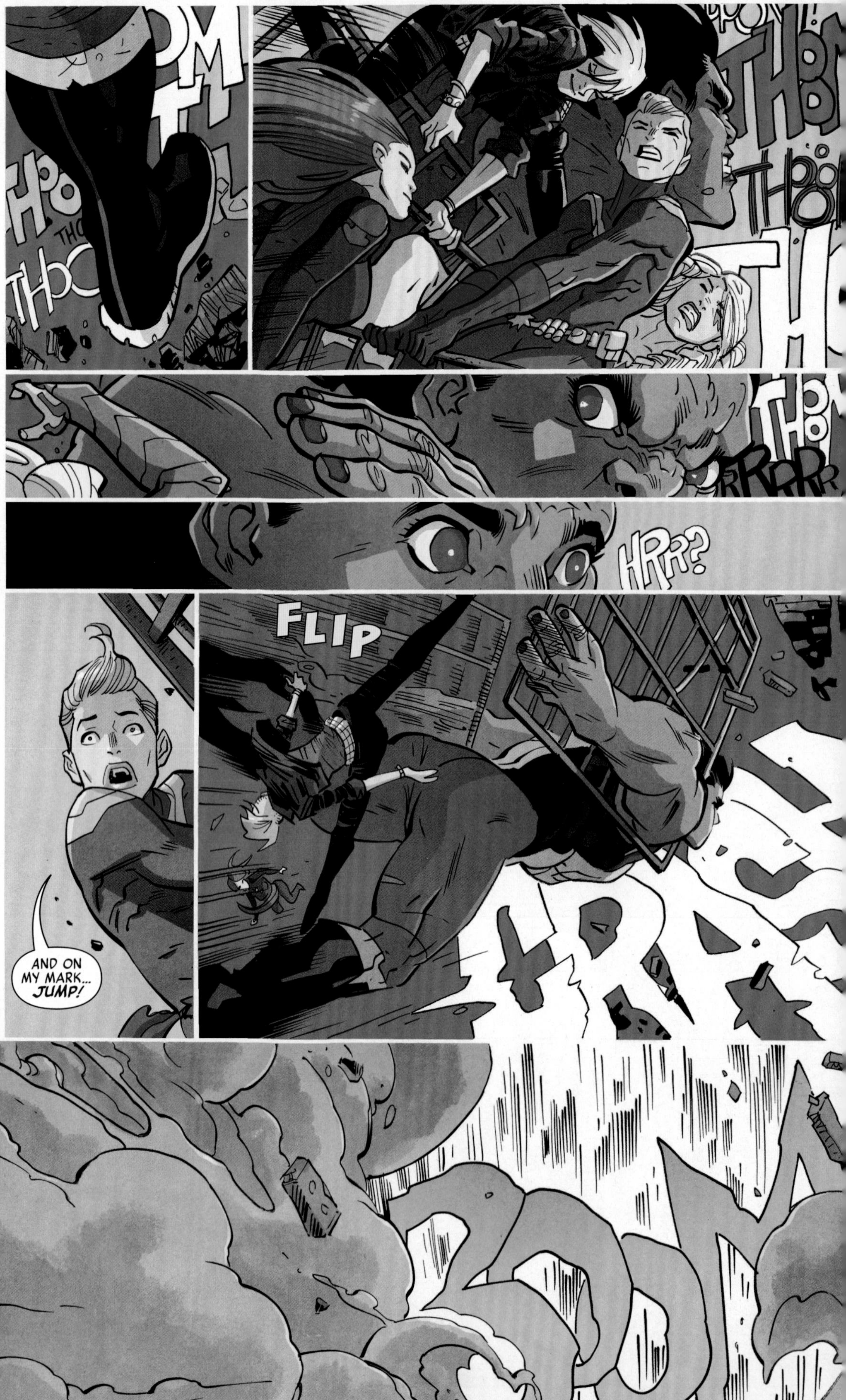
THOOM
THOOM
THOOM THOOM
THOOM
THOOM
THOOM
THOOM THOOM
THOOM
RRRRRRRR
HRRR?
FLIP
AND ON MY MARK... JUMP!
KRASH
BOOM

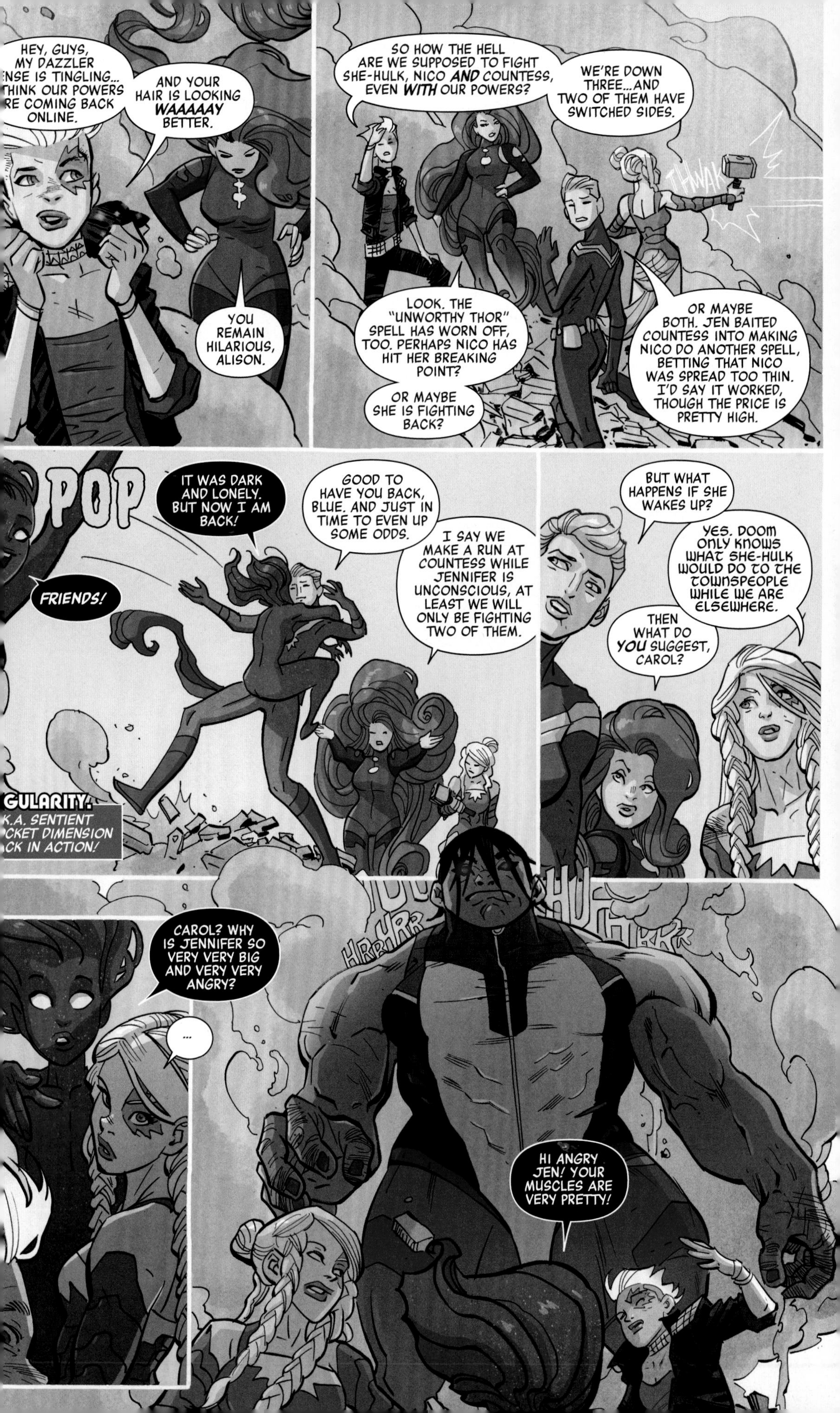
HEY, GUYS, MY DAZZLER ENSE IS TINGLING... THINK OUR POWERS RE COMING BACK ONLINE.
AND YOUR HAIR IS LOOKING WAAAAAY BETTER.
YOU REMAIN HILARIOUS, ALISON.
SO HOW THE HELL ARE WE SUPPOSED TO FIGHT SHE-HULK, NICO AND COUNTESS, EVEN WITH OUR POWERS?
WE'RE DOWN THREE...AND TWO OF THEM HAVE SWITCHED SIDES.
THWAK
LOOK. THE "UNWORTHY THOR" SPELL HAS WORN OFF, TOO. PERHAPS NICO HAS HIT HER BREAKING POINT?
OR MAYBE SHE IS FIGHTING BACK?
OR MAYBE BOTH. JEN BAITED COUNTESS INTO MAKING NICO DO ANOTHER SPELL, BETTING THAT NICO WAS SPREAD TOO THIN. I'D SAY IT WORKED, THOUGH THE PRICE IS PRETTY HIGH.
POP
IT WAS DARK AND LONELY. BUT NOW I AM BACK!
FRIENDS!
GOOD TO HAVE YOU BACK, BLUE. AND JUST IN TIME TO EVEN UP SOME ODDS.
I SAY WE MAKE A RUN AT COUNTESS WHILE JENNIFER IS UNCONSCIOUS, AT LEAST WE WILL ONLY BE FIGHTING TWO OF THEM.
GULARITY: K.A. SENTIENT CKET DIMENSION CK IN ACTION!
BUT WHAT HAPPENS IF SHE WAKES UP?
YES. DOOM ONLY KNOWS WHAT SHE-HULK WOULD DO TO THE TOWNSPEOPLE WHILE WE ARE ELSEWHERE.
THEN WHAT DO YOU SUGGEST, CAROL?
CAROL? WHY IS JENNIFER SO VERY VERY BIG AND VERY VERY ANGRY?
...
HRR HRR
HI ANGRY JEN! YOUR MUSCLES ARE VERY PRETTY!

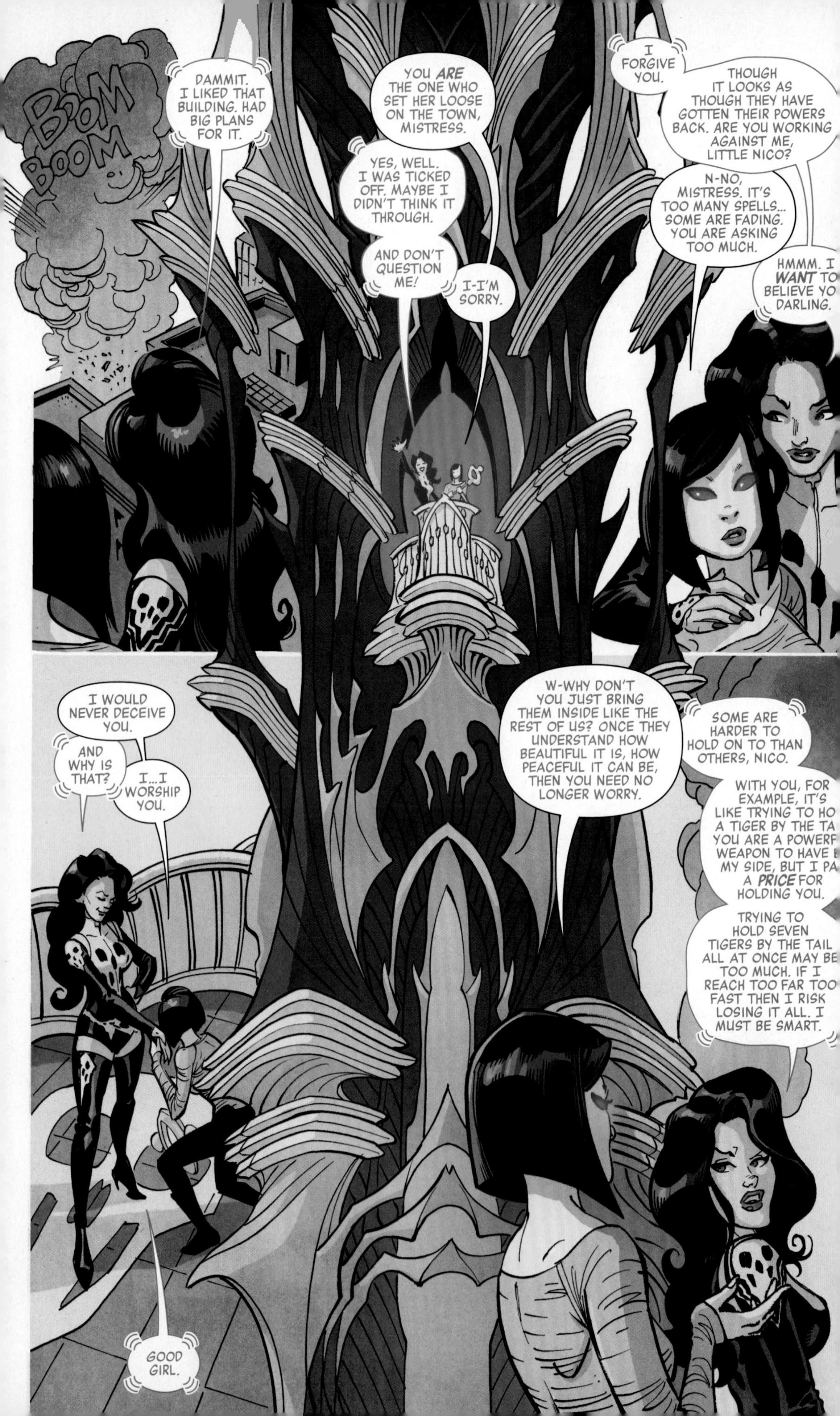
BOOM BOOM
DAMMIT. I LIKED THAT BUILDING. HAD BIG PLANS FOR IT.
YOU ARE THE ONE WHO SET HER LOOSE ON THE TOWN, MISTRESS.
YES, WELL. I WAS TICKED OFF. MAYBE I DIDN'T THINK IT THROUGH.
AND DON'T QUESTION ME!
I-I'M SORRY.
I FORGIVE YOU.
THOUGH IT LOOKS AS THOUGH THEY HAVE GOTTEN THEIR POWERS BACK. ARE YOU WORKING AGAINST ME, LITTLE NICO?
N-NO, MISTRESS. IT'S TOO MANY SPELLS... SOME ARE FADING. YOU ARE ASKING TOO MUCH.
HMMM. I WANT TO BELIEVE YO DARLING.
I WOULD NEVER DECEIVE YOU.
AND WHY IS THAT?
I...I WORSHIP YOU.
GOOD GIRL.
W-WHY DON'T YOU JUST BRING THEM INSIDE LIKE THE REST OF US? ONCE THEY UNDERSTAND HOW BEAUTIFUL IT IS, HOW PEACEFUL IT CAN BE, THEN YOU NEED NO LONGER WORRY.
SOME ARE HARDER TO HOLD ON TO THAN OTHERS, NICO.
WITH YOU, FOR EXAMPLE, IT'S LIKE TRYING TO HO A TIGER BY THE TA YOU ARE A POWERF WEAPON TO HAVE MY SIDE, BUT I PA A PRICE FOR HOLDING YOU.
TRYING TO HOLD SEVEN TIGERS BY THE TAIL ALL AT ONCE MAY BE TOO MUCH. IF I REACH TOO FAR TOO FAST THEN I RISK LOSING IT ALL. I MUST BE SMART.

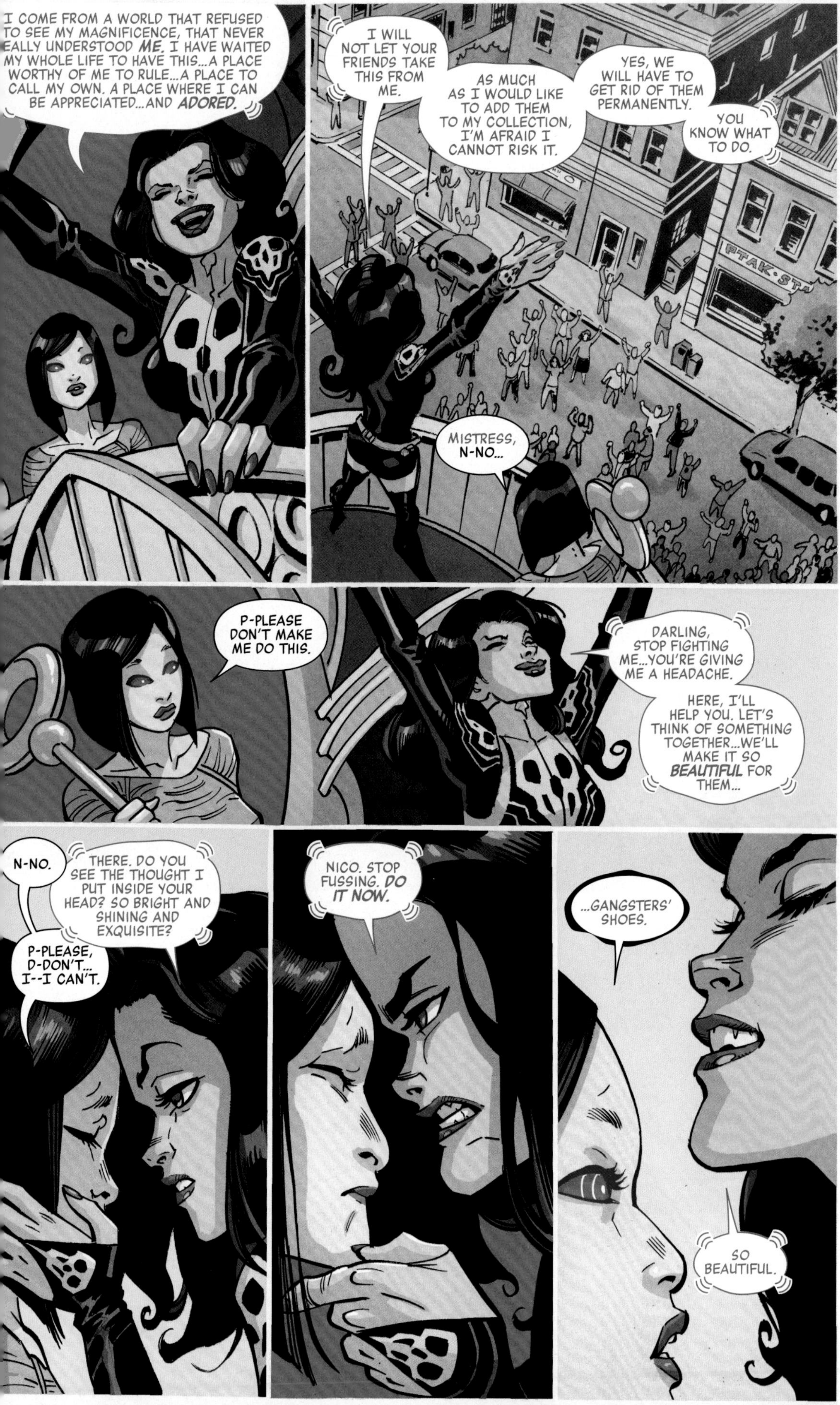
I COME FROM A WORLD THAT REFUSED TO SEE MY MAGNIFICENCE, THAT NEVER EALLY UNDERSTOOD ME. I HAVE WAITED MY WHOLE LIFE TO HAVE THIS...A PLACE WORTHY OF ME TO RULE...A PLACE TO CALL MY OWN. A PLACE WHERE I CAN BE APPRECIATED...AND ADORED.
I WILL NOT LET YOUR FRIENDS TAKE THIS FROM ME.
AS MUCH AS I WOULD LIKE TO ADD THEM TO MY COLLECTION, I'M AFRAID I CANNOT RISK IT.
YES, WE WILL HAVE TO GET RID OF THEM PERMANENTLY.
YOU KNOW WHAT TO DO.
PTAK·ST
MISTRESS, N-NO...
P-PLEASE DON'T MAKE ME DO THIS.
DARLING, STOP FIGHTING ME...YOU'RE GIVING ME A HEADACHE.
HERE, I'LL HELP YOU. LET'S THINK OF SOMETHING TOGETHER...WE'LL MAKE IT SO BEAUTIFUL FOR THEM...
N-NO.
THERE. DO YOU SEE THE THOUGHT I PUT INSIDE YOUR HEAD? SO BRIGHT AND SHINING AND EXQUISITE?
P-PLEASE, D-DON'T... I--I CAN'T.
NICO. STOP FUSSING. DO IT NOW.
...GANGSTERS' SHOES.
SO BEAUTIFUL.

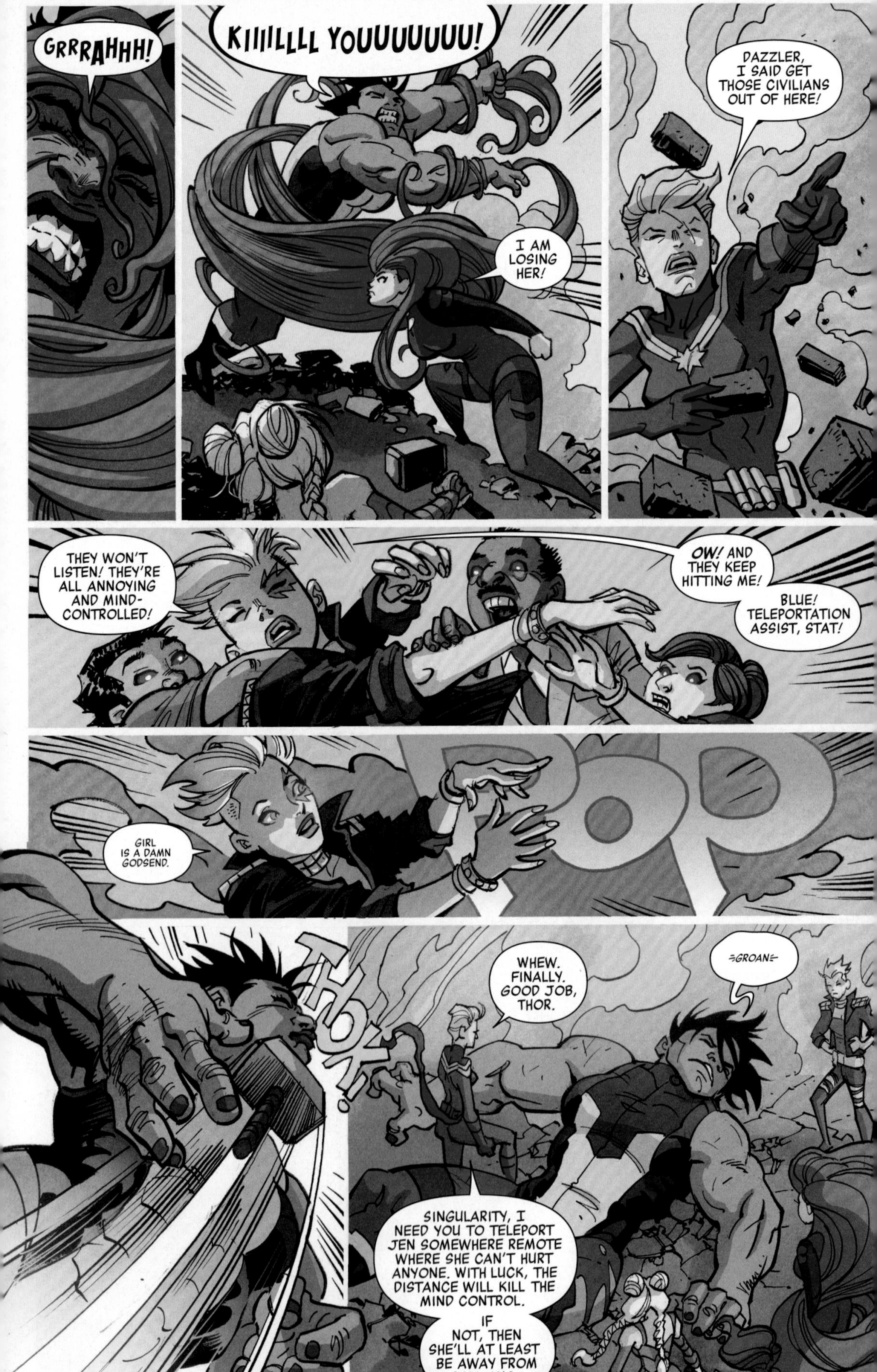

GRRRAHHH!
KIIIILLLL YOUUUUUUU!
I AM LOSING HER!
DAZZLER, I SAID GET THOSE CIVILIANS OUT OF HERE!
THEY WON'T LISTEN! THEY'RE ALL ANNOYING AND MIND-CONTROLLED!
OW! AND THEY KEEP HITTING ME!
BLUE! TELEPORTATION ASSIST, STAT!
GIRL IS A DAMN GODSEND.
THOK!
WHEW. FINALLY. GOOD JOB, THOR.
GROAN
SINGULARITY, I NEED YOU TO TELEPORT JEN SOMEWHERE REMOTE WHERE SHE CAN'T HURT ANYONE. WITH LUCK, THE DISTANCE WILL KILL THE MIND CONTROL.
IF NOT, THEN SHE'LL AT LEAST BE AWAY FROM CIVILIANS...

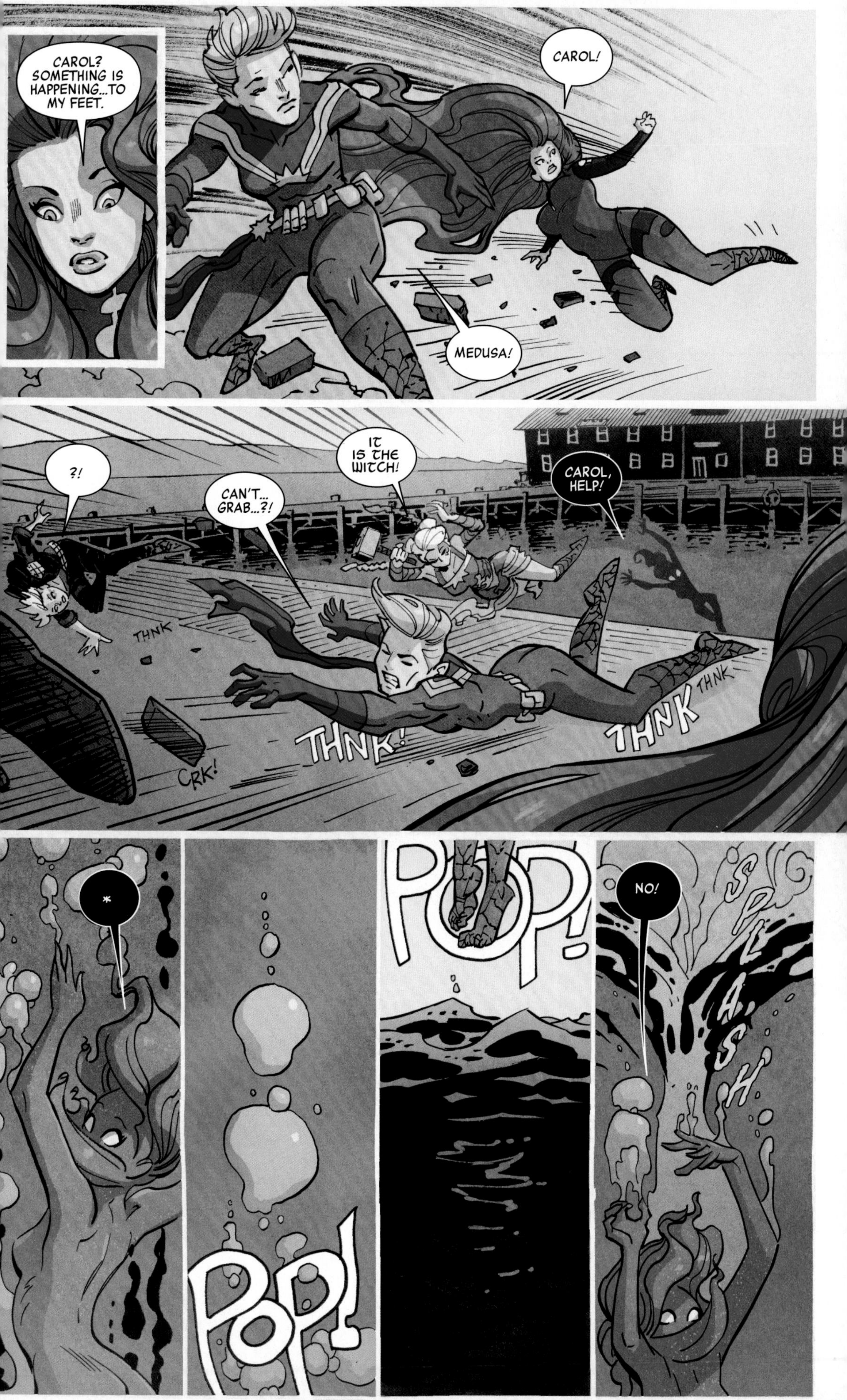
CAROL? SOMETHING IS HAPPENING...TO MY FEET.
CAROL!
MEDUSA!
?!
CAN'T... GRAB...?!
IT IS THE WITCH!
CAROL, HELP!
THNK
THNK!
THNK
THNK
CRK!
*
POP!
POP!
NO!
SPLASH

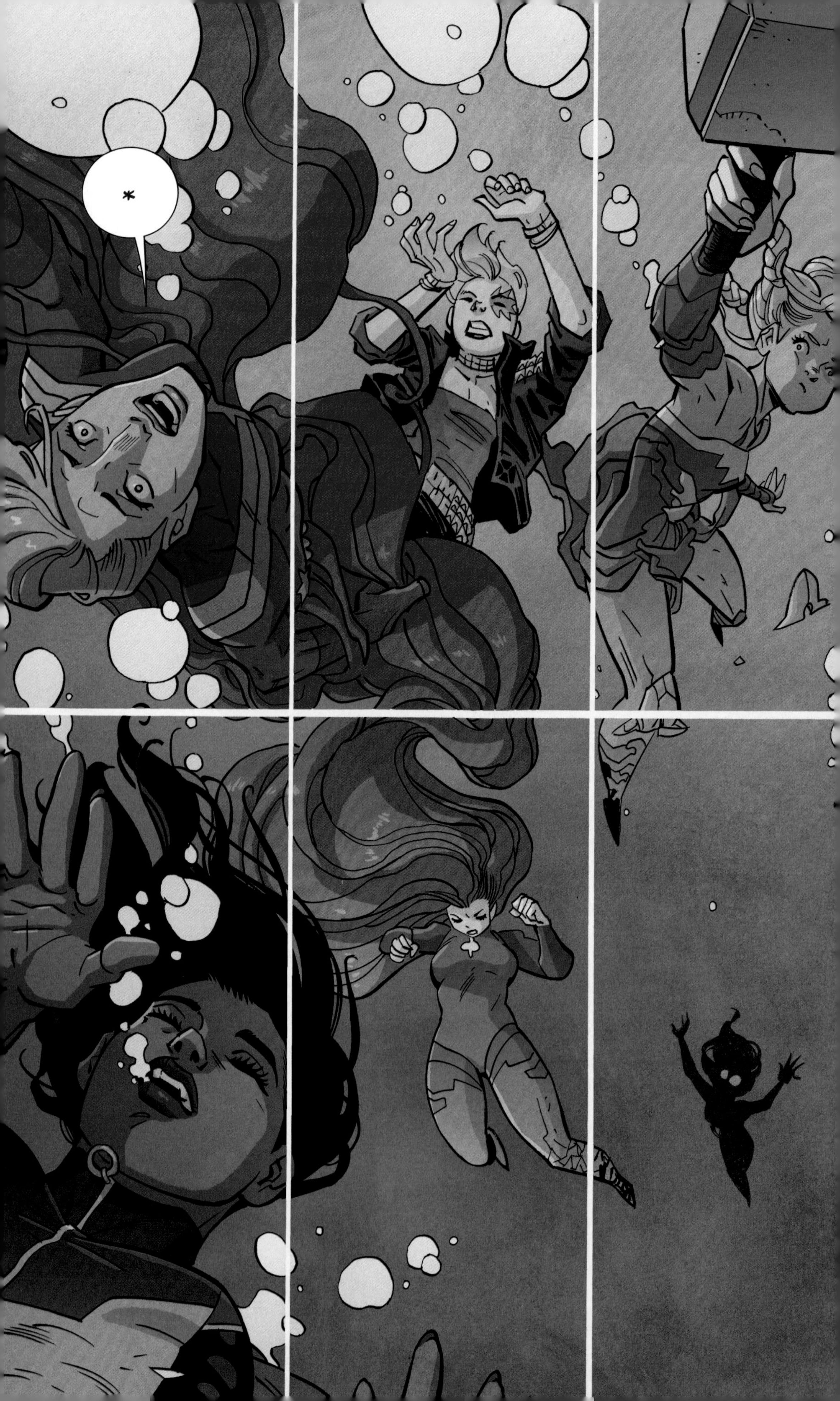
*

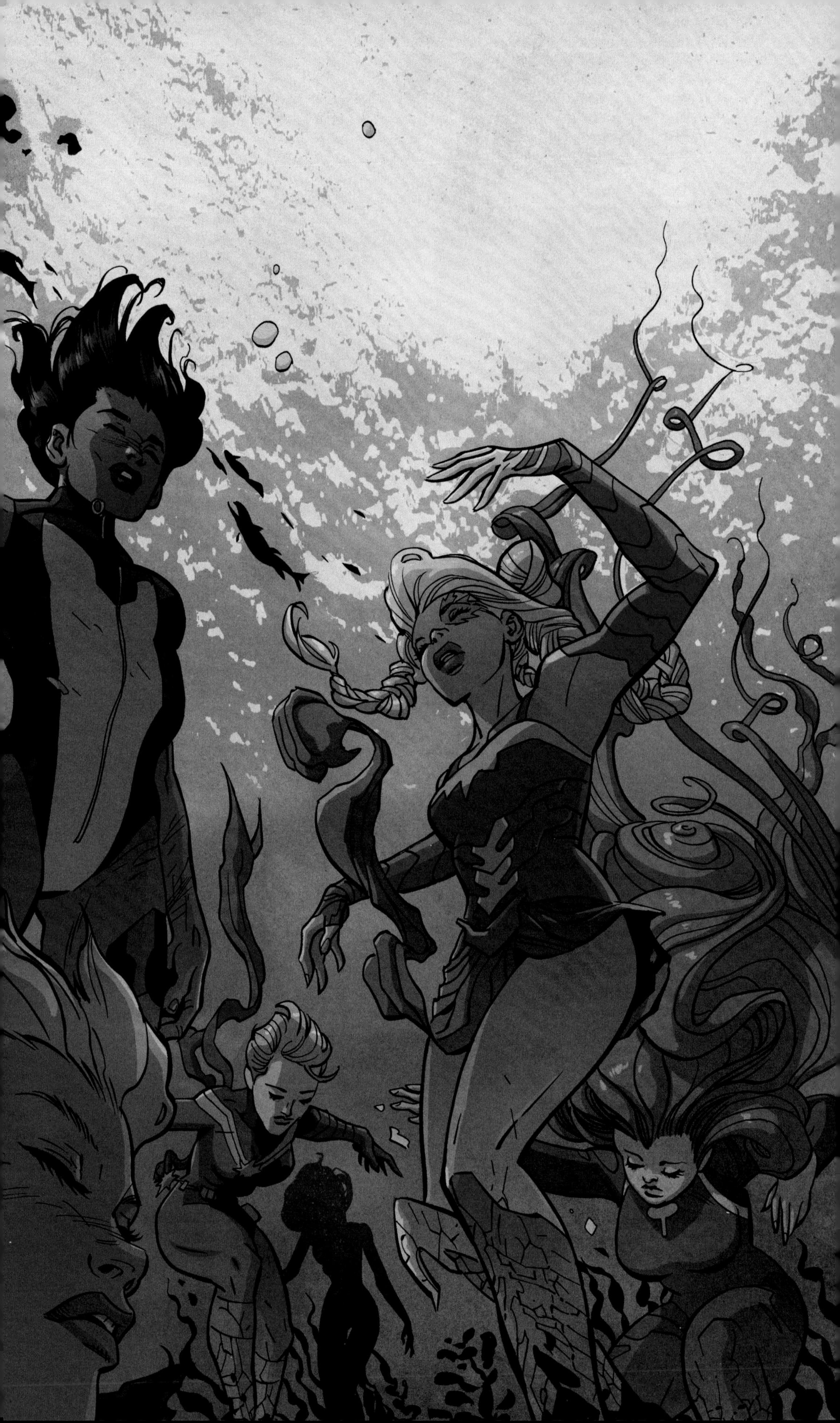

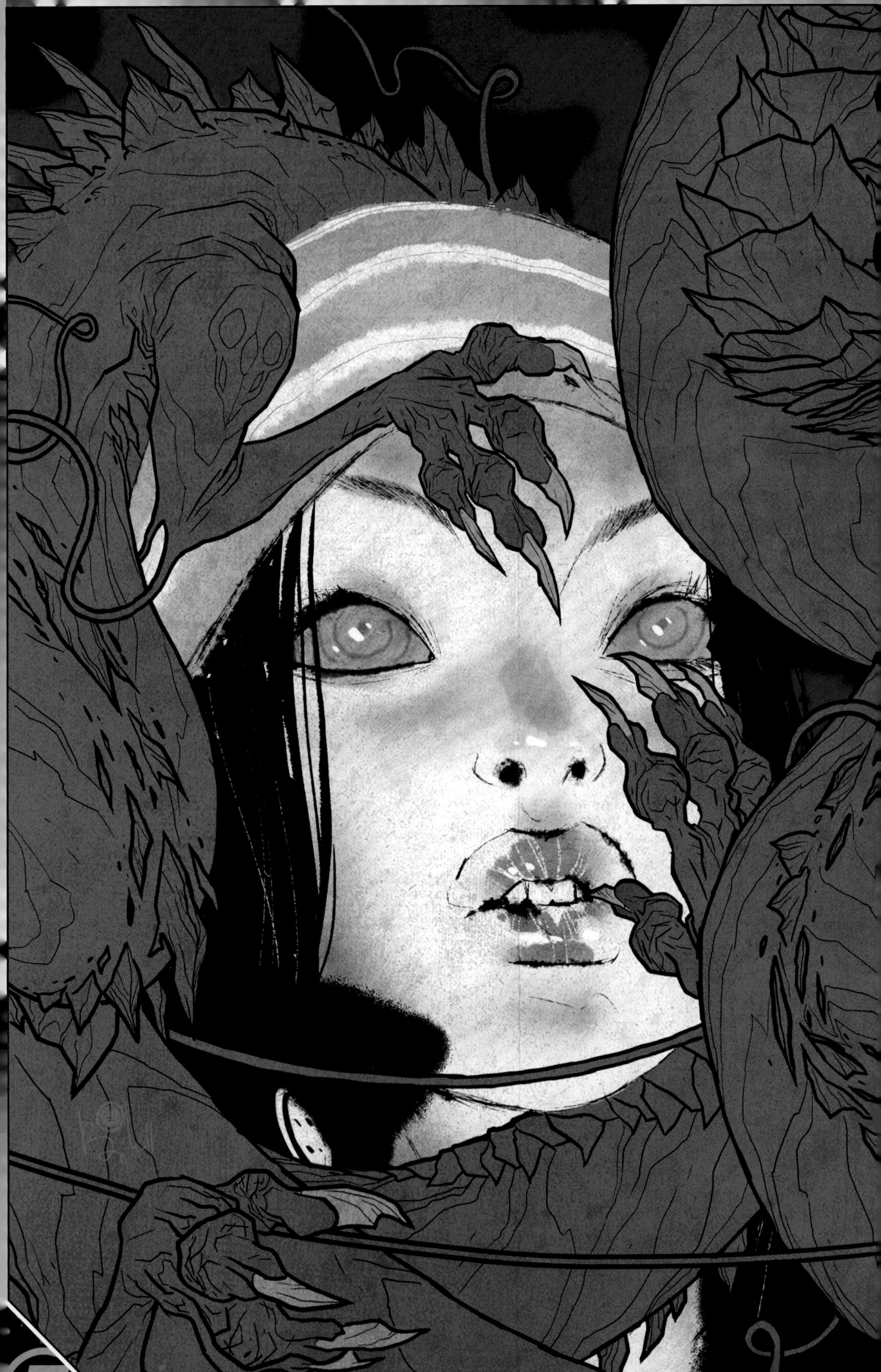

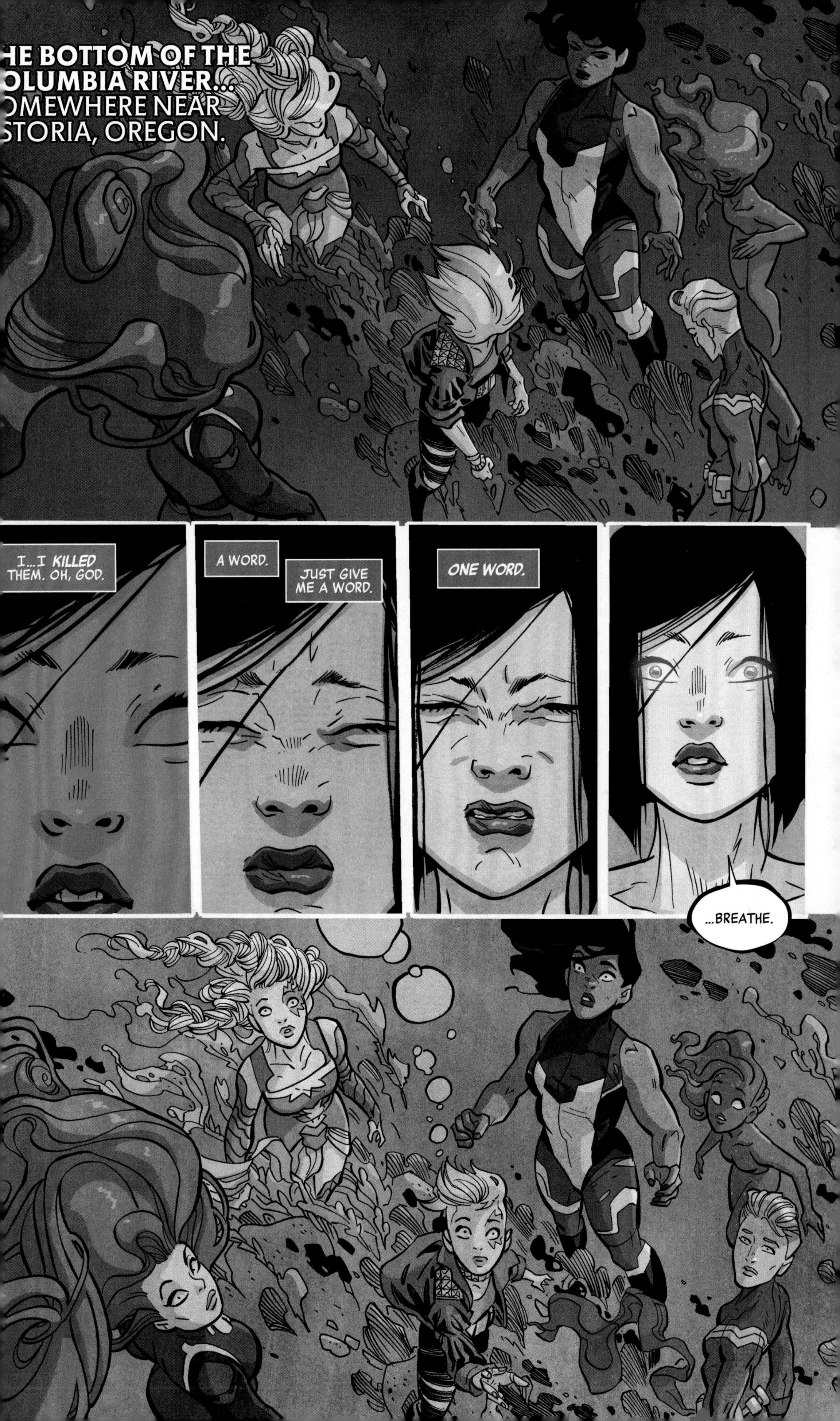

HE BOTTOM OF THE OLUMBIA RIVER... OMEWHERE NEAR STORIA, OREGON.
I...I KILLED THEM. OH, GOD.
A WORD.
JUST GIVE ME A WORD.
ONE WORD.
...BREATHE.

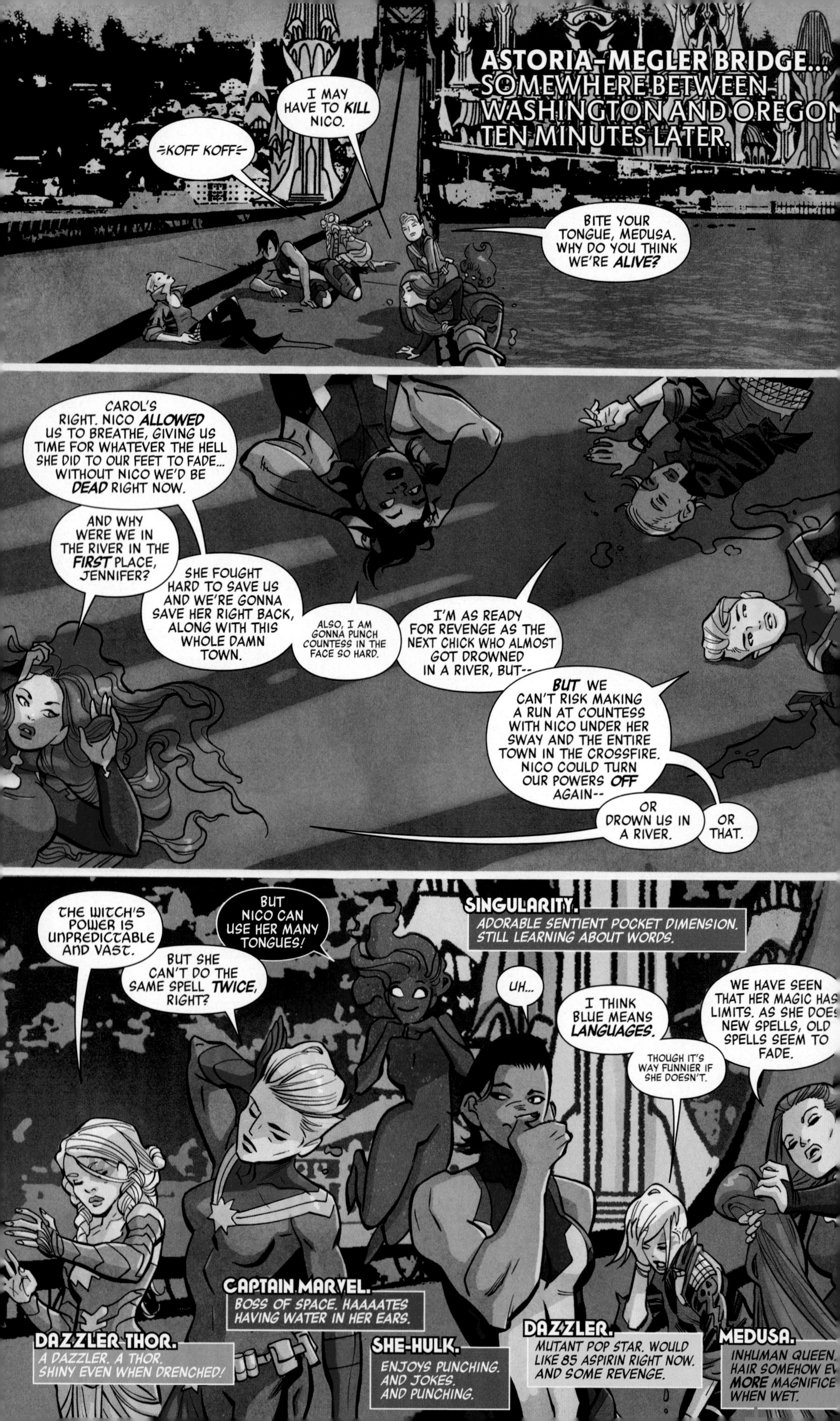

ASTORIA-MEGLER BRIDGE... SOMEWHERE BETWEEN WASHINGTON AND OREGON TEN MINUTES LATER.
=KOFF KOFF=
I MAY HAVE TO KILL NICO.
BITE YOUR TONGUE, MEDUSA. WHY DO YOU THINK WE'RE ALIVE?
CAROL'S RIGHT. NICO ALLOWED US TO BREATHE, GIVING US TIME FOR WHATEVER THE HELL SHE DID TO OUR FEET TO FADE... WITHOUT NICO WE'D BE DEAD RIGHT NOW.
AND WHY WERE WE IN THE RIVER IN THE FIRST PLACE, JENNIFER?
SHE FOUGHT HARD TO SAVE US AND WE'RE GONNA SAVE HER RIGHT BACK, ALONG WITH THIS WHOLE DAMN TOWN.
ALSO, I AM GONNA PUNCH COUNTESS IN THE FACE SO HARD.
I'M AS READY FOR REVENGE AS THE NEXT CHICK WHO ALMOST GOT DROWNED IN A RIVER, BUT--
BUT WE CAN'T RISK MAKING A RUN AT COUNTESS WITH NICO UNDER HER SWAY AND THE ENTIRE TOWN IN THE CROSSFIRE. NICO COULD TURN OUR POWERS OFF AGAIN--
OR DROWN US IN A RIVER.
OR THAT.
THE WITCH'S POWER IS UNPREDICTABLE AND VAST.
BUT NICO CAN USE HER MANY TONGUES!
BUT SHE CAN'T DO THE SAME SPELL TWICE, RIGHT?
SINGULARITY. ADORABLE SENTIENT POCKET DIMENSION. STILL LEARNING ABOUT WORDS.
UH...
I THINK BLUE MEANS LANGUAGES.
THOUGH IT'S WAY FUNNIER IF SHE DOESN'T.
WE HAVE SEEN THAT HER MAGIC HAS LIMITS. AS SHE DOES NEW SPELLS, OLD SPELLS SEEM TO FADE.
CAPTAIN MARVEL. BOSS OF SPACE. HAAAATES HAVING WATER IN HER EARS.
DAZZLER THOR. A DAZZLER. A THOR. SHINY EVEN WHEN DRENCHED!
SHE-HULK. ENJOYS PUNCHING. AND JOKES. AND PUNCHING.
DAZZLER. MUTANT POP STAR. WOULD LIKE 85 ASPIRIN RIGHT NOW. AND SOME REVENGE.
MEDUSA. INHUMAN QUEEN. HAIR SOMEHOW EV MORE MAGNIFICE WHEN WET.

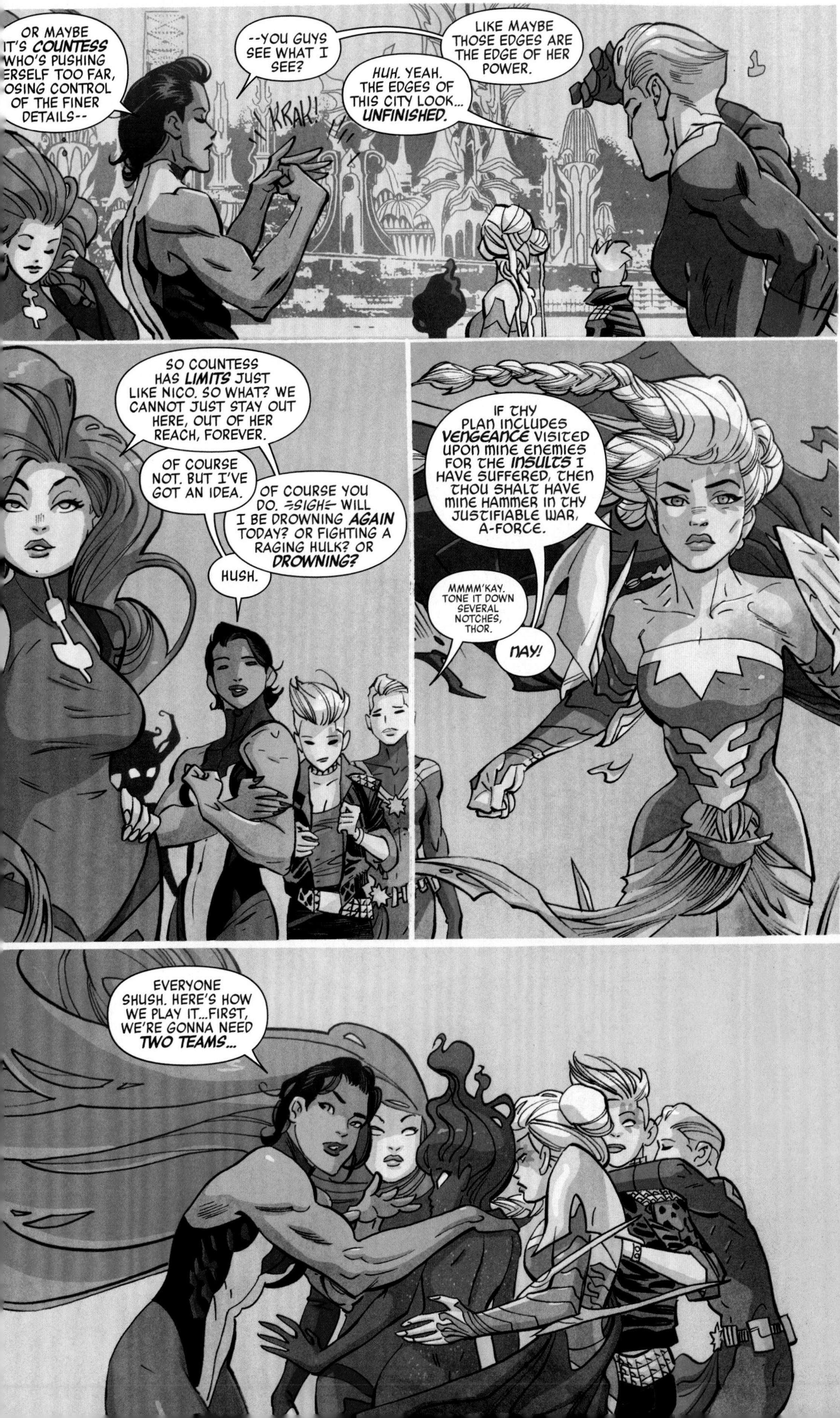
OR MAYBE IT'S COUNTESS WHO'S PUSHING ERSELF TOO FAR, OSING CONTROL OF THE FINER DETAILS--
--YOU GUYS SEE WHAT I SEE?
LIKE MAYBE THOSE EDGES ARE THE EDGE OF HER POWER.
HUH. YEAH. THE EDGES OF THIS CITY LOOK... UNFINISHED.
KRAK!
SO COUNTESS HAS LIMITS JUST LIKE NICO. SO WHAT? WE CANNOT JUST STAY OUT HERE, OUT OF HER REACH, FOREVER.
OF COURSE NOT. BUT I'VE GOT AN IDEA.
OF COURSE YOU DO. =SIGH= WILL I BE DROWNING AGAIN TODAY? OR FIGHTING A RAGING HULK? OR DROWNING?
HUSH.
IF THY PLAN INCLUDES VENGEANCE VISITED UPON MINE ENEMIES FOR THE INSULTS I HAVE SUFFERED, THEN THOU SHALT HAVE MINE HAMMER IN THY JUSTIFIABLE WAR, A-FORCE.
MMMM'KAY. TONE IT DOWN SEVERAL NOTCHES, THOR.
NAY!
EVERYONE SHUSH. HERE'S HOW WE PLAY IT...FIRST, WE'RE GONNA NEED TWO TEAMS...

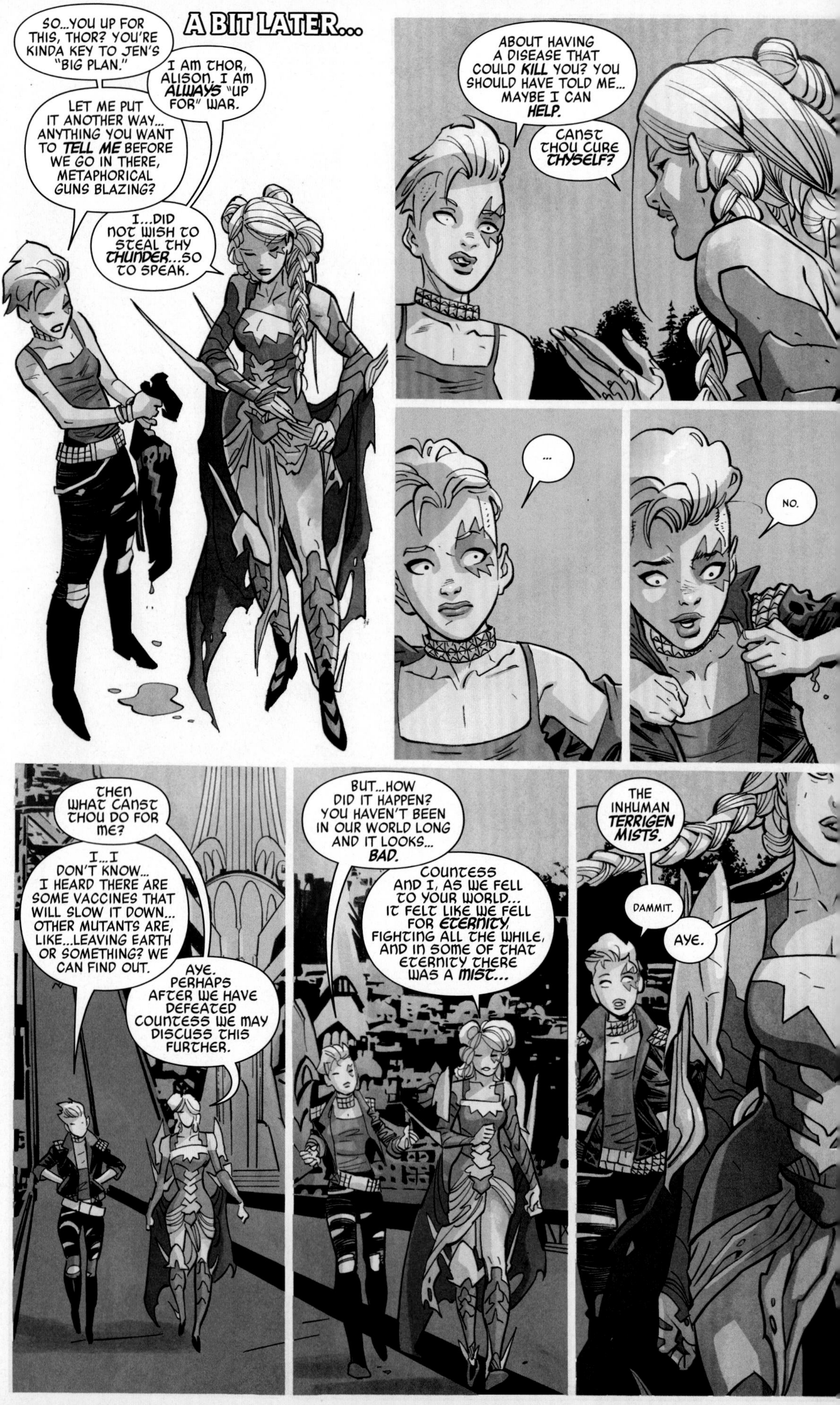
A BIT LATER...
SO...YOU UP FOR THIS, THOR? YOU'RE KINDA KEY TO JEN'S "BIG PLAN."
I AM THOR, ALISON. I AM ALWAYS "UP FOR" WAR.
LET ME PUT IT ANOTHER WAY... ANYTHING YOU WANT TO TELL ME BEFORE WE GO IN THERE, METAPHORICAL GUNS BLAZING?
I...DID NOT WISH TO STEAL THY THUNDER...SO TO SPEAK.
ABOUT HAVING A DISEASE THAT COULD KILL YOU? YOU SHOULD HAVE TOLD ME... MAYBE I CAN HELP.
CANST THOU CURE THYSELF?
...
NO.
THEN WHAT CANST THOU DO FOR ME?
I...I DON'T KNOW... I HEARD THERE ARE SOME VACCINES THAT WILL SLOW IT DOWN... OTHER MUTANTS ARE, LIKE...LEAVING EARTH OR SOMETHING? WE CAN FIND OUT.
AYE. PERHAPS AFTER WE HAVE DEFEATED COUNTESS WE MAY DISCUSS THIS FURTHER.
BUT...HOW DID IT HAPPEN? YOU HAVEN'T BEEN IN OUR WORLD LONG AND IT LOOKS... BAD.
COUNTESS AND I, AS WE FELL TO YOUR WORLD... IT FELT LIKE WE FELL FOR ETERNITY, FIGHTING ALL THE WHILE, AND IN SOME OF THAT ETERNITY THERE WAS A MIST...
THE INHUMAN TERRIGEN MISTS.
DAMMIT.
AYE.

BUT YOU ARE CORRECT, ALISON. I SHOULD HAVE TOLD YOU, AND YOUR TEAM.

--I *KNOW* THE TEAMS ARE *UNEVEN*, MEDUSA, THAT'S THE WHOLE *POINT!* OR PART OF IT.

WERE YOU EVEN *LISTENING* TO THE PLAN?! I'LL SAY IT ONE MORE--

SHE-HULK, I MUST SPEAK.

--HUH? WHAT'S HAPPENING?

I AM GOING TO TELL THEM.

YOU SURE?

AYE.

YOU ARE MY TEAM NOW, AND IF WE ARE TO ENTER THE FIELD OF BATTLE AGAIN, YOU MUST KNOW MY STRENGTHS...AND WEAKNESSES.

I HAVE BEEN *INFECTED* BY THE... ALISON SAYS THEY ARE CALLED "TERRIBLE MISTS."

TERRIGEN.

AYE. TERRIBLE TERRIGEN MISTS.

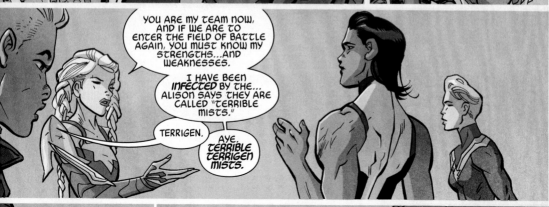

I TELL THEE NOT TO GAIN THY *PITY* BUT BECAUSE THE DISEASE APPEARS TO BE AFFECTING MY POWERS. NOT THE POWER I COMMAND AS THOR, BUT MY *MUTANT* POWERS...AT TIMES THEY FAIL ME, BECOMING WEAK, OR EVEN SURGING BEYOND MY CONTROL.

REGARDLESS, THOU WILT HAVE MY HAMMER IN THIS FIGHT.

UNTIL THE END.

IT WILL BE OKAY, SHINY THOR!

COME, SMALL ONE MADE OF STARS, LET US BEGIN SHE-HULK'S MASTER PLAN AND GET BACK OUR FELLOW WARRIOR...

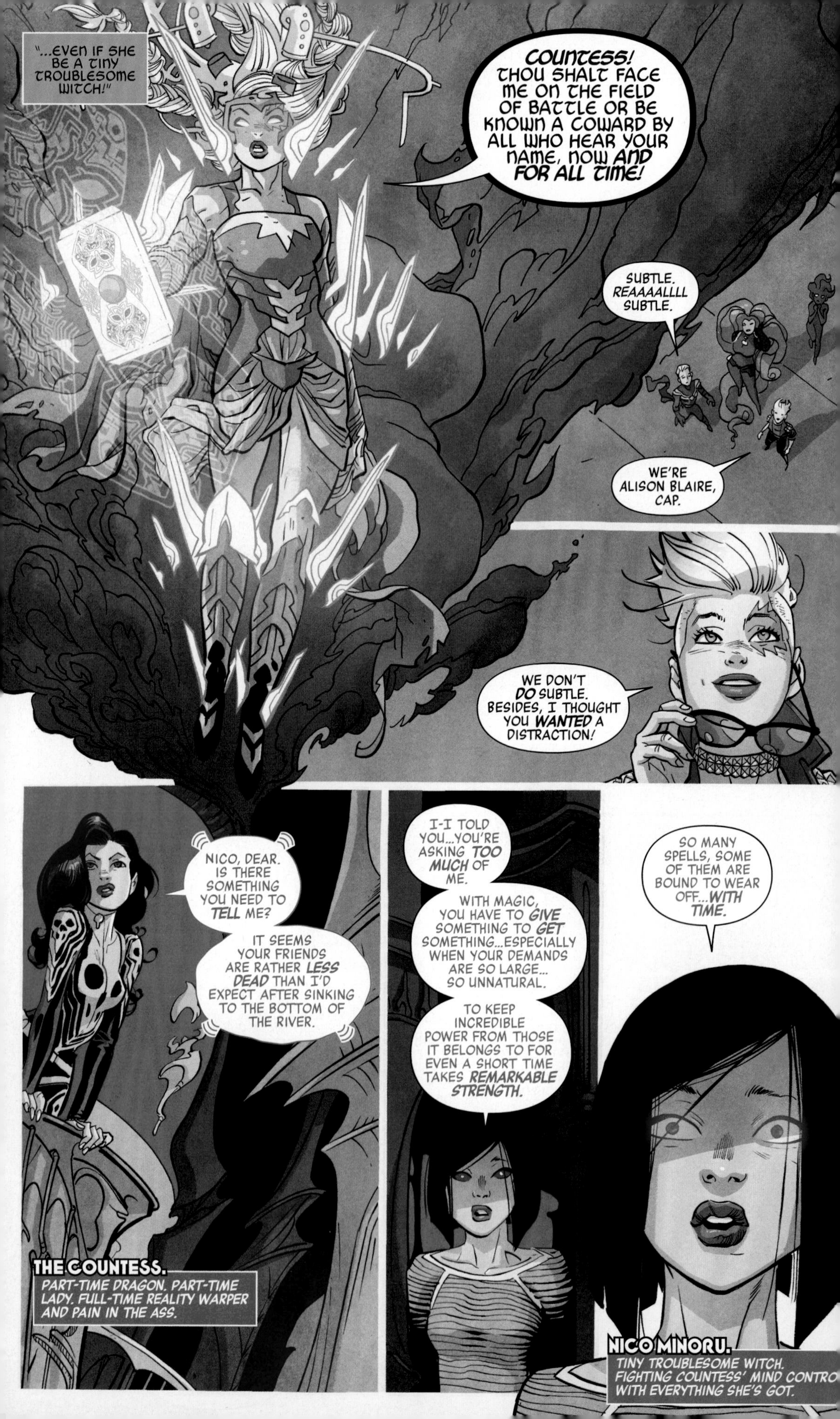
"...EVEN IF SHE BE A TINY TROUBLESOME WITCH!"
COUNTESS! THOU SHALT FACE ME ON THE FIELD OF BATTLE OR BE KNOWN A COWARD BY ALL WHO HEAR YOUR NAME, NOW AND FOR ALL TIME!
SUBTLE. REAAAALLLL SUBTLE.
WE'RE ALISON BLAIRE, CAP.
WE DON'T DO SUBTLE. BESIDES, I THOUGHT YOU WANTED A DISTRACTION!
NICO, DEAR. IS THERE SOMETHING YOU NEED TO TELL ME?
IT SEEMS YOUR FRIENDS ARE RATHER LESS DEAD THAN I'D EXPECT AFTER SINKING TO THE BOTTOM OF THE RIVER.
THE COUNTESS.
PART-TIME DRAGON. PART-TIME LADY. FULL-TIME REALITY WARPER AND PAIN IN THE ASS.
I-I TOLD YOU...YOU'RE ASKING TOO MUCH OF ME.
WITH MAGIC, YOU HAVE TO GIVE SOMETHING TO GET SOMETHING...ESPECIALLY WHEN YOUR DEMANDS ARE SO LARGE... SO UNNATURAL.
TO KEEP INCREDIBLE POWER FROM THOSE IT BELONGS TO FOR EVEN A SHORT TIME TAKES REMARKABLE STRENGTH.
SO MANY SPELLS, SOME OF THEM ARE BOUND TO WEAR OFF...WITH TIME.
NICO MINORU.
TINY TROUBLESOME WITCH. FIGHTING COUNTESS' MIND CONTRO WITH EVERYTHING SHE'S GOT.

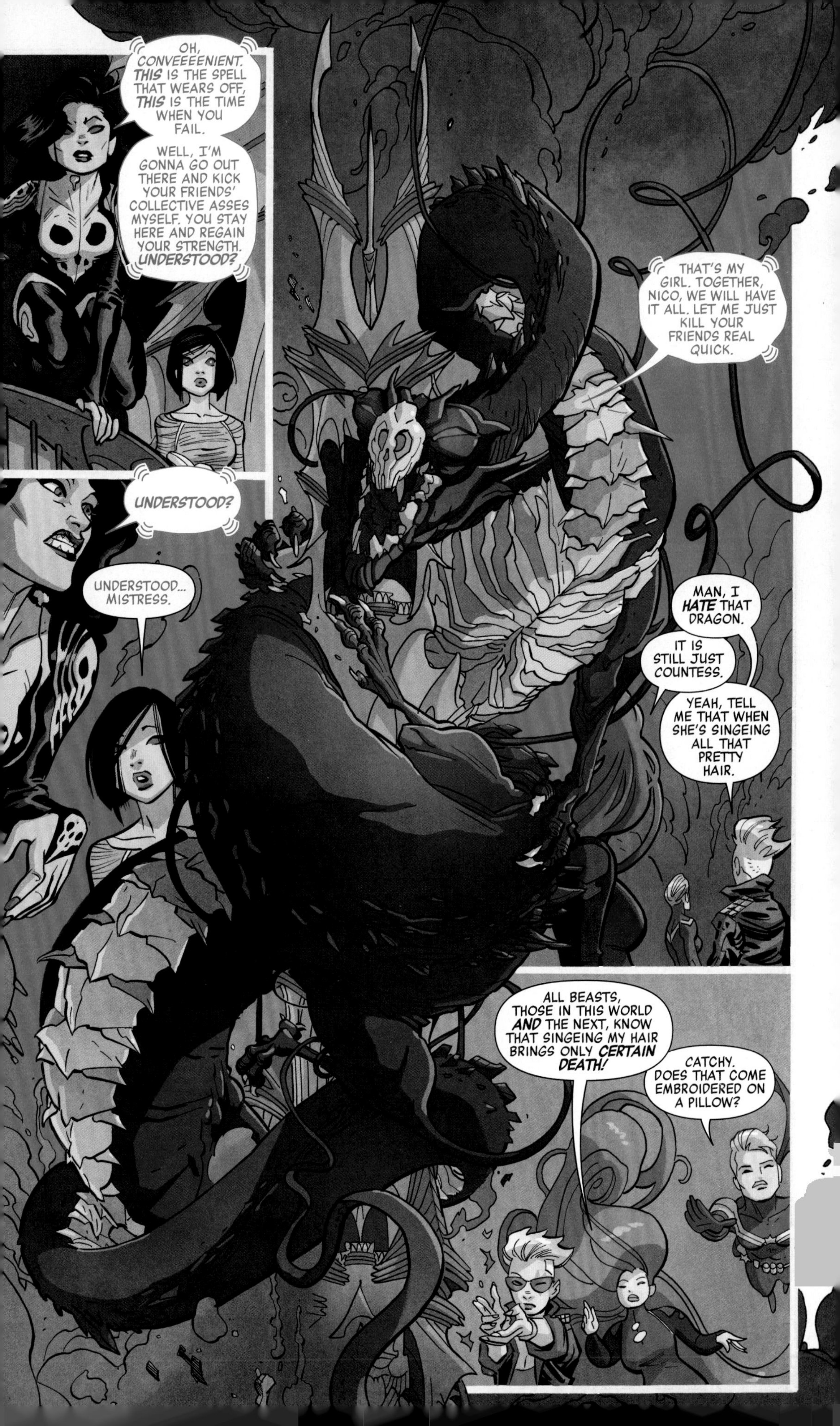

OH, CONVEEEEENIENT. THIS IS THE SPELL THAT WEARS OFF, THIS IS THE TIME WHEN YOU FAIL.
WELL, I'M GONNA GO OUT THERE AND KICK YOUR FRIENDS' COLLECTIVE ASSES MYSELF. YOU STAY HERE AND REGAIN YOUR STRENGTH. UNDERSTOOD?
UNDERSTOOD?
UNDERSTOOD... MISTRESS.
THAT'S MY GIRL. TOGETHER, NICO, WE WILL HAVE IT ALL. LET ME JUST KILL YOUR FRIENDS REAL QUICK.
MAN, I HATE THAT DRAGON.
IT IS STILL JUST COUNTESS.
YEAH, TELL ME THAT WHEN SHE'S SINGEING ALL THAT PRETTY HAIR.
ALL BEASTS, THOSE IN THIS WORLD AND THE NEXT, KNOW THAT SINGEING MY HAIR BRINGS ONLY CERTAIN DEATH!
CATCHY. DOES THAT COME EMBROIDERED ON A PILLOW?

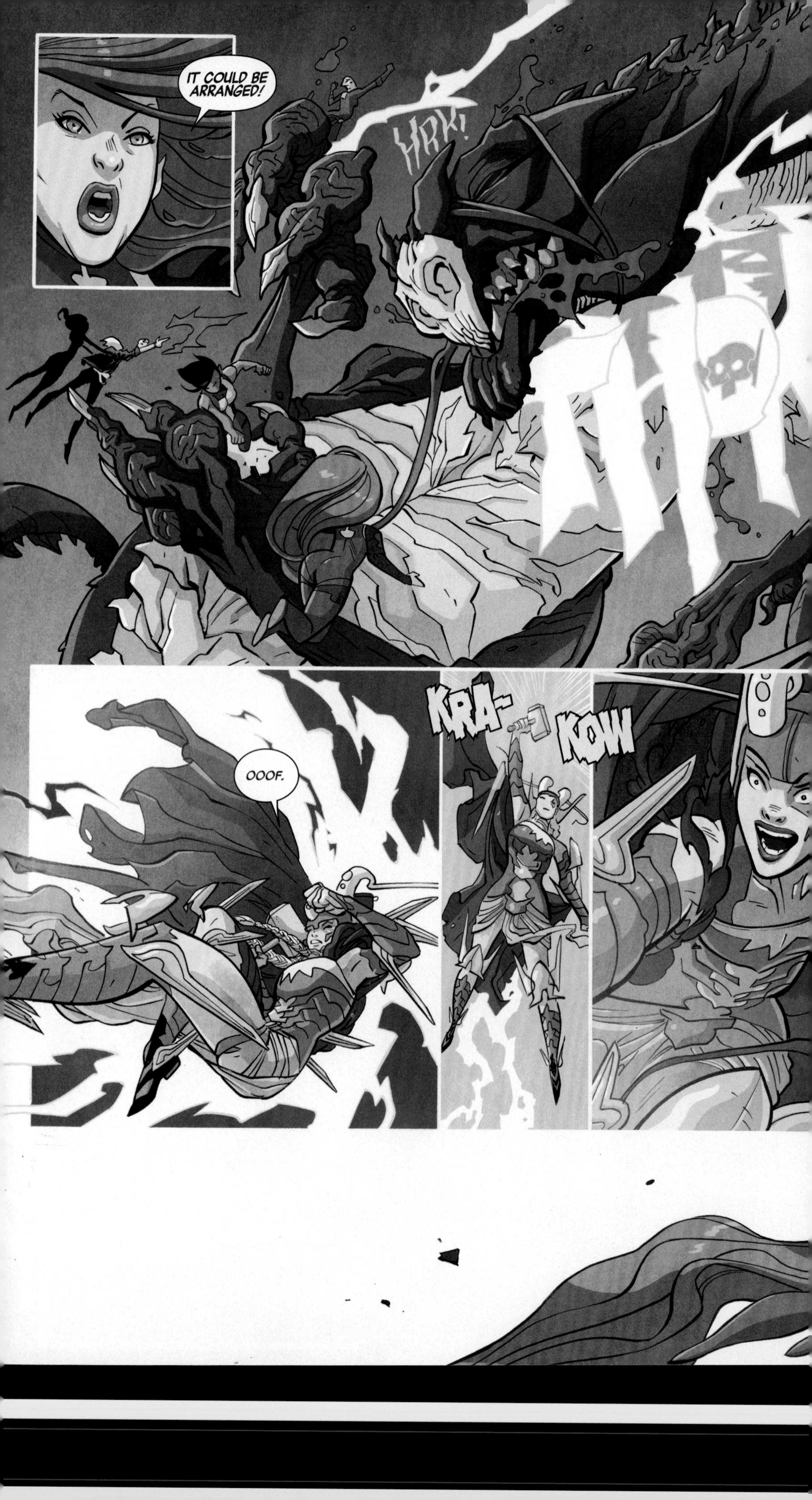
IT COULD BE ARRANGED!
HRK!
OOOF.
KRA-
KOW

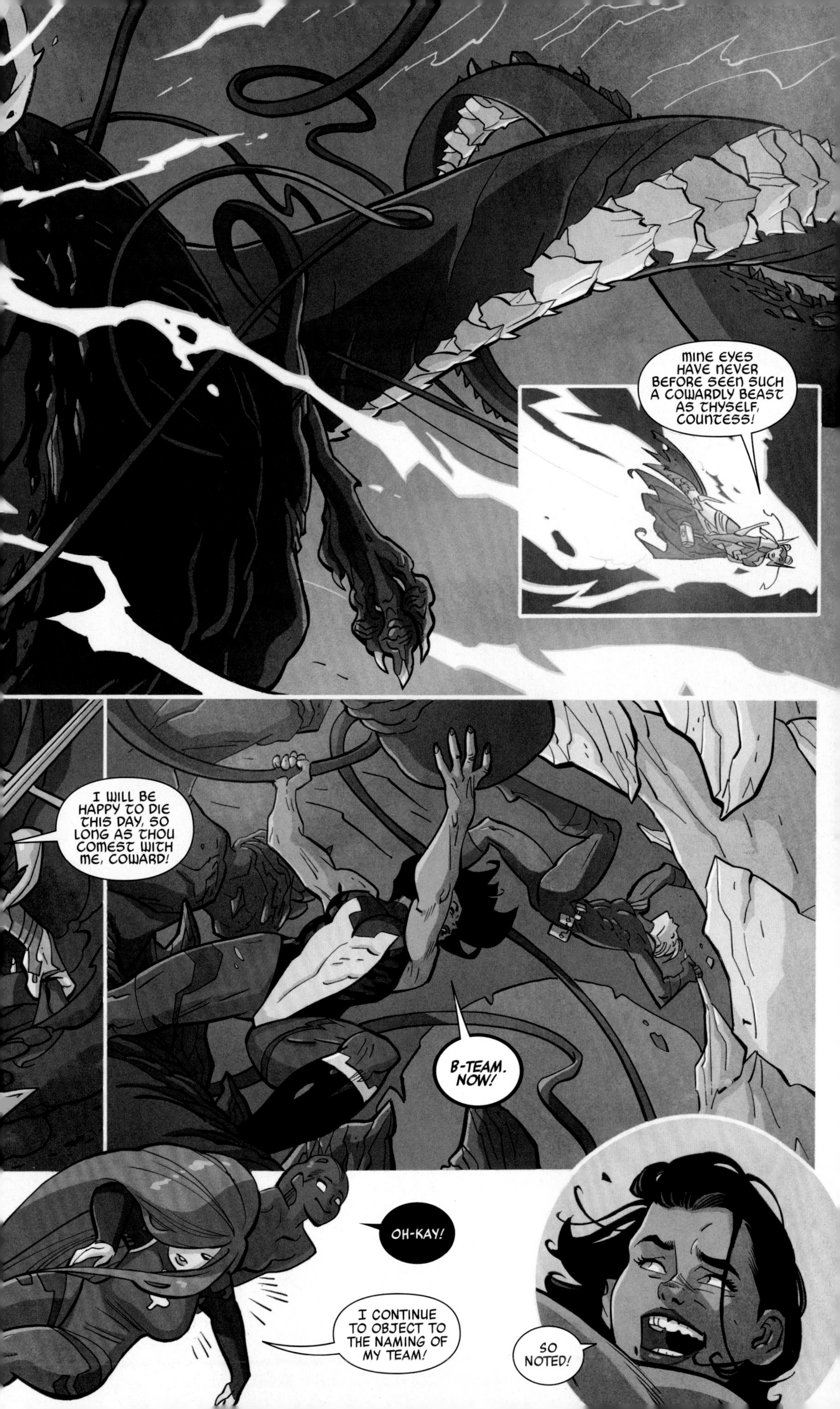

MINE EYES HAVE NEVER BEFORE SEEN SUCH A COWARDLY BEAST AS THYSELF, COUNTESS!
I WILL BE HAPPY TO DIE THIS DAY, SO LONG AS THOU COMEST WITH ME, COWARD!
B-TEAM. NOW!
OH-KAY!
I CONTINUE TO OBJECT TO THE NAMING OF MY TEAM!
SO NOTED!

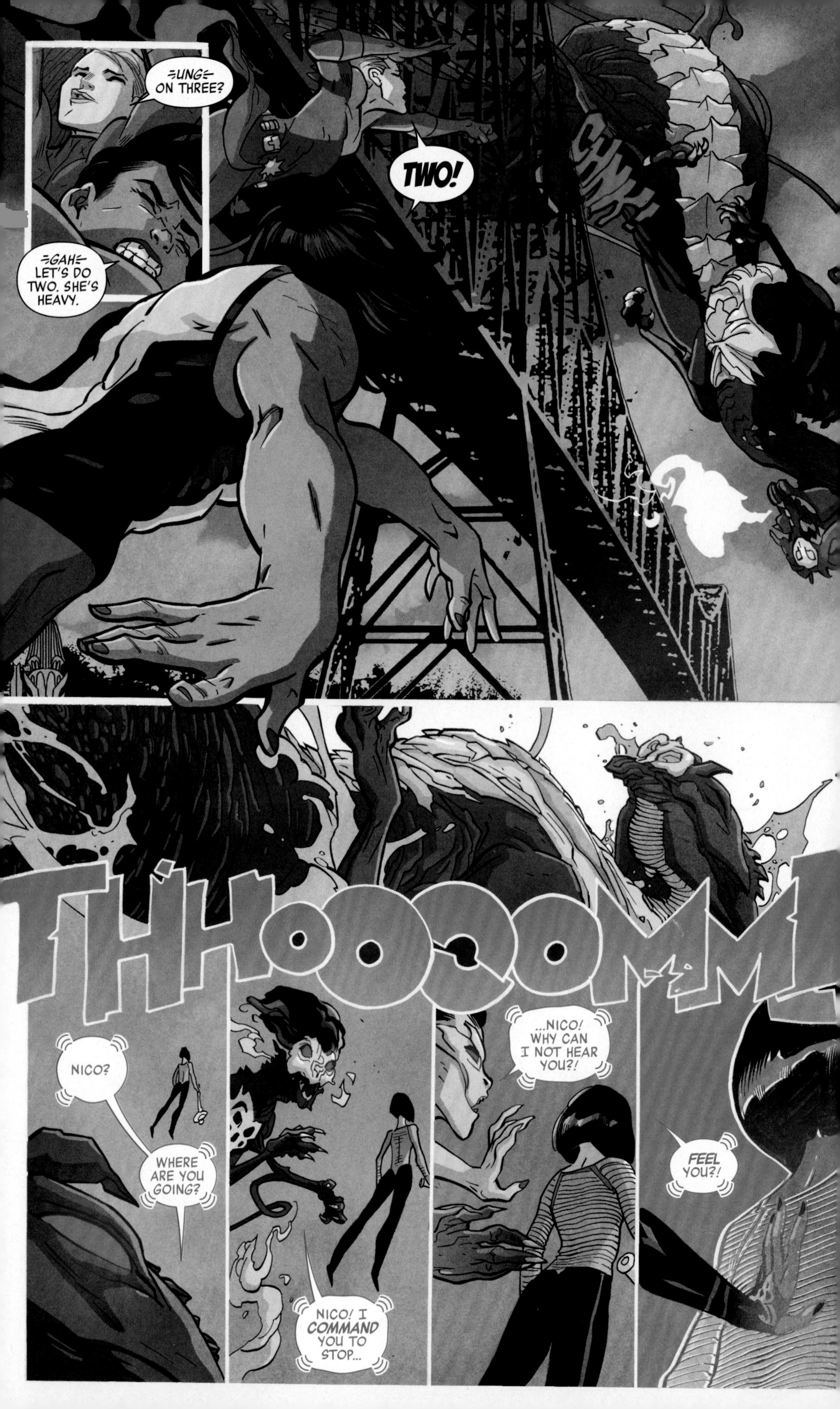

UNG
ON THREE?
GAH
LET'S DO TWO. SHE'S HEAVY.
TWO!
CHNK!
THOOOOMM
NICO?
WHERE ARE YOU GOING?
NICO! I COMMAND YOU TO STOP...
...NICO! WHY CAN I NOT HEAR YOU?!
FEEL YOU?!

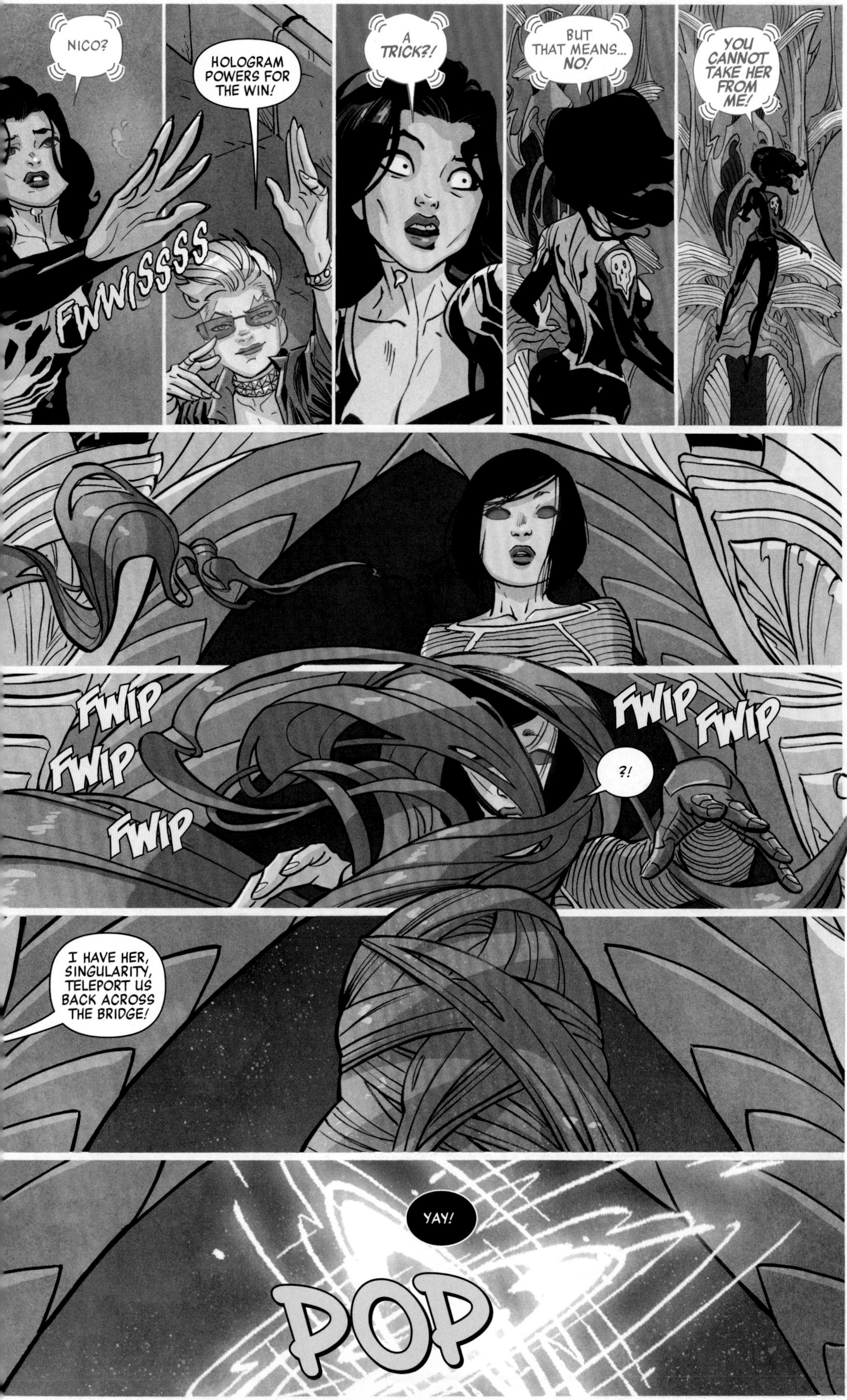
NICO?
HOLOGRAM POWERS FOR THE WIN!
FWWISSSSS
A TRICK?!
BUT THAT MEANS... NO!
YOU CANNOT TAKE HER FROM ME!
FWIP
FWIP
FWIP
FWIP
FWIP
?!
I HAVE HER, SINGULARITY, TELEPORT US BACK ACROSS THE BRIDGE!
YAY!
POP

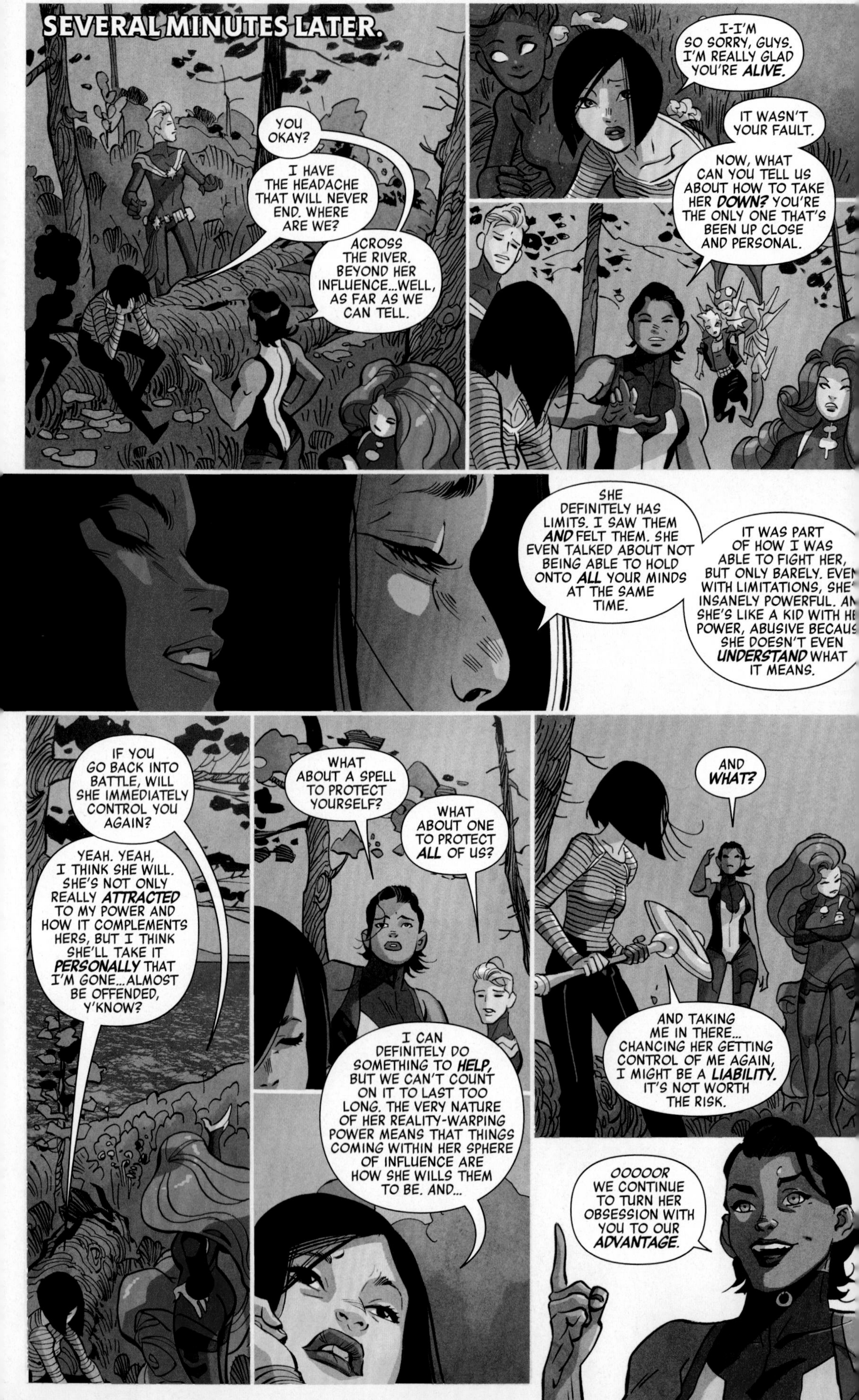
SEVERAL MINUTES LATER.
YOU OKAY?
I HAVE THE HEADACHE THAT WILL NEVER END. WHERE ARE WE?
ACROSS THE RIVER. BEYOND HER INFLUENCE...WELL, AS FAR AS WE CAN TELL.
I-I'M SO SORRY, GUYS. I'M REALLY GLAD YOU'RE ALIVE.
IT WASN'T YOUR FAULT.
NOW, WHAT CAN YOU TELL US ABOUT HOW TO TAKE HER DOWN? YOU'RE THE ONLY ONE THAT'S BEEN UP CLOSE AND PERSONAL.
SHE DEFINITELY HAS LIMITS. I SAW THEM AND FELT THEM. SHE EVEN TALKED ABOUT NOT BEING ABLE TO HOLD ONTO ALL YOUR MINDS AT THE SAME TIME.
IT WAS PART OF HOW I WAS ABLE TO FIGHT HER, BUT ONLY BARELY. EVEN WITH LIMITATIONS, SHE'S INSANELY POWERFUL. AND SHE'S LIKE A KID WITH HER POWER, ABUSIVE BECAUSE SHE DOESN'T EVEN UNDERSTAND WHAT IT MEANS.
IF YOU GO BACK INTO BATTLE, WILL SHE IMMEDIATELY CONTROL YOU AGAIN?
YEAH. YEAH, I THINK SHE WILL. SHE'S NOT ONLY REALLY ATTRACTED TO MY POWER AND HOW IT COMPLEMENTS HERS, BUT I THINK SHE'LL TAKE IT PERSONALLY THAT I'M GONE...ALMOST BE OFFENDED, Y'KNOW?
WHAT ABOUT A SPELL TO PROTECT YOURSELF?
WHAT ABOUT ONE TO PROTECT ALL OF US?
I CAN DEFINITELY DO SOMETHING TO HELP, BUT WE CAN'T COUNT ON IT TO LAST TOO LONG. THE VERY NATURE OF HER REALITY-WARPING POWER MEANS THAT THINGS COMING WITHIN HER SPHERE OF INFLUENCE ARE HOW SHE WILLS THEM TO BE. AND...
AND WHAT?
AND TAKING ME IN THERE... CHANCING HER GETTING CONTROL OF ME AGAIN, I MIGHT BE A LIABILITY. IT'S NOT WORTH THE RISK.
OOOOOR WE CONTINUE TO TURN HER OBSESSION WITH YOU TO OUR ADVANTAGE.

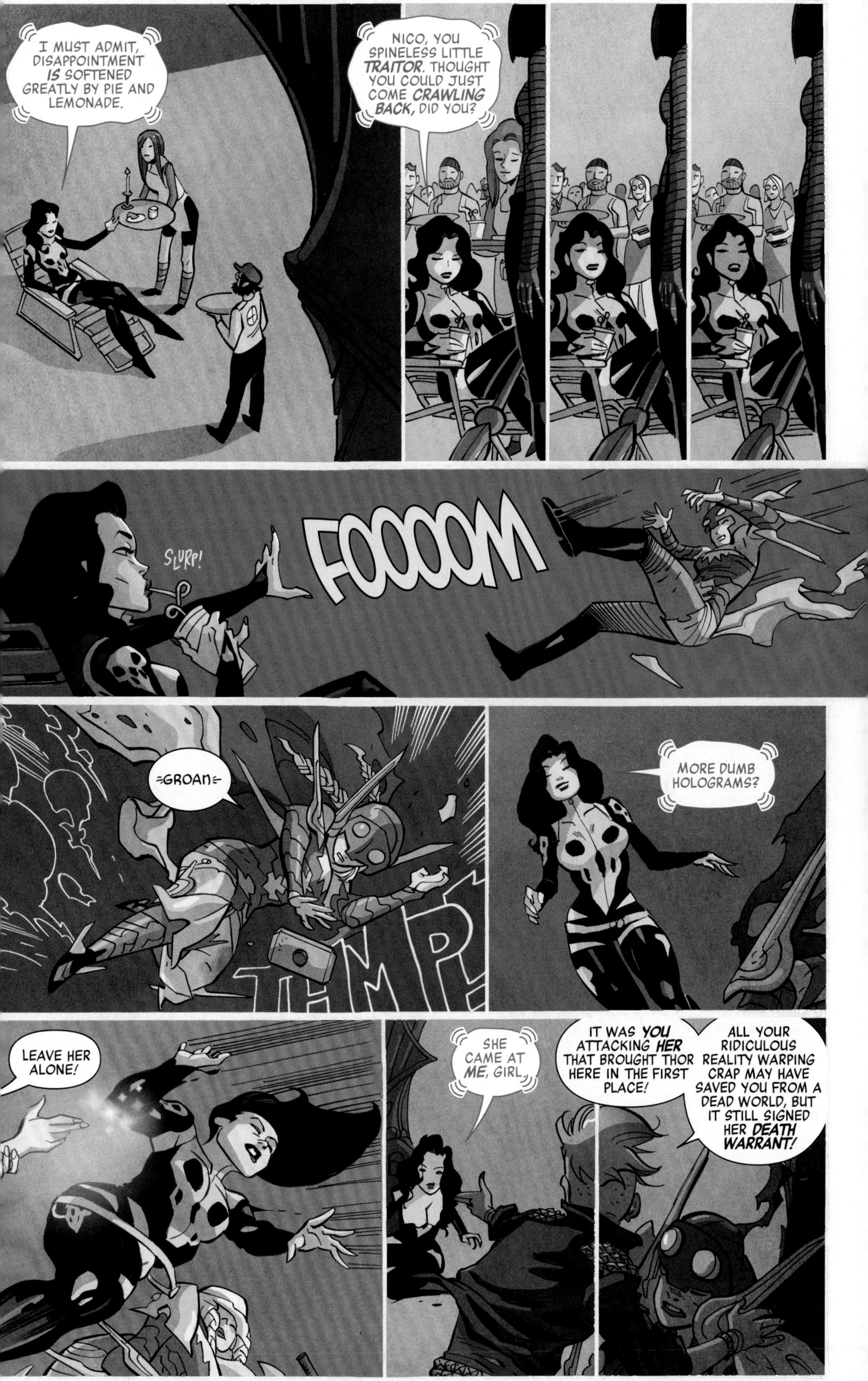
I MUST ADMIT, DISAPPOINTMENT IS SOFTENED GREATLY BY PIE AND LEMONADE.
NICO, YOU SPINELESS LITTLE TRAITOR. THOUGHT YOU COULD JUST COME CRAWLING BACK, DID YOU?
SLURP!
FOOOOM
GROAN
THMP!
MORE DUMB HOLOGRAMS?
LEAVE HER ALONE!
SHE CAME AT ME, GIRL.
IT WAS YOU ATTACKING HER THAT BROUGHT THOR HERE IN THE FIRST PLACE!
ALL YOUR RIDICULOUS REALITY WARPING CRAP MAY HAVE SAVED YOU FROM A DEAD WORLD, BUT IT STILL SIGNED HER DEATH WARRANT!

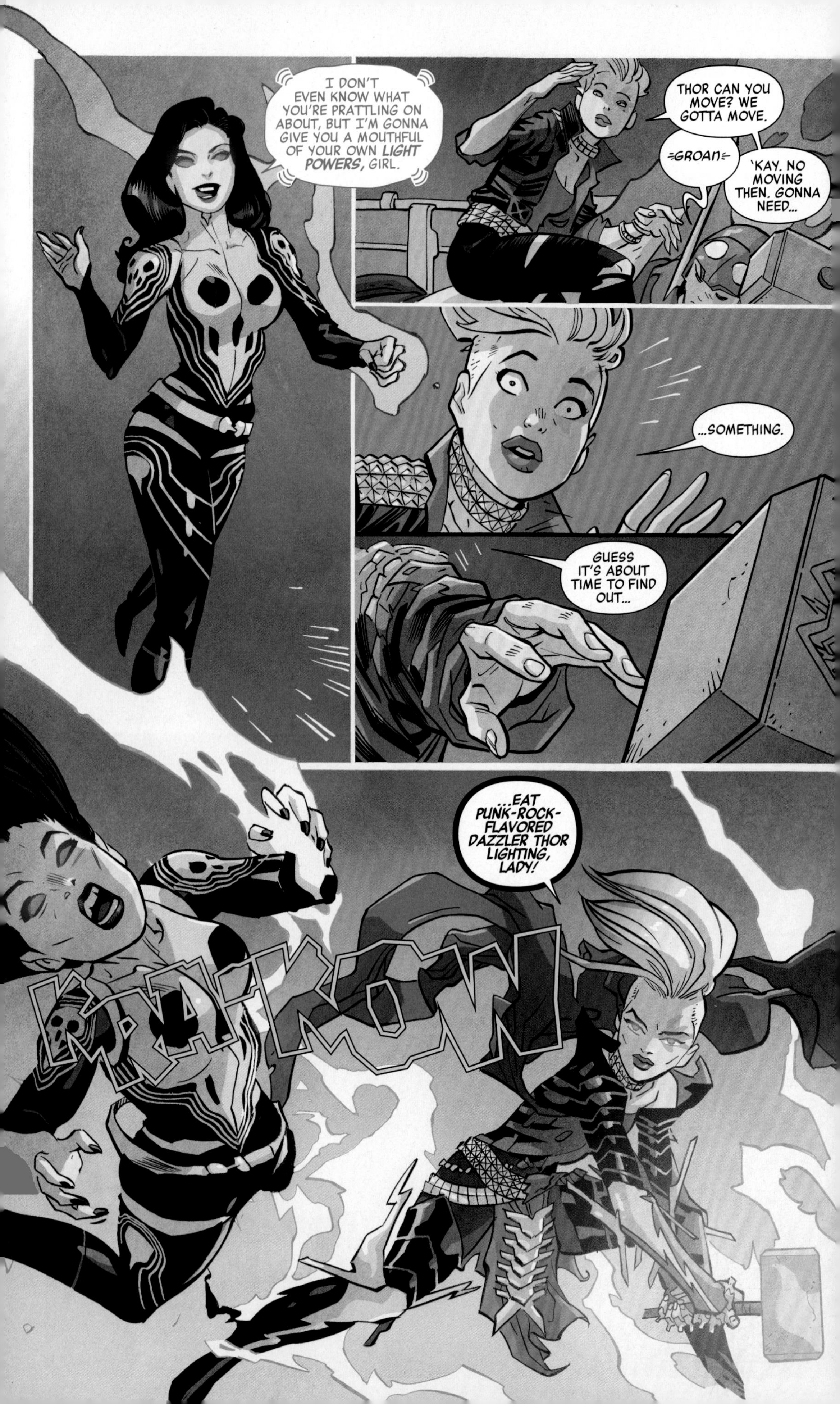

I DON'T EVEN KNOW WHAT YOU'RE PRATTLING ON ABOUT, BUT I'M GONNA GIVE YOU A MOUTHFUL OF YOUR OWN LIGHT POWERS, GIRL.
THOR CAN YOU MOVE? WE GOTTA MOVE.
=GROAN=
'KAY. NO MOVING THEN. GONNA NEED...
...SOMETHING.
GUESS IT'S ABOUT TIME TO FIND OUT...
...EAT PUNK-ROCK-FLAVORED DAZZLER THOR LIGHTING, LADY!
KRAKOOM

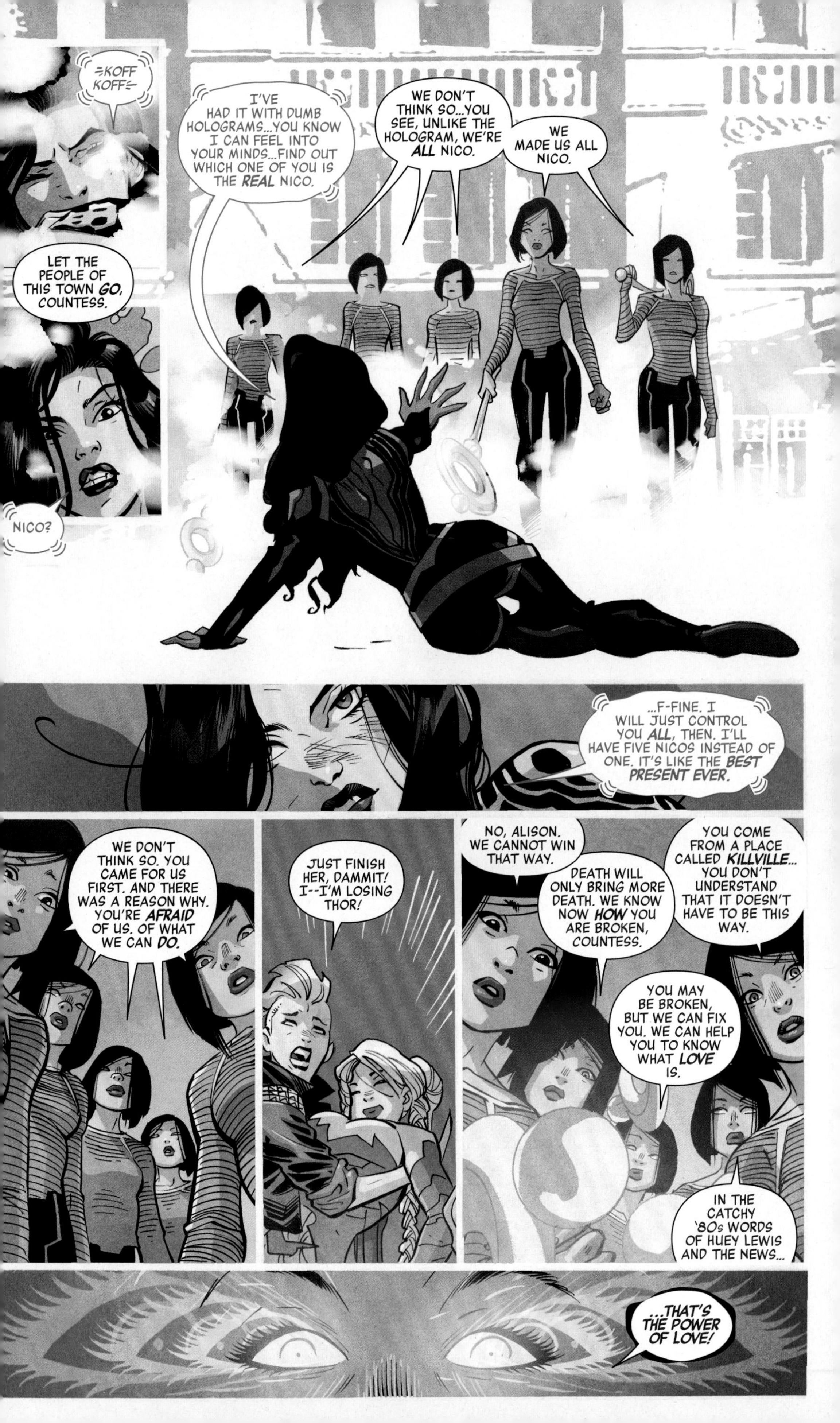

≠KOFF KOFF≠
LET THE PEOPLE OF THIS TOWN GO, COUNTESS.
NICO?
I'VE HAD IT WITH DUMB HOLOGRAMS...YOU KNOW I CAN FEEL INTO YOUR MINDS...FIND OUT WHICH ONE OF YOU IS THE REAL NICO.
WE DON'T THINK SO...YOU SEE, UNLIKE THE HOLOGRAM, WE'RE ALL NICO.
WE MADE US ALL NICO.
...F-FINE. I WILL JUST CONTROL YOU ALL, THEN. I'LL HAVE FIVE NICOS INSTEAD OF ONE. IT'S LIKE THE BEST PRESENT EVER.
WE DON'T THINK SO. YOU CAME FOR US FIRST. AND THERE WAS A REASON WHY. YOU'RE AFRAID OF US. OF WHAT WE CAN DO.
JUST FINISH HER, DAMMIT! I--I'M LOSING THOR!
NO, ALISON. WE CANNOT WIN THAT WAY.
DEATH WILL ONLY BRING MORE DEATH. WE KNOW NOW HOW YOU ARE BROKEN, COUNTESS.
YOU COME FROM A PLACE CALLED KILLVILLE... YOU DON'T UNDERSTAND THAT IT DOESN'T HAVE TO BE THIS WAY.
YOU MAY BE BROKEN, BUT WE CAN FIX YOU. WE CAN HELP YOU TO KNOW WHAT LOVE IS.
IN THE CATCHY '80s WORDS OF HUEY LEWIS AND THE NEWS...
...THAT'S THE POWER OF LOVE!

IT'S STRONG AND IT'S SUDDEN AND IT'S CRUEL SOMETIMES..
BUT IT MIGHT JUST SAVE YOUR LIFE....
...THAT'S THE POWER OF LOVE

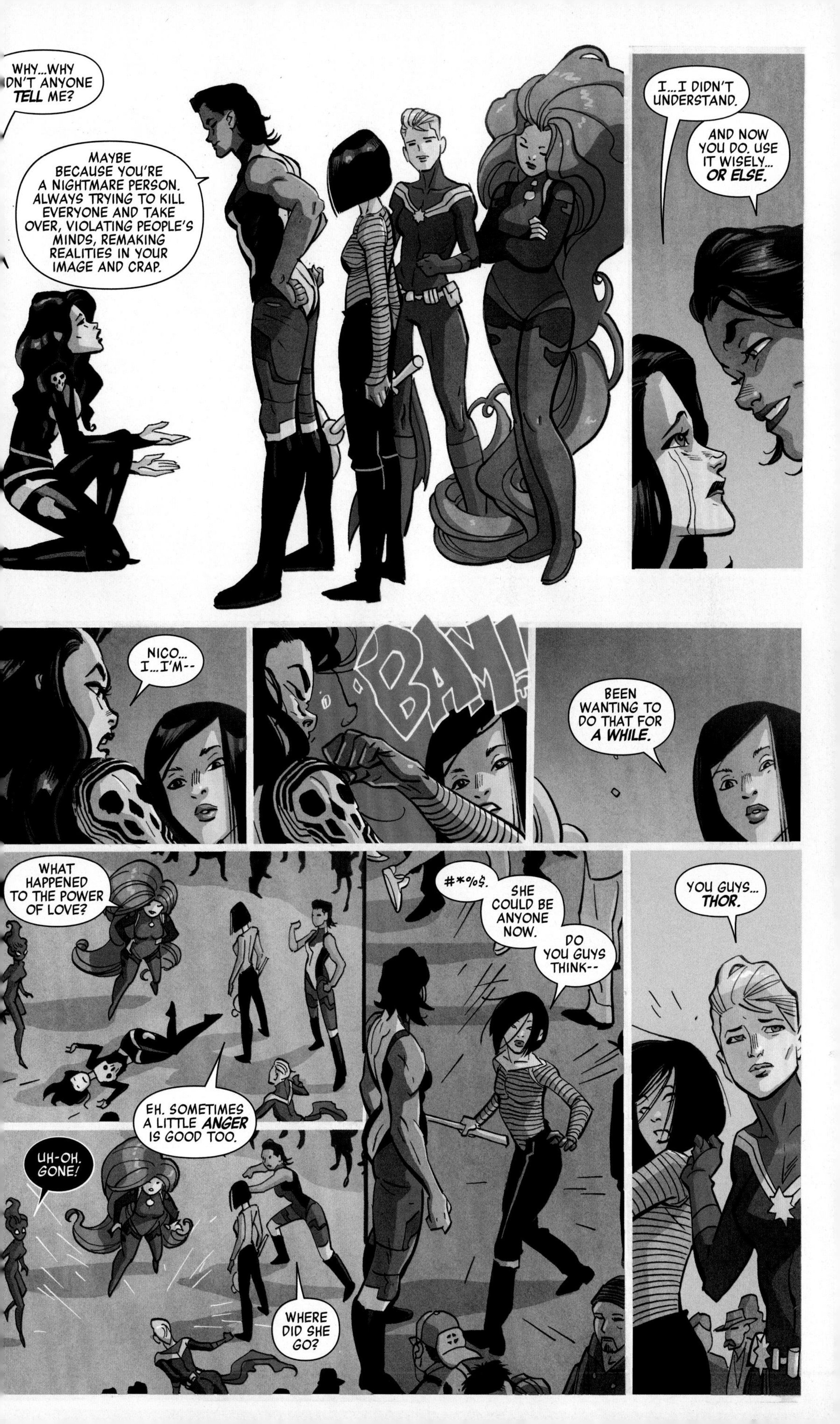
WHY...WHY DN'T ANYONE TELL ME?
MAYBE BECAUSE YOU'RE A NIGHTMARE PERSON. ALWAYS TRYING TO KILL EVERYONE AND TAKE OVER, VIOLATING PEOPLE'S MINDS, REMAKING REALITIES IN YOUR IMAGE AND CRAP.
I...I DIDN'T UNDERSTAND.
AND NOW YOU DO. USE IT WISELY... OR ELSE.
NICO... I...I'M--
BAM!
BEEN WANTING TO DO THAT FOR A WHILE.
WHAT HAPPENED TO THE POWER OF LOVE?
EH. SOMETIMES A LITTLE ANGER IS GOOD TOO.
UH-OH. GONE!
WHERE DID SHE GO?
#*%$.
SHE COULD BE ANYONE NOW.
DO YOU GUYS THINK--
YOU GUYS... THOR.

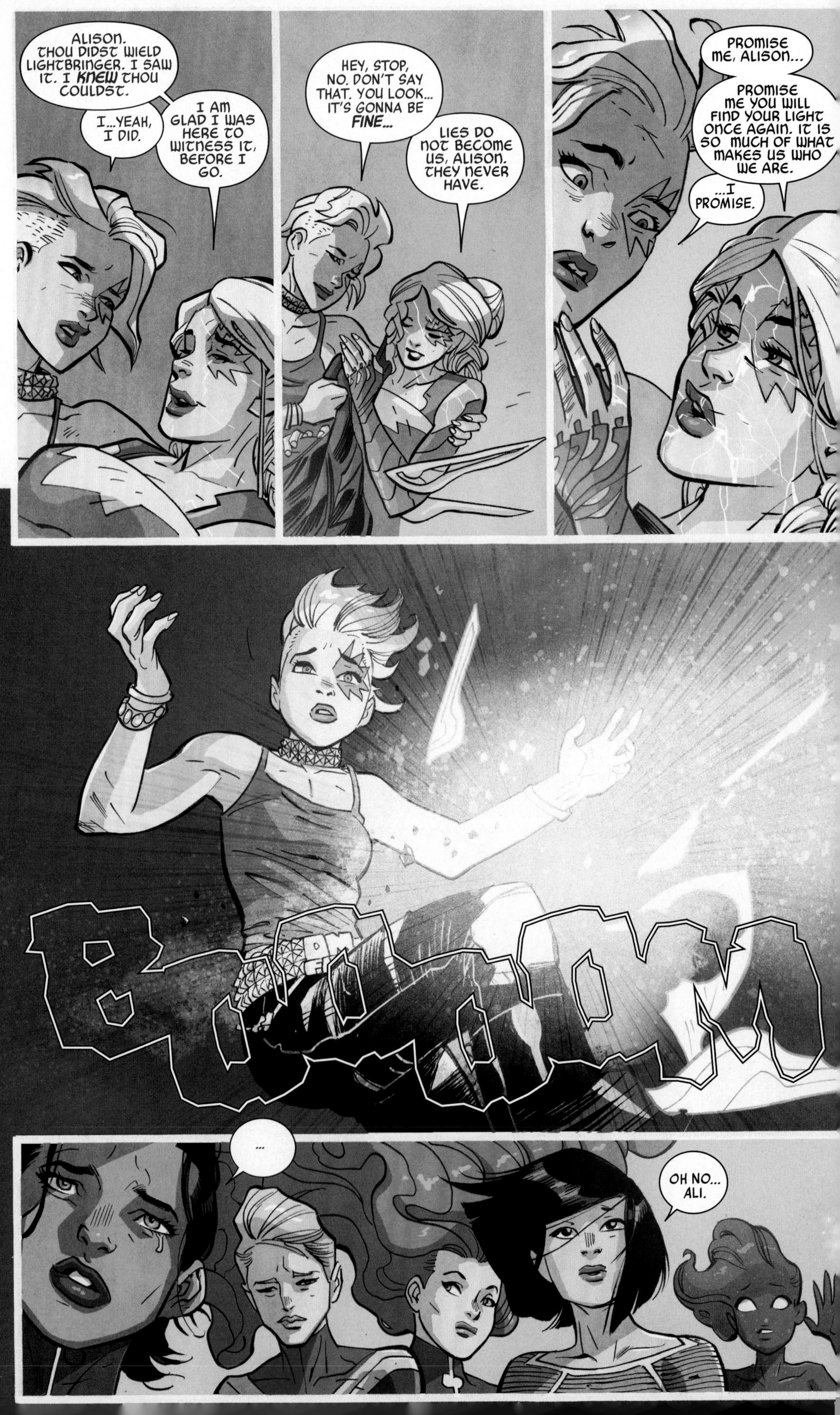

ALISON. THOU DIDST WIELD LIGHTBRINGER. I SAW IT. I KNEW THOU COULDST.
I...YEAH, I DID.
I AM GLAD I WAS HERE TO WITNESS IT, BEFORE I GO.
HEY, STOP, NO. DON'T SAY THAT. YOU LOOK... IT'S GONNA BE FINE...
LIES DO NOT BECOME US, ALISON. THEY NEVER HAVE.
PROMISE ME, ALISON...
PROMISE ME YOU WILL FIND YOUR LIGHT ONCE AGAIN. IT IS SO MUCH OF WHAT MAKES US WHO WE ARE.
...I PROMISE.
...
OH NO... ALI.

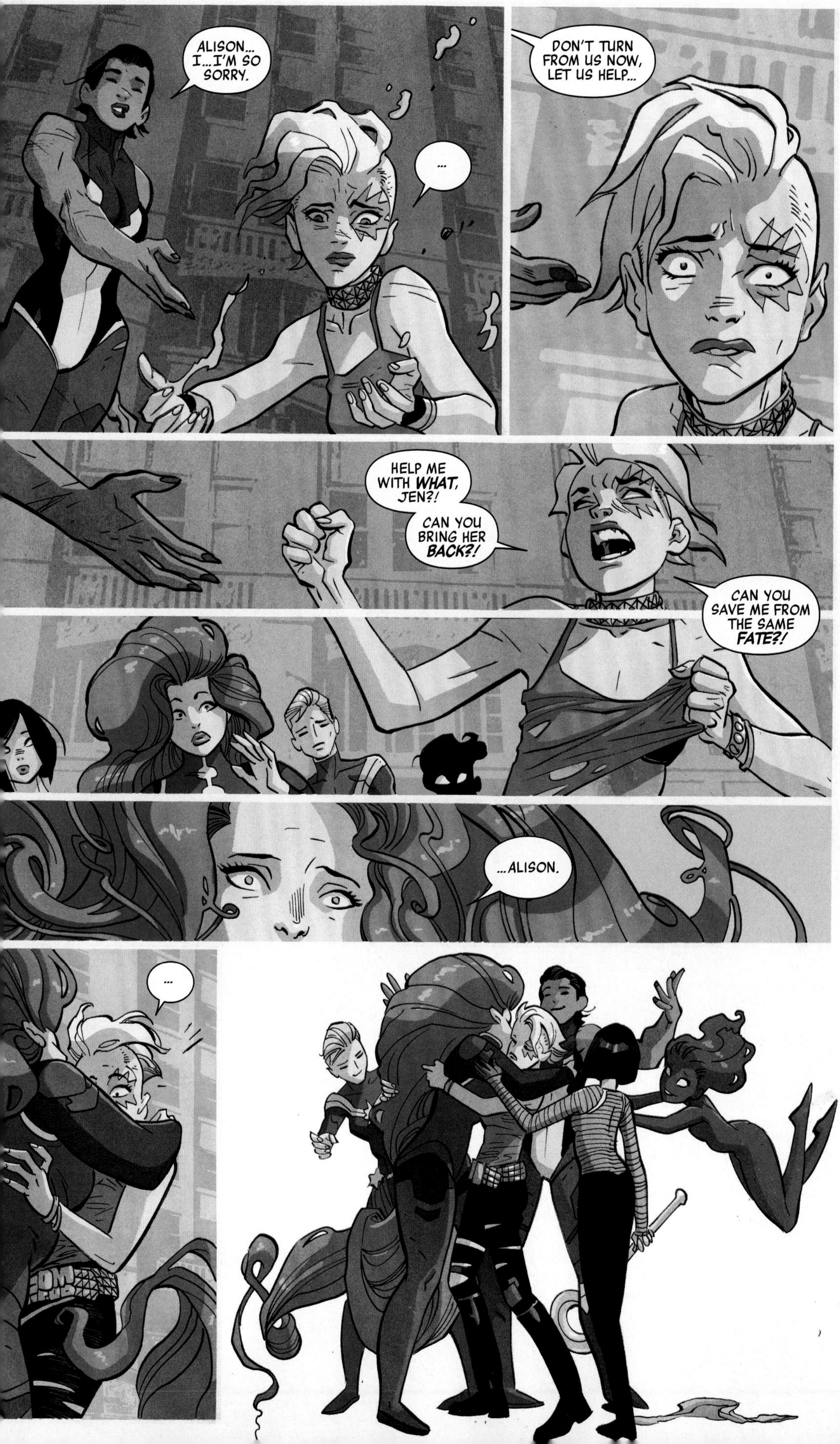
ALISON... I...I'M SO SORRY.
...
DON'T TURN FROM US NOW, LET US HELP...
HELP ME WITH **WHAT**, JEN?!
CAN YOU BRING HER **BACK?!**
CAN YOU SAVE ME FROM THE SAME **FATE?!**
...ALISON.
...

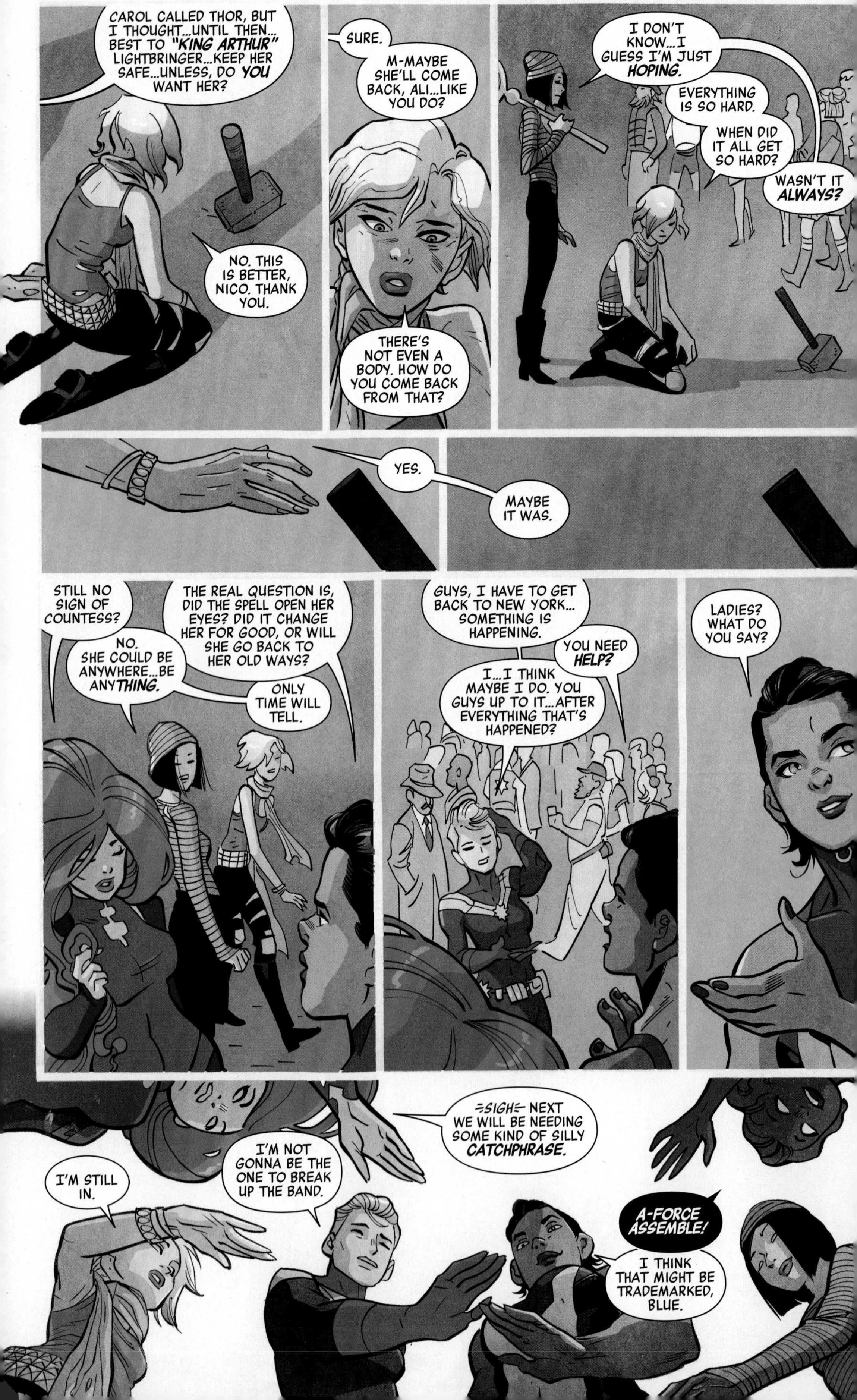
CAROL CALLED THOR, BUT I THOUGHT...UNTIL THEN... BEST TO "KING ARTHUR" LIGHTBRINGER...KEEP HER SAFE...UNLESS, DO YOU WANT HER?
NO. THIS IS BETTER, NICO. THANK YOU.
SURE.
M-MAYBE SHE'LL COME BACK, ALI...LIKE YOU DO?
THERE'S NOT EVEN A BODY. HOW DO YOU COME BACK FROM THAT?
I DON'T KNOW...I GUESS I'M JUST HOPING.
EVERYTHING IS SO HARD.
WHEN DID IT ALL GET SO HARD?
WASN'T IT ALWAYS?
YES.
MAYBE IT WAS.
STILL NO SIGN OF COUNTESS?
NO. SHE COULD BE ANYWHERE...BE ANYTHING.
THE REAL QUESTION IS, DID THE SPELL OPEN HER EYES? DID IT CHANGE HER FOR GOOD, OR WILL SHE GO BACK TO HER OLD WAYS?
ONLY TIME WILL TELL.
GUYS, I HAVE TO GET BACK TO NEW YORK... SOMETHING IS HAPPENING.
YOU NEED HELP?
I...I THINK MAYBE I DO. YOU GUYS UP TO IT...AFTER EVERYTHING THAT'S HAPPENED?
LADIES? WHAT DO YOU SAY?
I'M STILL IN.
I'M NOT GONNA BE THE ONE TO BREAK UP THE BAND.
=SIGH= NEXT WE WILL BE NEEDING SOME KIND OF SILLY CATCHPHRASE.
A-FORCE ASSEMBLE!
I THINK THAT MIGHT BE TRADEMARKED, BLUE.

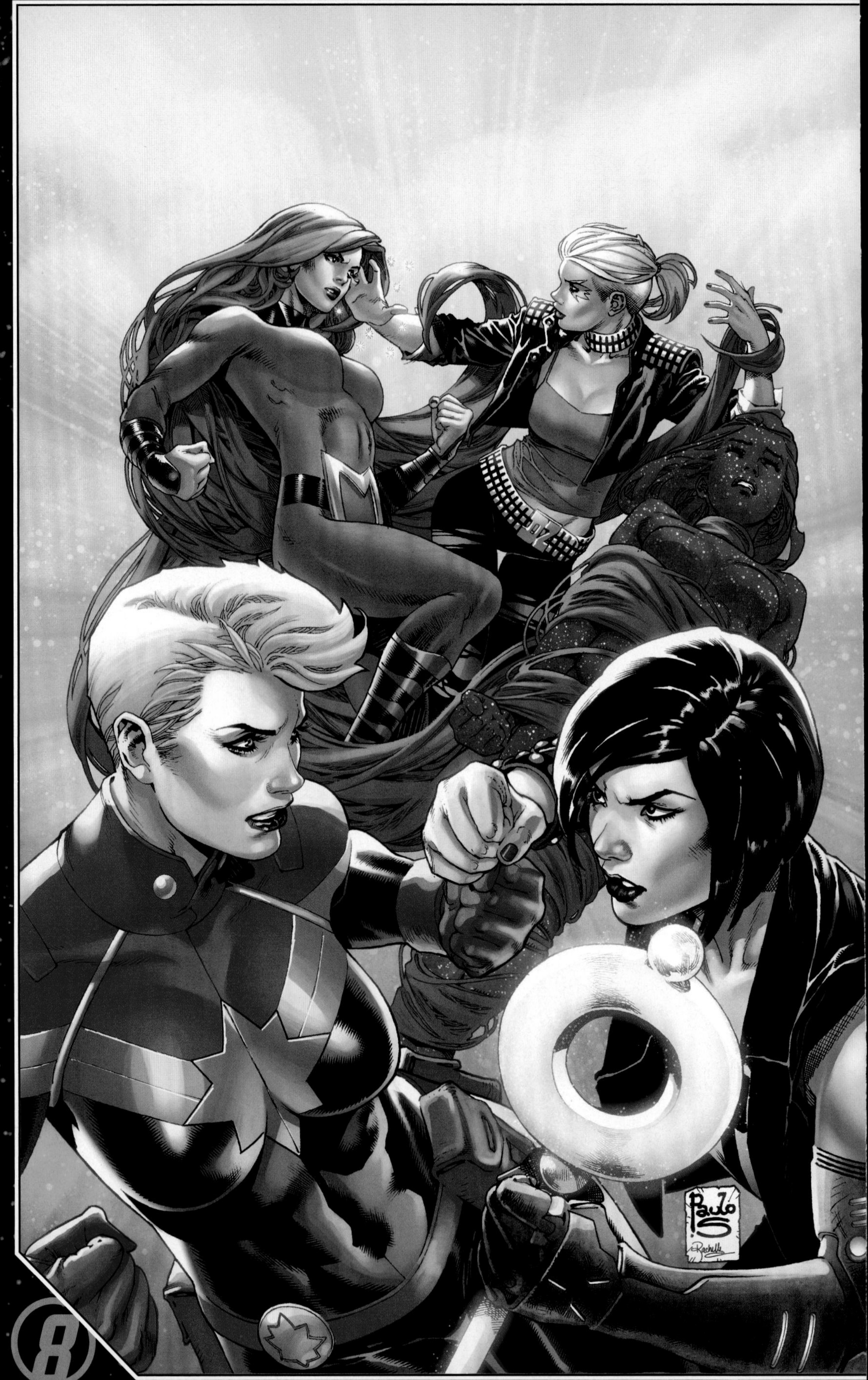

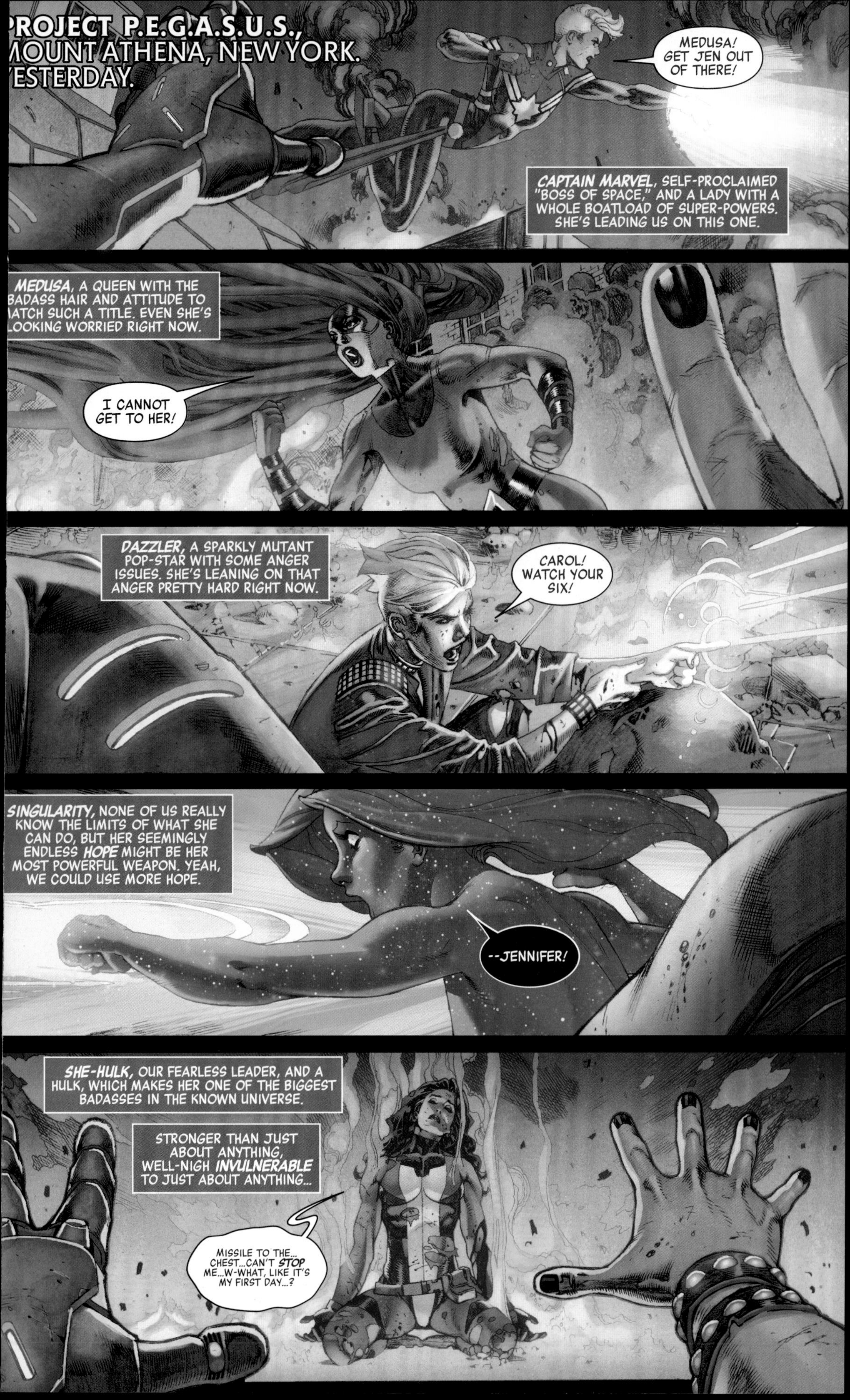

PROJECT P.E.G.A.S.U.S., MOUNT ATHENA, NEW YORK. YESTERDAY.
MEDUSA! GET JEN OUT OF THERE!
CAPTAIN MARVEL, SELF-PROCLAIMED "BOSS OF SPACE," AND A LADY WITH A WHOLE BOATLOAD OF SUPER-POWERS. SHE'S LEADING US ON THIS ONE.
MEDUSA, A QUEEN WITH THE BADASS HAIR AND ATTITUDE TO MATCH SUCH A TITLE. EVEN SHE'S LOOKING WORRIED RIGHT NOW.
I CANNOT GET TO HER!
DAZZLER, A SPARKLY MUTANT POP-STAR WITH SOME ANGER ISSUES. SHE'S LEANING ON THAT ANGER PRETTY HARD RIGHT NOW.
CAROL! WATCH YOUR SIX!
SINGULARITY, NONE OF US REALLY KNOW THE LIMITS OF WHAT SHE CAN DO, BUT HER SEEMINGLY ENDLESS HOPE MIGHT BE HER MOST POWERFUL WEAPON. YEAH, WE COULD USE MORE HOPE.
--JENNIFER!
SHE-HULK, OUR FEARLESS LEADER, AND A HULK, WHICH MAKES HER ONE OF THE BIGGEST BADASSES IN THE KNOWN UNIVERSE.
STRONGER THAN JUST ABOUT ANYTHING, WELL-NIGH INVULNERABLE TO JUST ABOUT ANYTHING...
MISSILE TO THE... CHEST...CAN'T STOP ME...W-WHAT, LIKE IT'S MY FIRST DAY...?

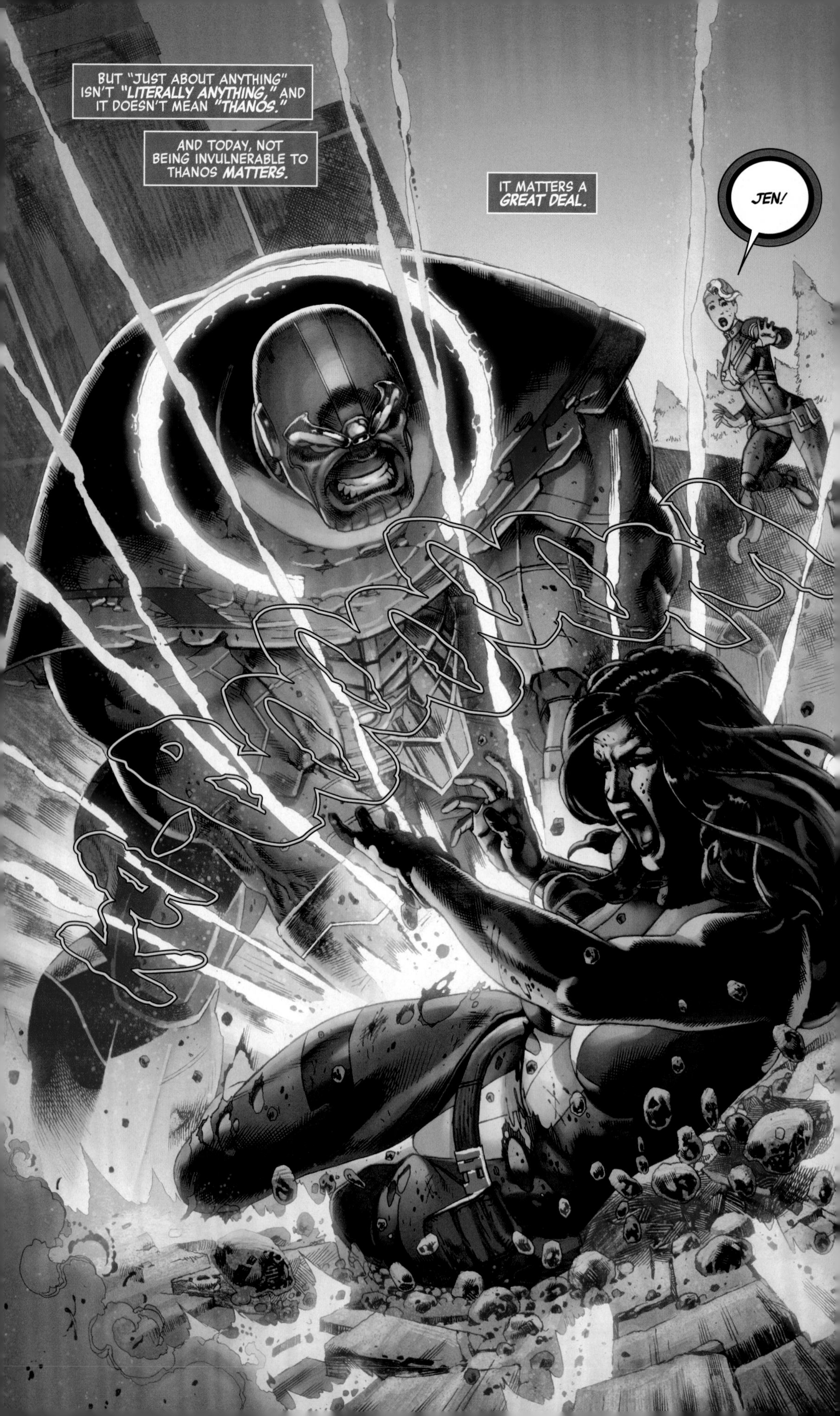
BUT "JUST ABOUT ANYTHING" ISN'T "LITERALLY ANYTHING," AND IT DOESN'T MEAN "THANOS."
AND TODAY, NOT BEING INVULNERABLE TO THANOS MATTERS.
IT MATTERS A GREAT DEAL.
JEN!

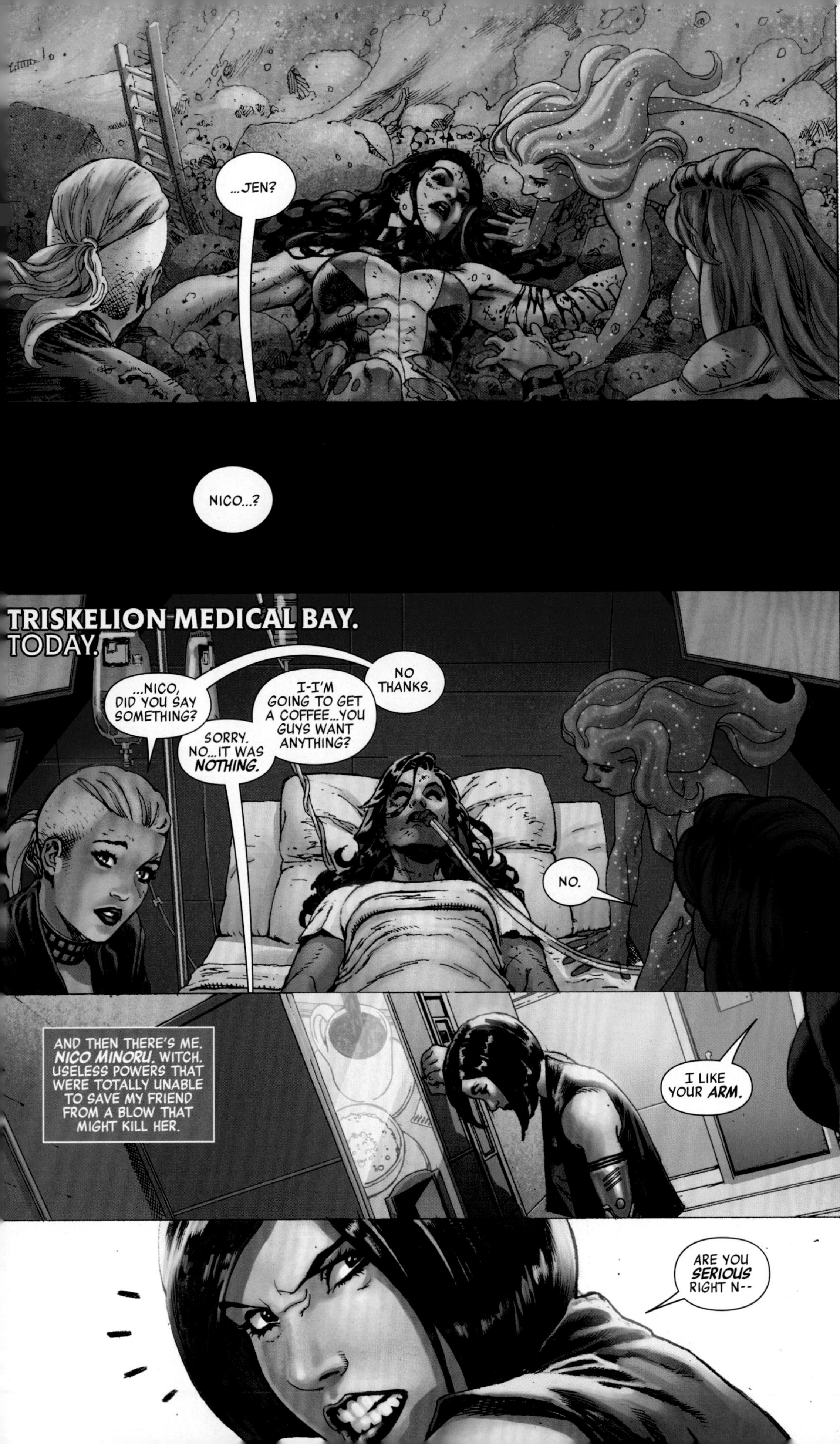

...JEN?
NICO...?
TRISKELION MEDICAL BAY. TODAY.
...NICO, DID YOU SAY SOMETHING?
SORRY. NO...IT WAS NOTHING.
I-I'M GOING TO GET A COFFEE...YOU GUYS WANT ANYTHING?
NO THANKS.
NO.
AND THEN THERE'S ME. NICO MINORU. WITCH. USELESS POWERS THAT WERE TOTALLY UNABLE TO SAVE MY FRIEND FROM A BLOW THAT MIGHT KILL HER.
I LIKE YOUR ARM.
ARE YOU SERIOUS RIGHT N--

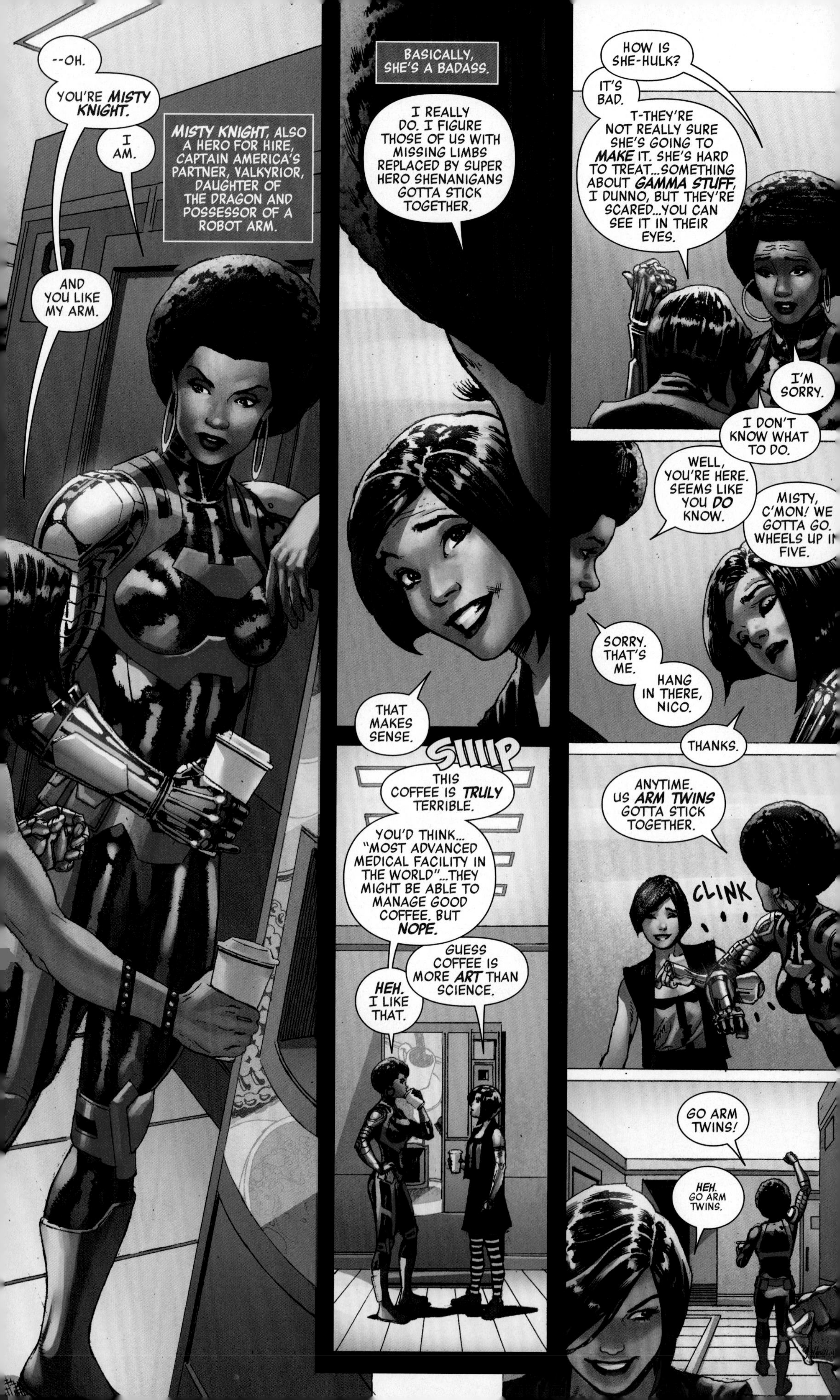
--OH.
YOU'RE MISTY KNIGHT.
I AM.
MISTY KNIGHT, ALSO A HERO FOR HIRE, CAPTAIN AMERICA'S PARTNER, VALKYRIOR, DAUGHTER OF THE DRAGON AND POSSESSOR OF A ROBOT ARM.
AND YOU LIKE MY ARM.
BASICALLY, SHE'S A BADASS.
I REALLY DO. I FIGURE THOSE OF US WITH MISSING LIMBS REPLACED BY SUPER HERO SHENANIGANS GOTTA STICK TOGETHER.
THAT MAKES SENSE.
SIIIIP
THIS COFFEE IS TRULY TERRIBLE.
YOU'D THINK... "MOST ADVANCED MEDICAL FACILITY IN THE WORLD"...THEY MIGHT BE ABLE TO MANAGE GOOD COFFEE. BUT NOPE.
GUESS COFFEE IS MORE ART THAN SCIENCE.
HEH. I LIKE THAT.
HOW IS SHE-HULK?
IT'S BAD.
T-THEY'RE NOT REALLY SURE SHE'S GOING TO MAKE IT. SHE'S HARD TO TREAT...SOMETHING ABOUT GAMMA STUFF, I DUNNO, BUT THEY'RE SCARED...YOU CAN SEE IT IN THEIR EYES.
I'M SORRY.
I DON'T KNOW WHAT TO DO.
WELL, YOU'RE HERE. SEEMS LIKE YOU DO KNOW.
MISTY, C'MON! WE GOTTA GO. WHEELS UP I
FIVE.
SORRY. THAT'S ME.
HANG IN THERE, NICO.
THANKS.
ANYTIME. US ARM TWINS GOTTA STICK TOGETHER.
CLINK
GO ARM TWINS!
HEH. GO ARM TWINS.

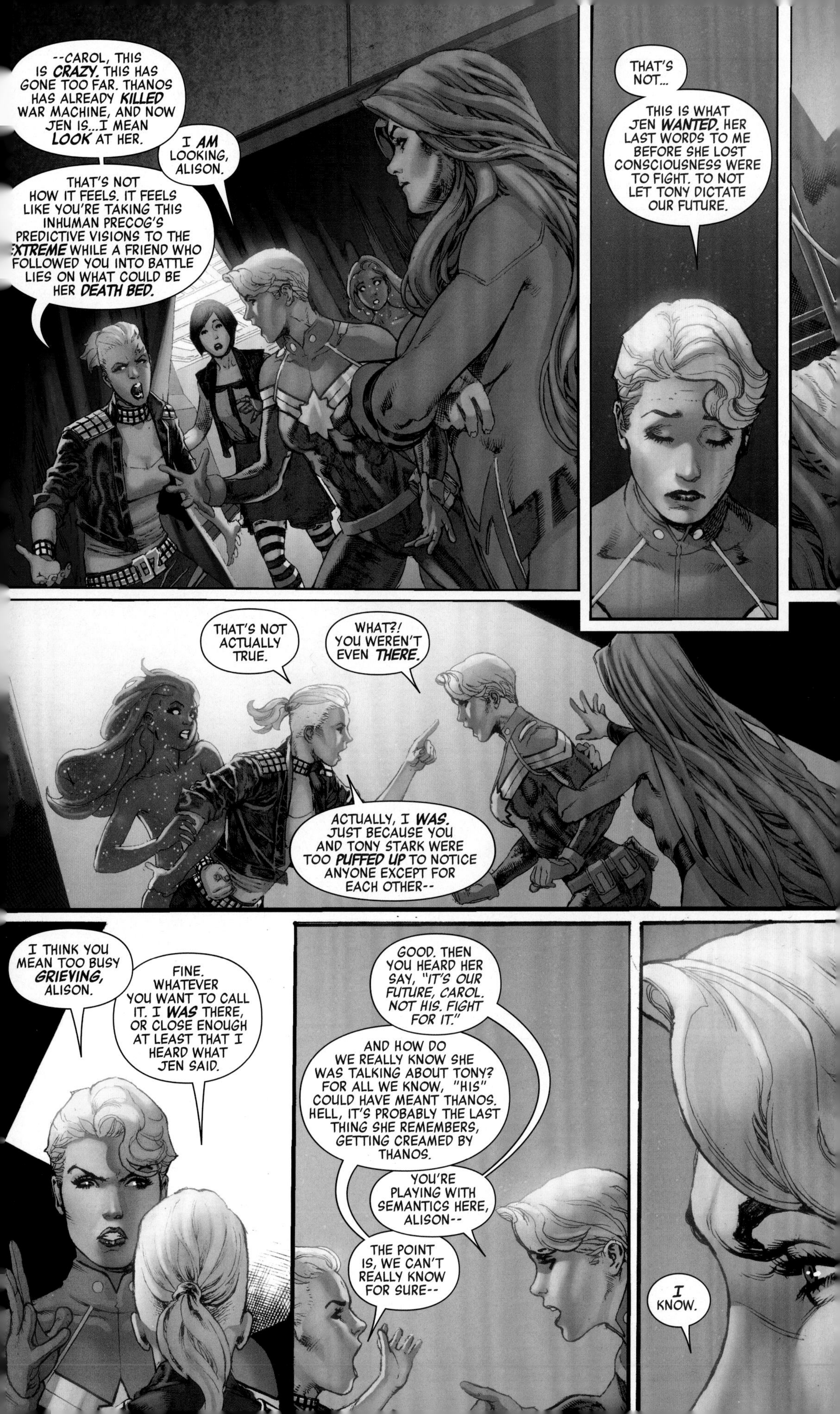
--CAROL, THIS IS CRAZY. THIS HAS GONE TOO FAR. THANOS HAS ALREADY KILLED WAR MACHINE, AND NOW JEN IS...I MEAN LOOK AT HER.
I AM LOOKING, ALISON.
THAT'S NOT HOW IT FEELS. IT FEELS LIKE YOU'RE TAKING THIS INHUMAN PRECOG'S PREDICTIVE VISIONS TO THE EXTREME WHILE A FRIEND WHO FOLLOWED YOU INTO BATTLE LIES ON WHAT COULD BE HER DEATH BED.
THAT'S NOT...
THIS IS WHAT JEN WANTED. HER LAST WORDS TO ME BEFORE SHE LOST CONSCIOUSNESS WERE TO FIGHT. TO NOT LET TONY DICTATE OUR FUTURE.
THAT'S NOT ACTUALLY TRUE.
WHAT?! YOU WEREN'T EVEN THERE.
ACTUALLY, I WAS. JUST BECAUSE YOU AND TONY STARK WERE TOO PUFFED UP TO NOTICE ANYONE EXCEPT FOR EACH OTHER--
I THINK YOU MEAN TOO BUSY GRIEVING, ALISON.
FINE. WHATEVER YOU WANT TO CALL IT. I WAS THERE, OR CLOSE ENOUGH AT LEAST THAT I HEARD WHAT JEN SAID.
GOOD. THEN YOU HEARD HER SAY, "IT'S OUR FUTURE, CAROL. NOT HIS. FIGHT FOR IT."
AND HOW DO WE REALLY KNOW SHE WAS TALKING ABOUT TONY? FOR ALL WE KNOW, "HIS" COULD HAVE MEANT THANOS. HELL, IT'S PROBABLY THE LAST THING SHE REMEMBERS, GETTING CREAMED BY THANOS.
YOU'RE PLAYING WITH SEMANTICS HERE, ALISON--
THE POINT IS, WE CAN'T REALLY KNOW FOR SURE--
I KNOW.

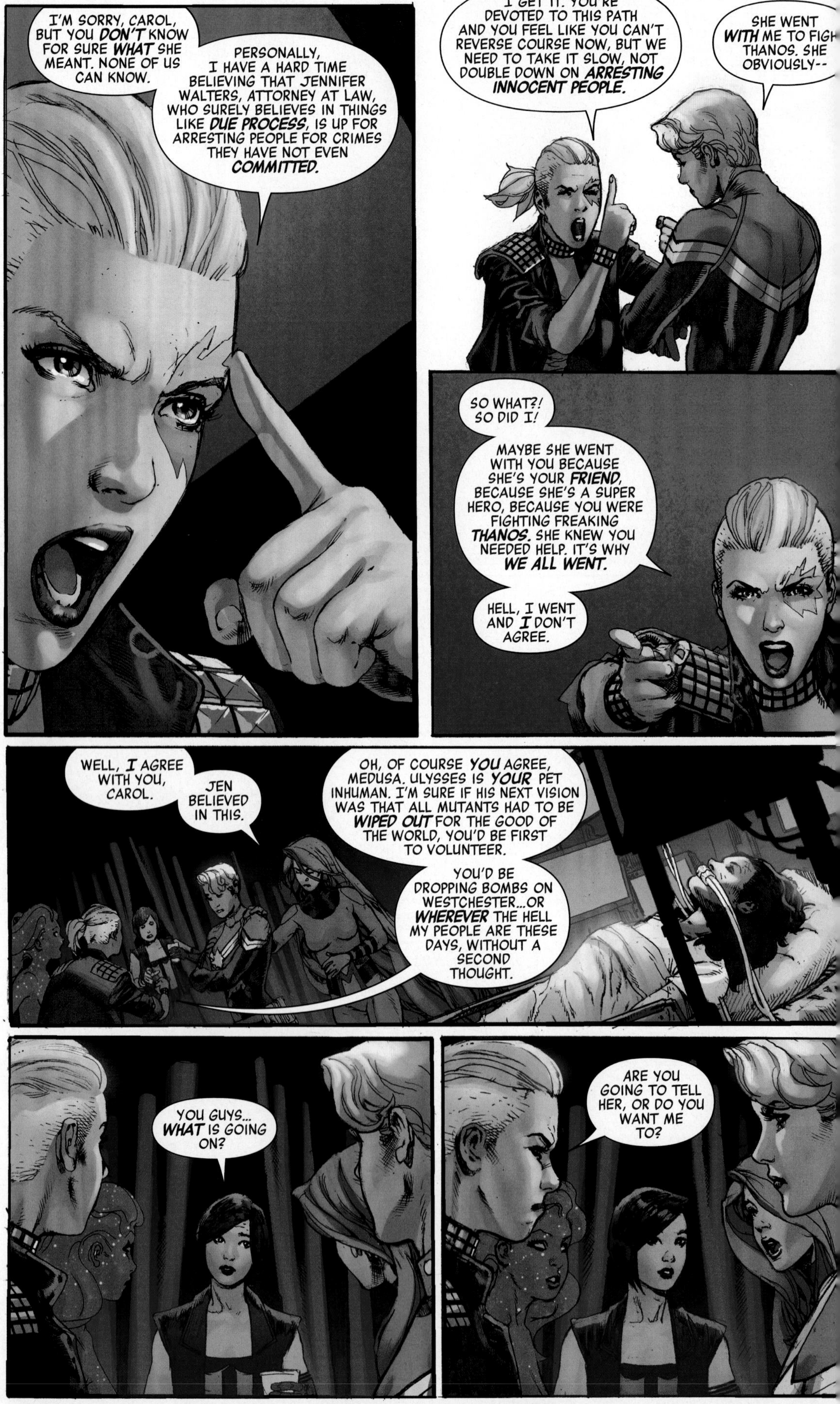
I'M SORRY, CAROL, BUT YOU DON'T KNOW FOR SURE WHAT SHE MEANT. NONE OF US CAN KNOW.
PERSONALLY, I HAVE A HARD TIME BELIEVING THAT JENNIFER WALTERS, ATTORNEY AT LAW, WHO SURELY BELIEVES IN THINGS LIKE DUE PROCESS, IS UP FOR ARRESTING PEOPLE FOR CRIMES THEY HAVE NOT EVEN COMMITTED.
I GET IT. YOU'RE DEVOTED TO THIS PATH AND YOU FEEL LIKE YOU CAN'T REVERSE COURSE NOW, BUT WE NEED TO TAKE IT SLOW, NOT DOUBLE DOWN ON ARRESTING INNOCENT PEOPLE.
SHE WENT WITH ME TO FIGH THANOS. SHE OBVIOUSLY--
SO WHAT?! SO DID I!
MAYBE SHE WENT WITH YOU BECAUSE SHE'S YOUR FRIEND, BECAUSE SHE'S A SUPER HERO, BECAUSE YOU WERE FIGHTING FREAKING THANOS. SHE KNEW YOU NEEDED HELP. IT'S WHY WE ALL WENT.
HELL, I WENT AND I DON'T AGREE.
WELL, I AGREE WITH YOU, CAROL.
JEN BELIEVED IN THIS.
OH, OF COURSE YOU AGREE, MEDUSA. ULYSSES IS YOUR PET INHUMAN. I'M SURE IF HIS NEXT VISION WAS THAT ALL MUTANTS HAD TO BE WIPED OUT FOR THE GOOD OF THE WORLD, YOU'D BE FIRST TO VOLUNTEER.
YOU'D BE DROPPING BOMBS ON WESTCHESTER...OR WHEREVER THE HELL MY PEOPLE ARE THESE DAYS, WITHOUT A SECOND THOUGHT.
YOU GUYS... WHAT IS GOING ON?
ARE YOU GOING TO TELL HER, OR DO YOU WANT ME TO?

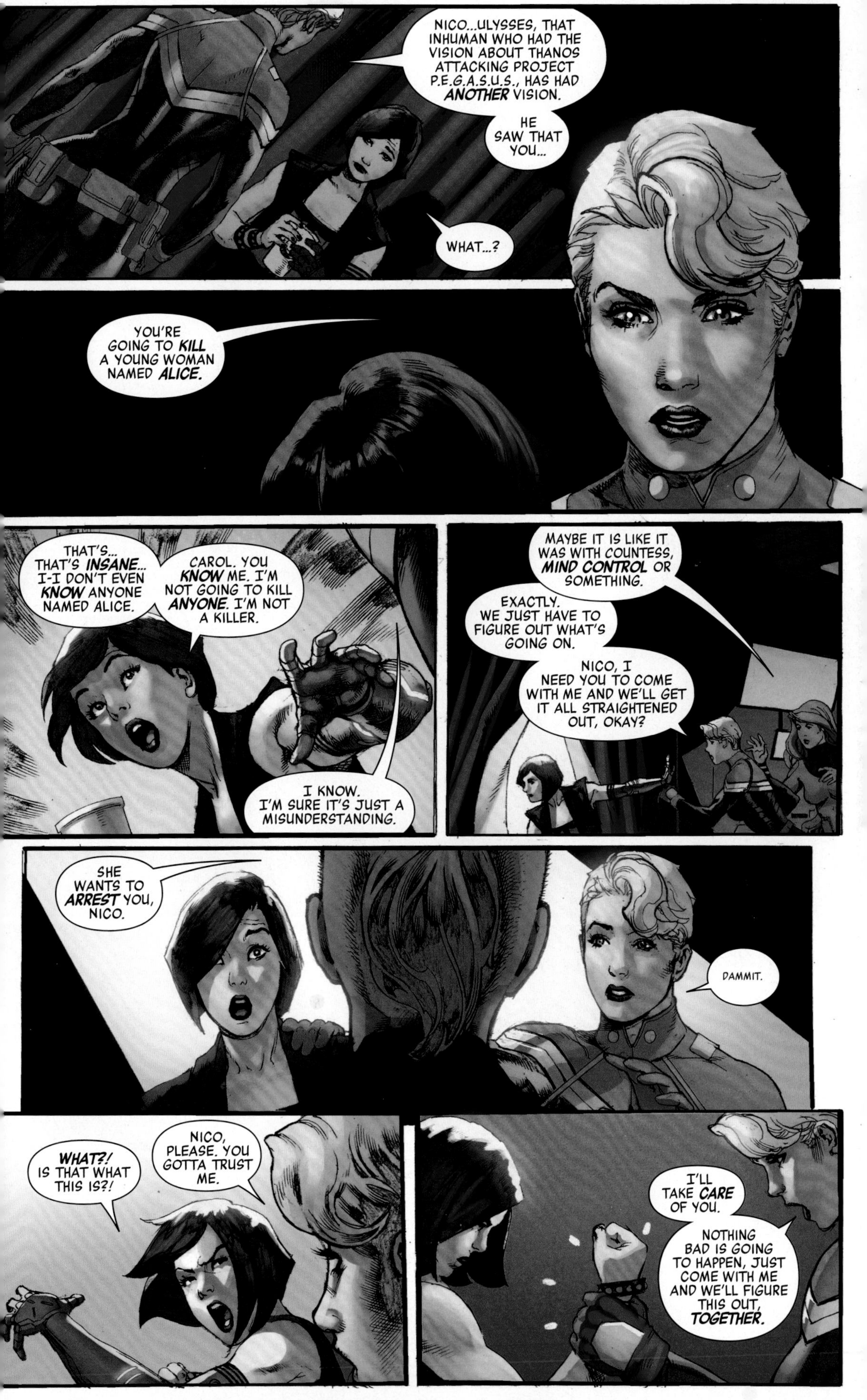

NICO...ULYSSES, THAT INHUMAN WHO HAD THE VISION ABOUT THANOS ATTACKING PROJECT P.E.G.A.S.U.S., HAS HAD ANOTHER VISION.
HE SAW THAT YOU...
WHAT...?
YOU'RE GOING TO KILL A YOUNG WOMAN NAMED ALICE.
THAT'S... THAT'S INSANE... I-I DON'T EVEN KNOW ANYONE NAMED ALICE.
CAROL. YOU KNOW ME. I'M NOT GOING TO KILL ANYONE. I'M NOT A KILLER.
I KNOW. I'M SURE IT'S JUST A MISUNDERSTANDING.
MAYBE IT IS LIKE IT WAS WITH COUNTESS, MIND CONTROL OR SOMETHING.
EXACTLY. WE JUST HAVE TO FIGURE OUT WHAT'S GOING ON.
NICO, I NEED YOU TO COME WITH ME AND WE'LL GET IT ALL STRAIGHTENED OUT, OKAY?
SHE WANTS TO ARREST YOU, NICO.
DAMMIT.
WHAT?! IS THAT WHAT THIS IS?!
NICO, PLEASE. YOU GOTTA TRUST ME.
I'LL TAKE CARE OF YOU.
NOTHING BAD IS GOING TO HAPPEN, JUST COME WITH ME AND WE'LL FIGURE THIS OUT, TOGETHER.

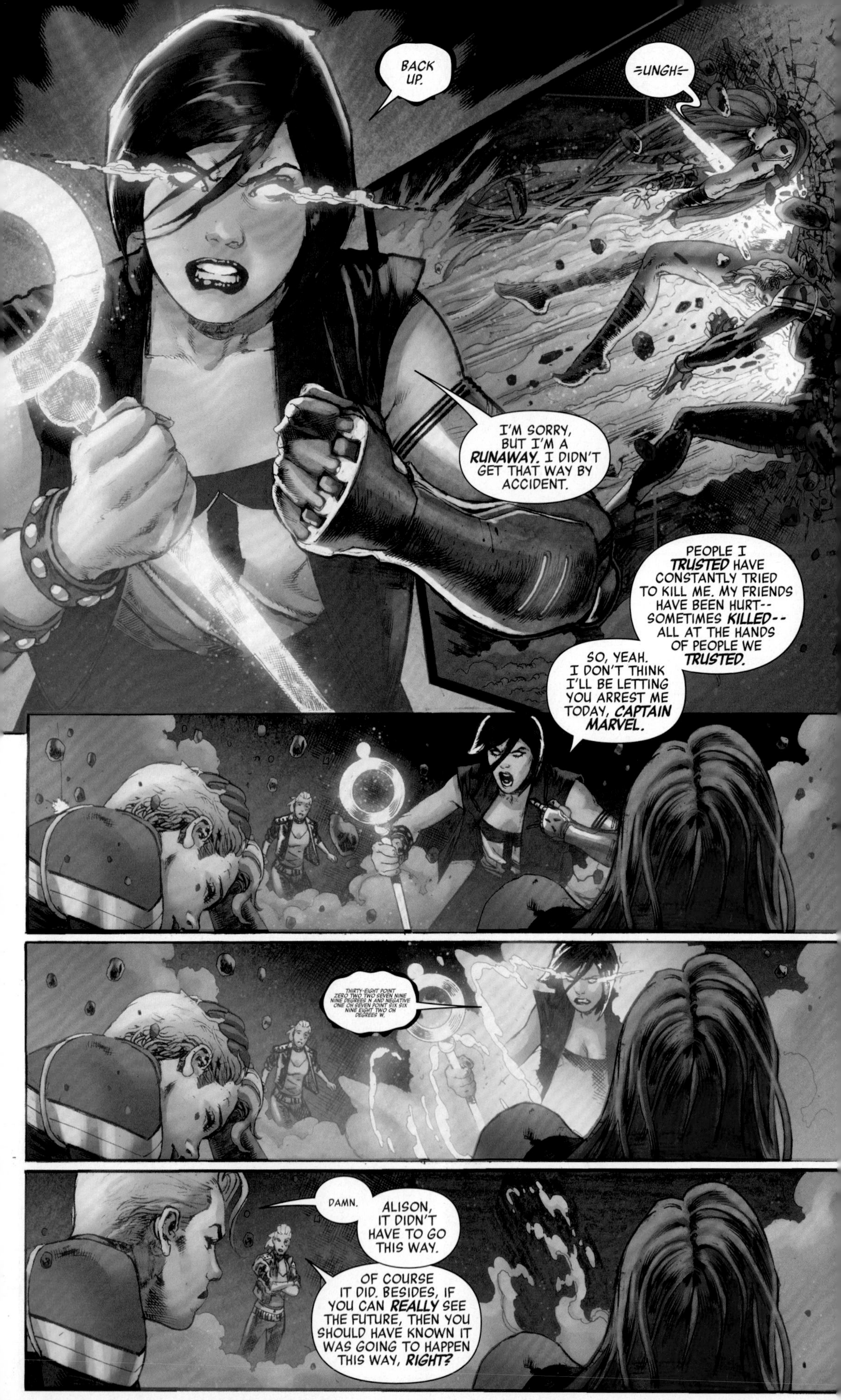
BACK UP.
=UNGH=
I'M SORRY, BUT I'M A RUNAWAY. I DIDN'T GET THAT WAY BY ACCIDENT.
PEOPLE I TRUSTED HAVE CONSTANTLY TRIED TO KILL ME. MY FRIENDS HAVE BEEN HURT-- SOMETIMES KILLED-- ALL AT THE HANDS OF PEOPLE WE TRUSTED.
SO, YEAH. I DON'T THINK I'LL BE LETTING YOU ARREST ME TODAY, CAPTAIN MARVEL.
THIRTY-EIGHT POINT ZERO TWO TWO SEVEN NINE NINE DEGREES N AND NEGATIVE ONE OH SEVEN POINT SIX SIX NINE EIGHT TWO OH DEGREES W.
DAMN.
ALISON, IT DIDN'T HAVE TO GO THIS WAY.
OF COURSE IT DID. BESIDES, IF YOU CAN REALLY SEE THE FUTURE, THEN YOU SHOULD HAVE KNOWN IT WAS GOING TO HAPPEN THIS WAY, RIGHT?

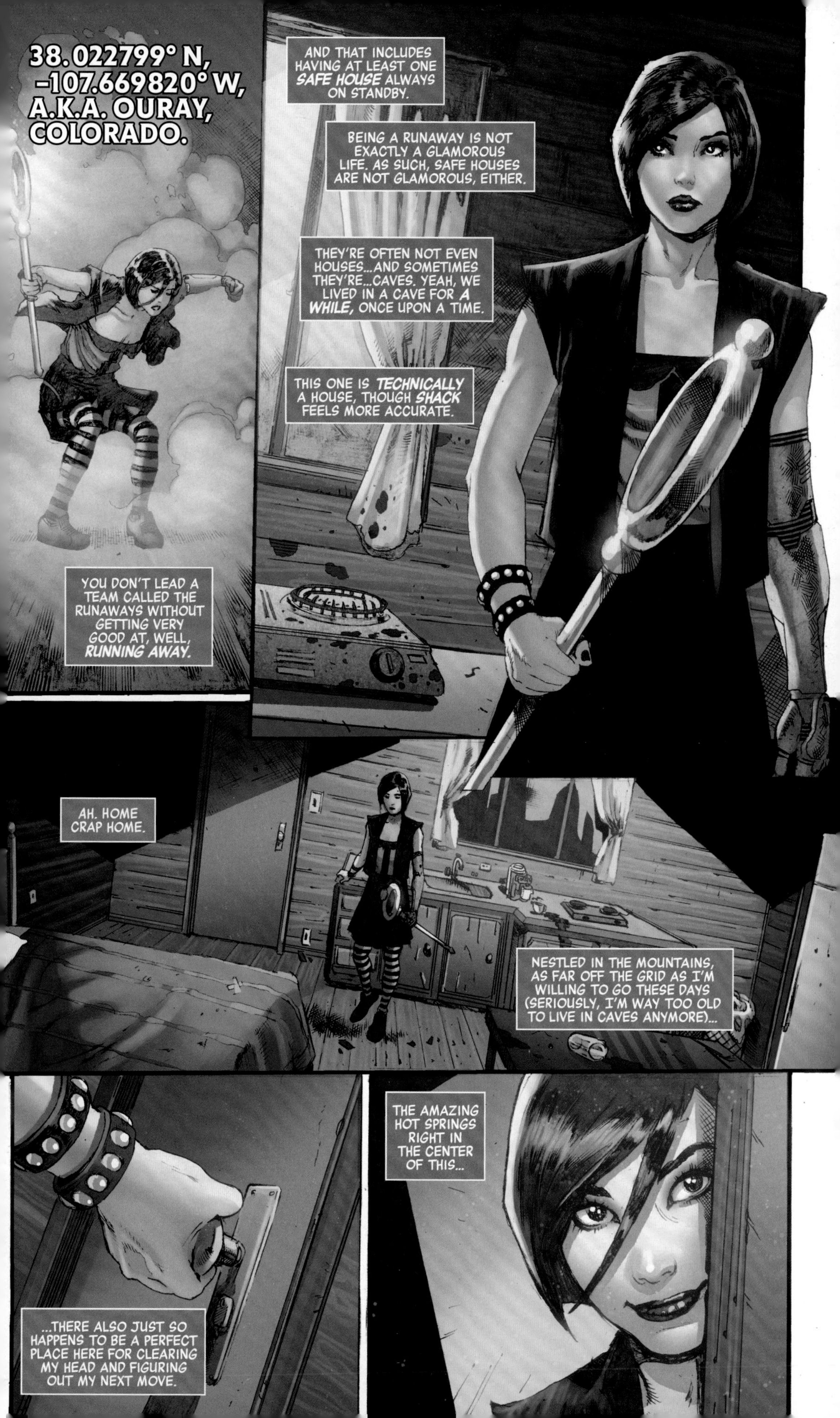
38.022799° N,
–107.669820° W,
A.K.A. OURAY,
COLORADO.
YOU DON'T LEAD A TEAM CALLED THE RUNAWAYS WITHOUT GETTING VERY GOOD AT, WELL, RUNNING AWAY.
AND THAT INCLUDES HAVING AT LEAST ONE SAFE HOUSE ALWAYS ON STANDBY.
BEING A RUNAWAY IS NOT EXACTLY A GLAMOROUS LIFE. AS SUCH, SAFE HOUSES ARE NOT GLAMOROUS, EITHER.
THEY'RE OFTEN NOT EVEN HOUSES...AND SOMETIMES THEY'RE...CAVES. YEAH, WE LIVED IN A CAVE FOR A WHILE, ONCE UPON A TIME.
THIS ONE IS TECHNICALLY A HOUSE, THOUGH SHACK FEELS MORE ACCURATE.
AH. HOME CRAP HOME.
NESTLED IN THE MOUNTAINS, AS FAR OFF THE GRID AS I'M WILLING TO GO THESE DAYS (SERIOUSLY, I'M WAY TOO OLD TO LIVE IN CAVES ANYMORE)...
THE AMAZING HOT SPRINGS RIGHT IN THE CENTER OF THIS...
...THERE ALSO JUST SO HAPPENS TO BE A PERFECT PLACE HERE FOR CLEARING MY HEAD AND FIGURING OUT MY NEXT MOVE.

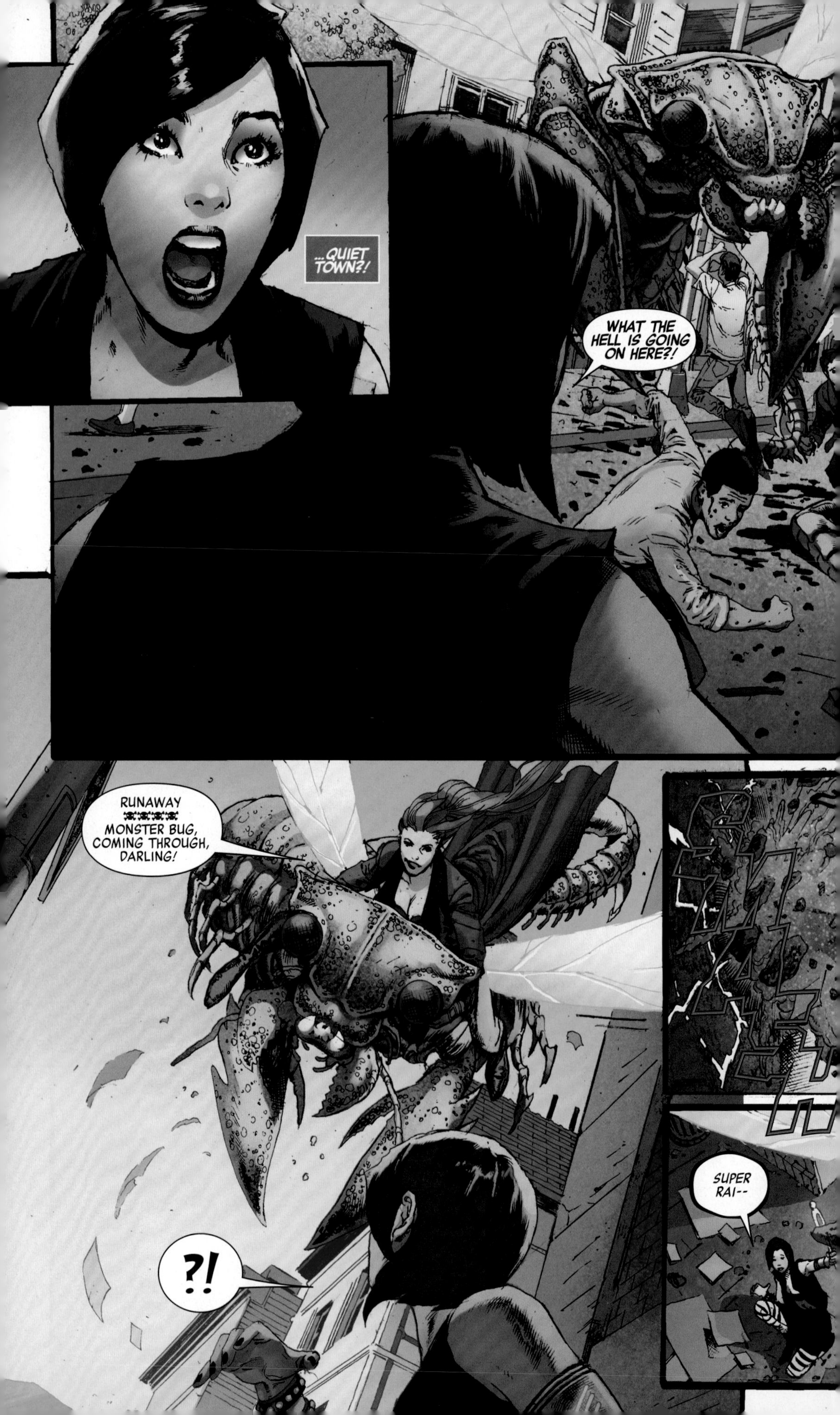
...QUIET TOWN?!
WHAT THE HELL IS GOING ON HERE?!
RUNAWAY MONSTER BUG, COMING THROUGH, DARLING!
?!
SUPER RAI--

WELL, MY "SAFE HOUSE" IS OFFICIALLY *UNSAFE.*

AH--!

GAH!

--HEY!

LEAVE THIS ONE TO THE FANCY BLOODSTONE HAND!

FOOOM

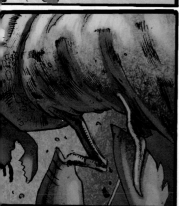

SORRY ABOUT THE TACKLE, DARLING. *NON-FATAL* BLASTS ONLY, I'M AFRAID. WASN'T SURE WHAT THAT WHAMMY YOU WERE COOKING UP WAS GOING TO DO...

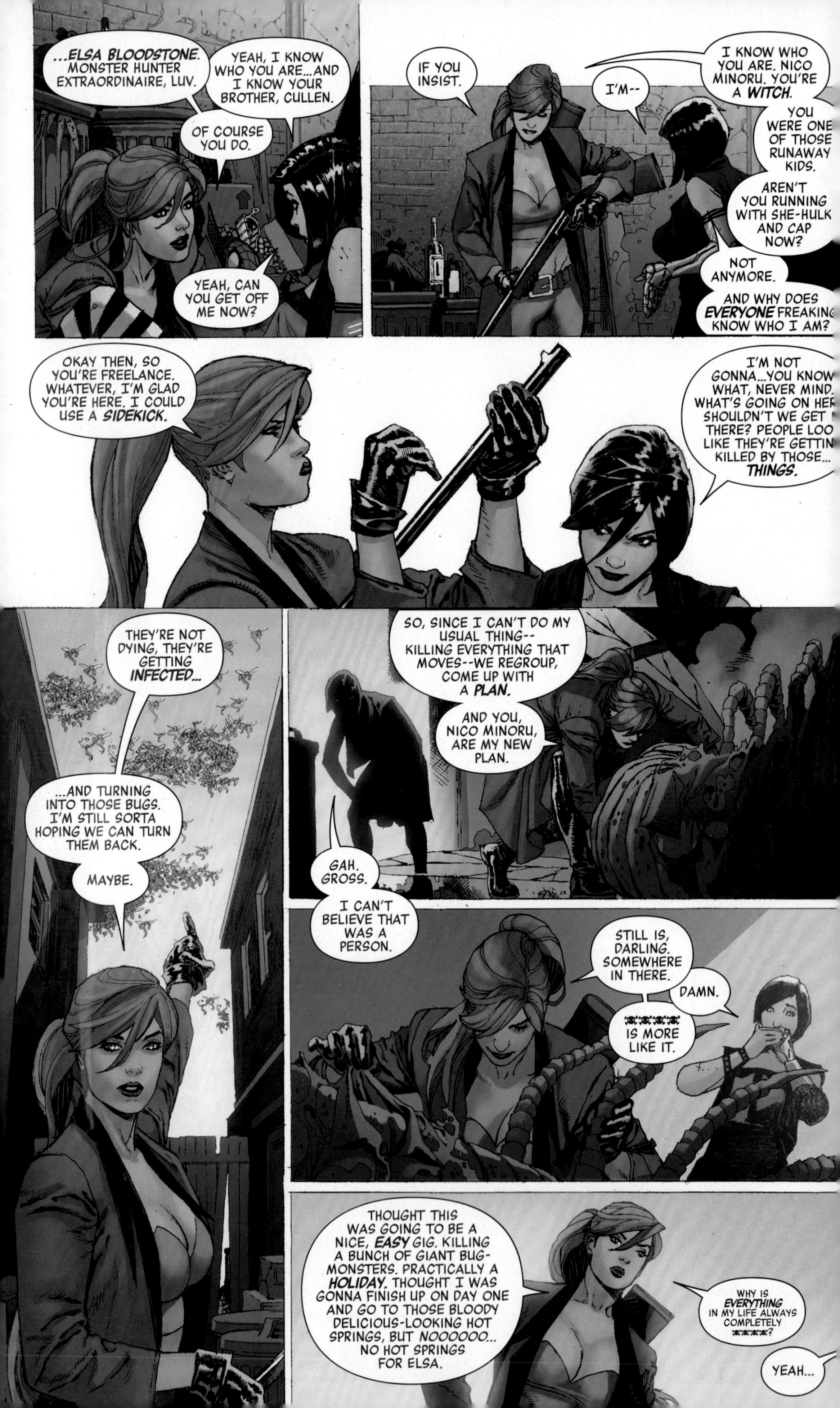

...ELSA BLOODSTONE. MONSTER HUNTER EXTRAORDINAIRE, LUV.
YEAH, I KNOW WHO YOU ARE...AND I KNOW YOUR BROTHER, CULLEN.
OF COURSE YOU DO.
YEAH, CAN YOU GET OFF ME NOW?
IF YOU INSIST.
I'M--
I KNOW WHO YOU ARE. NICO MINORU. YOU'RE A WITCH.
YOU WERE ONE OF THOSE RUNAWAY KIDS.
AREN'T YOU RUNNING WITH SHE-HULK AND CAP NOW?
NOT ANYMORE.
AND WHY DOES EVERYONE FREAKING KNOW WHO I AM?
OKAY THEN, SO YOU'RE FREELANCE. WHATEVER, I'M GLAD YOU'RE HERE. I COULD USE A SIDEKICK.
I'M NOT GONNA...YOU KNOW WHAT, NEVER MIND. WHAT'S GOING ON HER SHOULDN'T WE GET THERE? PEOPLE LOO LIKE THEY'RE GETTIN KILLED BY THOSE... THINGS.
THEY'RE NOT DYING, THEY'RE GETTING INFECTED...
...AND TURNING INTO THOSE BUGS. I'M STILL SORTA HOPING WE CAN TURN THEM BACK.
MAYBE.
SO, SINCE I CAN'T DO MY USUAL THING-- KILLING EVERYTHING THAT MOVES--WE REGROUP, COME UP WITH A PLAN.
AND YOU, NICO MINORU, ARE MY NEW PLAN.
GAH. GROSS.
I CAN'T BELIEVE THAT WAS A PERSON.
STILL IS, DARLING. SOMEWHERE IN THERE.
DAMN.
IS MORE LIKE IT.
THOUGHT THIS WAS GOING TO BE A NICE, EASY GIG. KILLING A BUNCH OF GIANT BUG-MONSTERS. PRACTICALLY A HOLIDAY. THOUGHT I WAS GONNA FINISH UP ON DAY ONE AND GO TO THOSE BLOODY DELICIOUS-LOOKING HOT SPRINGS, BUT NOOOOOO... NO HOT SPRINGS FOR ELSA.
WHY IS EVERYTHING IN MY LIFE ALWAYS COMPLETELY ?
YEAH...

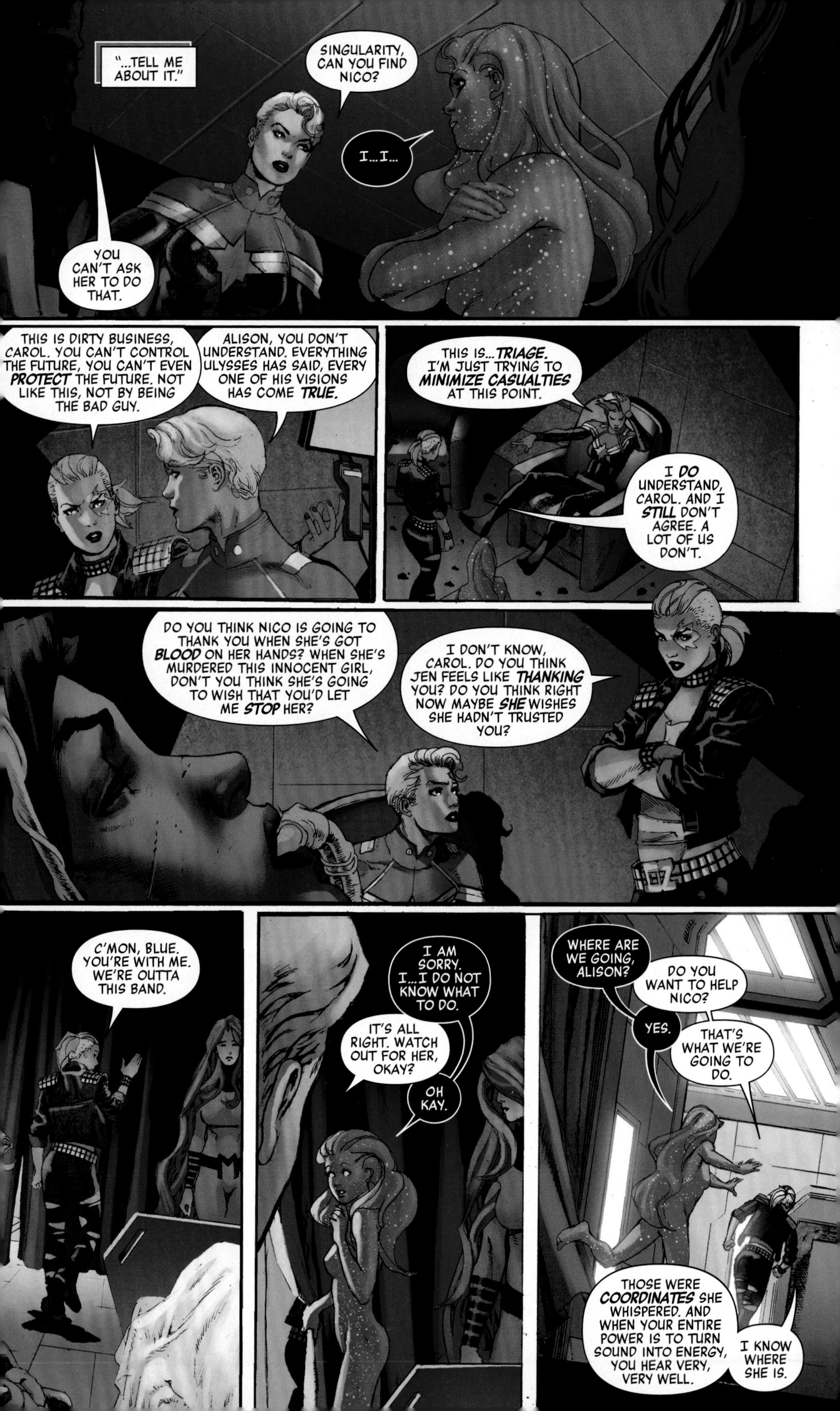
"...TELL ME ABOUT IT."
SINGULARITY, CAN YOU FIND NICO?
I...I...
YOU CAN'T ASK HER TO DO THAT.
THIS IS DIRTY BUSINESS, CAROL. YOU CAN'T CONTROL THE FUTURE, YOU CAN'T EVEN PROTECT THE FUTURE. NOT LIKE THIS, NOT BY BEING THE BAD GUY.
ALISON, YOU DON'T UNDERSTAND. EVERYTHING ULYSSES HAS SAID, EVERY ONE OF HIS VISIONS HAS COME TRUE.
THIS IS...TRIAGE. I'M JUST TRYING TO MINIMIZE CASUALTIES AT THIS POINT.
I DO UNDERSTAND, CAROL. AND I STILL DON'T AGREE. A LOT OF US DON'T.
DO YOU THINK NICO IS GOING TO THANK YOU WHEN SHE'S GOT BLOOD ON HER HANDS? WHEN SHE'S MURDERED THIS INNOCENT GIRL, DON'T YOU THINK SHE'S GOING TO WISH THAT YOU'D LET ME STOP HER?
I DON'T KNOW, CAROL. DO YOU THINK JEN FEELS LIKE THANKING YOU? DO YOU THINK RIGHT NOW MAYBE SHE WISHES SHE HADN'T TRUSTED YOU?
C'MON, BLUE. YOU'RE WITH ME. WE'RE OUTTA THIS BAND.
I AM SORRY. I...I DO NOT KNOW WHAT TO DO.
IT'S ALL RIGHT. WATCH OUT FOR HER, OKAY?
OH KAY.
WHERE ARE WE GOING, ALISON?
DO YOU WANT TO HELP NICO?
YES.
THAT'S WHAT WE'RE GOING TO DO.
THOSE WERE COORDINATES SHE WHISPERED. AND WHEN YOUR ENTIRE POWER IS TO TURN SOUND INTO ENERGY, YOU HEAR VERY, VERY WELL.
I KNOW WHERE SHE IS.

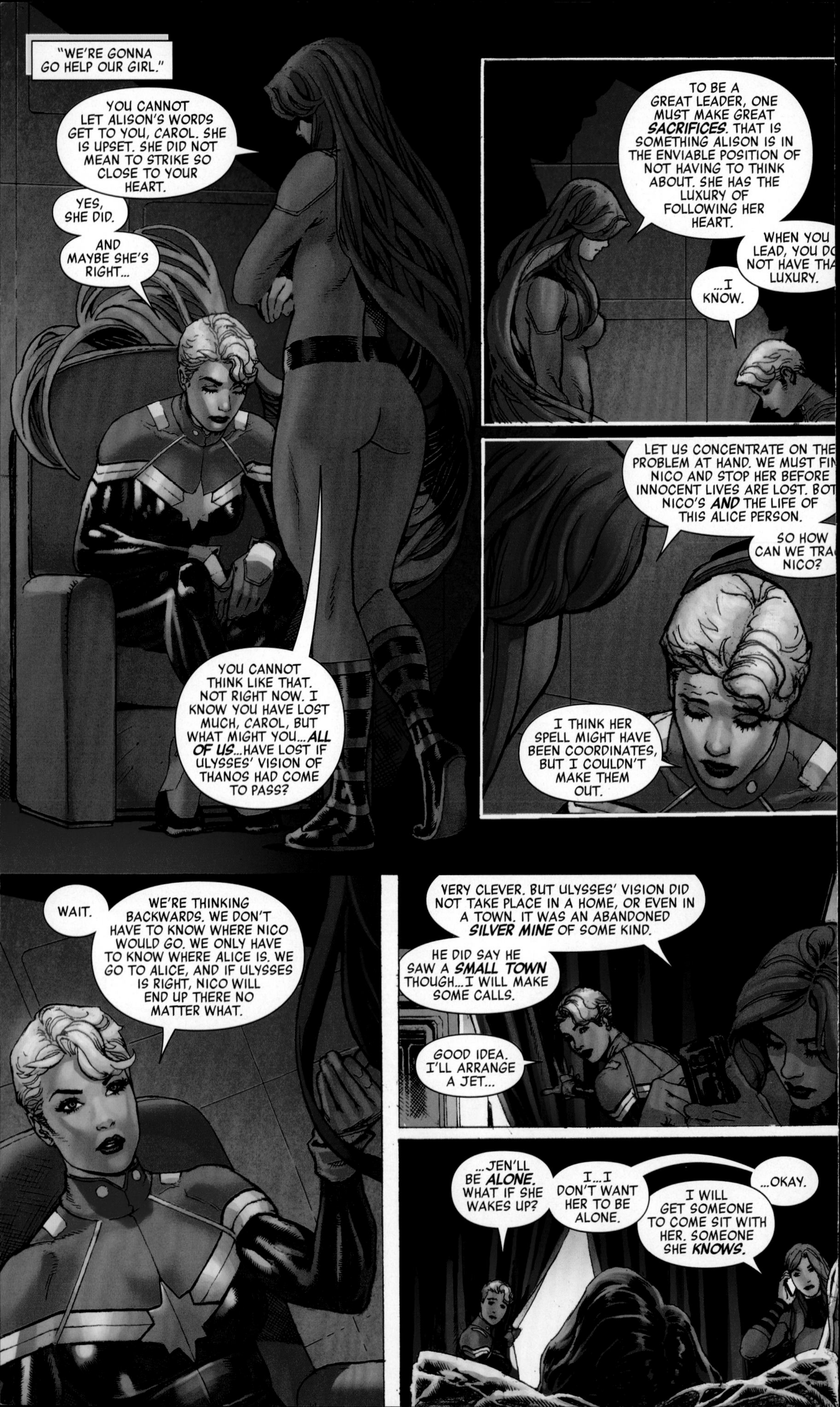
"WE'RE GONNA GO HELP OUR GIRL."
YOU CANNOT LET ALISON'S WORDS GET TO YOU, CAROL. SHE IS UPSET. SHE DID NOT MEAN TO STRIKE SO CLOSE TO YOUR HEART.
YES, SHE DID.
AND MAYBE SHE'S RIGHT...
YOU CANNOT THINK LIKE THAT. NOT RIGHT NOW. I KNOW YOU HAVE LOST MUCH, CAROL, BUT WHAT MIGHT YOU...ALL OF US...HAVE LOST IF ULYSSES' VISION OF THANOS HAD COME TO PASS?
TO BE A GREAT LEADER, ONE MUST MAKE GREAT SACRIFICES. THAT IS SOMETHING ALISON IS IN THE ENVIABLE POSITION OF NOT HAVING TO THINK ABOUT. SHE HAS THE LUXURY OF FOLLOWING HER HEART.
WHEN YOU LEAD, YOU DO NOT HAVE THA LUXURY.
...I KNOW.
LET US CONCENTRATE ON THE PROBLEM AT HAND. WE MUST FIN NICO AND STOP HER BEFORE INNOCENT LIVES ARE LOST. BOT NICO'S AND THE LIFE OF THIS ALICE PERSON.
SO HOW CAN WE TRA NICO?
I THINK HER SPELL MIGHT HAVE BEEN COORDINATES, BUT I COULDN'T MAKE THEM OUT.
WAIT.
WE'RE THINKING BACKWARDS. WE DON'T HAVE TO KNOW WHERE NICO WOULD GO. WE ONLY HAVE TO KNOW WHERE ALICE IS. WE GO TO ALICE, AND IF ULYSSES IS RIGHT, NICO WILL END UP THERE NO MATTER WHAT.
VERY CLEVER. BUT ULYSSES' VISION DID NOT TAKE PLACE IN A HOME, OR EVEN IN A TOWN. IT WAS AN ABANDONED SILVER MINE OF SOME KIND.
HE DID SAY HE SAW A SMALL TOWN THOUGH...I WILL MAKE SOME CALLS.
GOOD IDEA. I'LL ARRANGE A JET...
...JEN'LL BE ALONE. WHAT IF SHE WAKES UP?
I...I DON'T WANT HER TO BE ALONE.
...OKAY.
I WILL GET SOMEONE TO COME SIT WITH HER. SOMEONE SHE KNOWS.

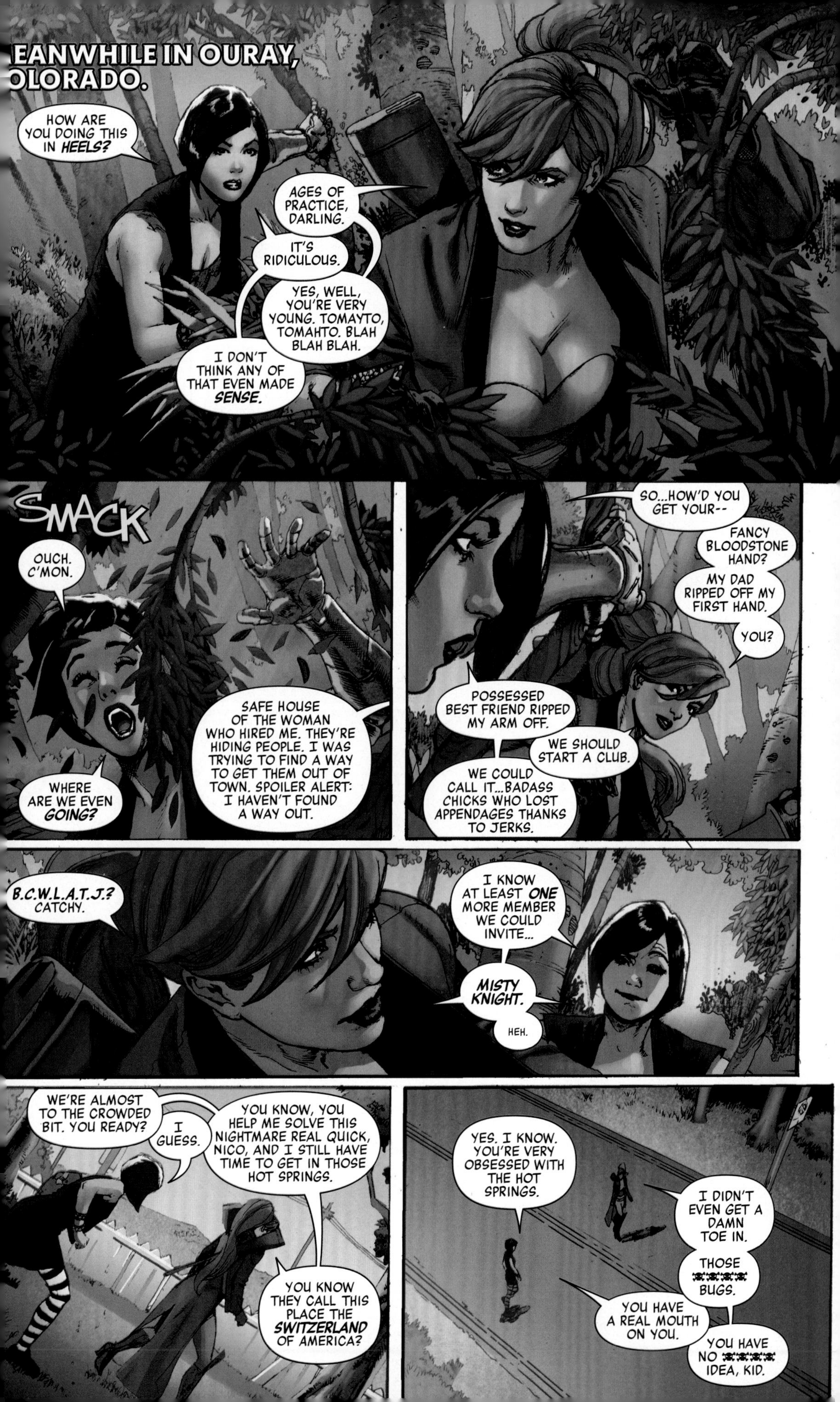
EANWHILE IN OURAY, OLORADO.
HOW ARE YOU DOING THIS IN HEELS?
AGES OF PRACTICE, DARLING.
IT'S RIDICULOUS.
YES, WELL, YOU'RE VERY YOUNG. TOMAYTO, TOMAHTO. BLAH BLAH BLAH.
I DON'T THINK ANY OF THAT EVEN MADE SENSE.
SMACK
OUCH. C'MON.
WHERE ARE WE EVEN GOING?
SAFE HOUSE OF THE WOMAN WHO HIRED ME. THEY'RE HIDING PEOPLE. I WAS TRYING TO FIND A WAY TO GET THEM OUT OF TOWN. SPOILER ALERT: I HAVEN'T FOUND A WAY OUT.
SO...HOW'D YOU GET YOUR--
FANCY BLOODSTONE HAND?
MY DAD RIPPED OFF MY FIRST HAND.
YOU?
POSSESSED BEST FRIEND RIPPED MY ARM OFF.
WE SHOULD START A CLUB.
WE COULD CALL IT...BADASS CHICKS WHO LOST APPENDAGES THANKS TO JERKS.
B.C.W.L.A.T.J.? CATCHY.
I KNOW AT LEAST ONE MORE MEMBER WE COULD INVITE...
MISTY KNIGHT.
HEH.
WE'RE ALMOST TO THE CROWDED BIT. YOU READY?
I GUESS.
YOU KNOW, YOU HELP ME SOLVE THIS NIGHTMARE REAL QUICK, NICO, AND I STILL HAVE TIME TO GET IN THOSE HOT SPRINGS.
YOU KNOW THEY CALL THIS PLACE THE SWITZERLAND OF AMERICA?
YES. I KNOW. YOU'RE VERY OBSESSED WITH THE HOT SPRINGS.
I DIDN'T EVEN GET A DAMN TOE IN.
THOSE ☠☠☠ BUGS.
YOU HAVE A REAL MOUTH ON YOU.
YOU HAVE NO ☠☠☠ IDEA, KID.

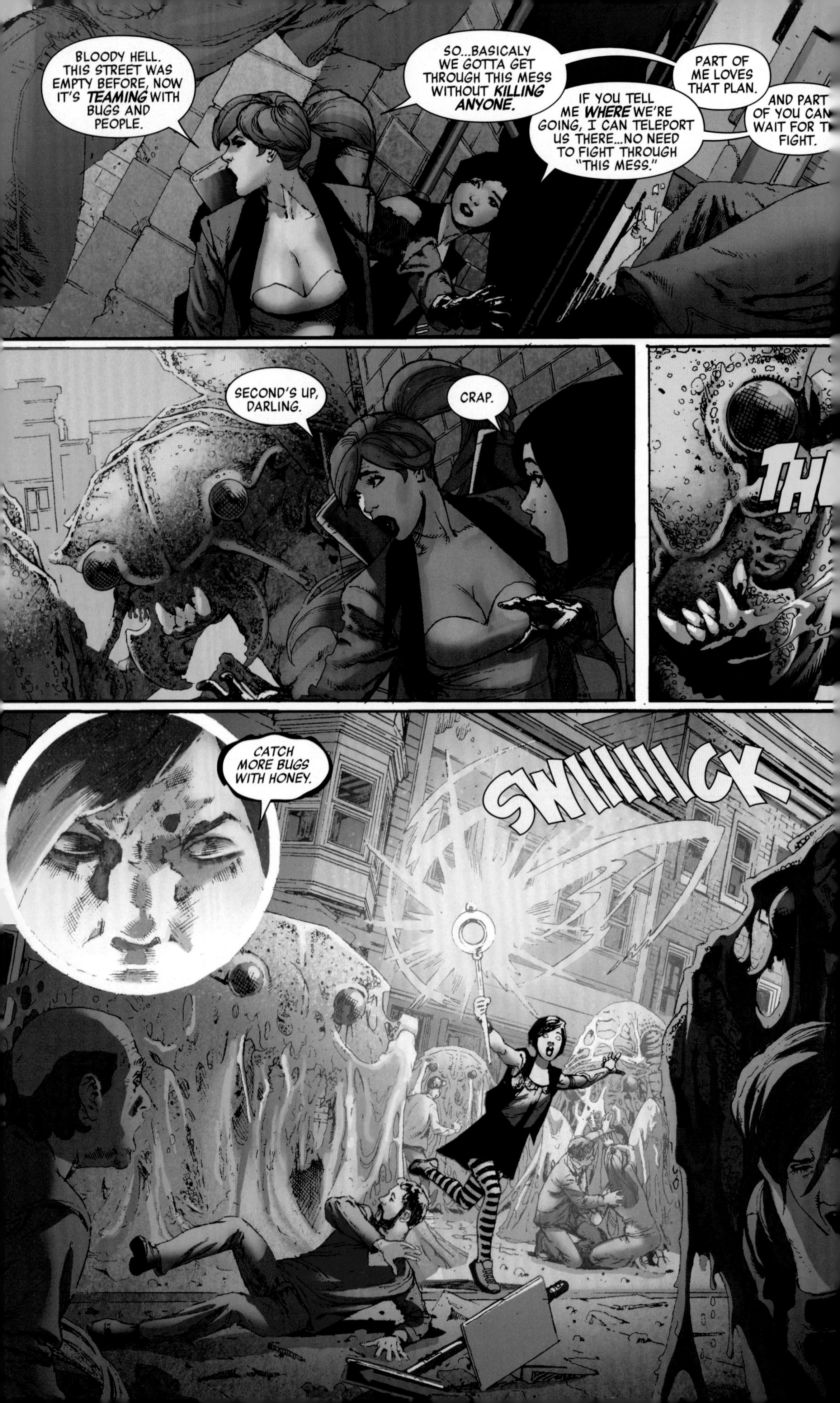
BLOODY HELL. THIS STREET WAS EMPTY BEFORE, NOW IT'S TEAMING WITH BUGS AND PEOPLE.
SO...BASICALY WE GOTTA GET THROUGH THIS MESS WITHOUT KILLING ANYONE.
PART OF ME LOVES THAT PLAN.
AND PART OF YOU CAN WAIT FOR T FIGHT.
IF YOU TELL ME WHERE WE'RE GOING, I CAN TELEPORT US THERE...NO NEED TO FIGHT THROUGH "THIS MESS."
SECOND'S UP, DARLING.
CRAP.
TH
CATCH MORE BUGS WITH HONEY.
SWIIIIICK

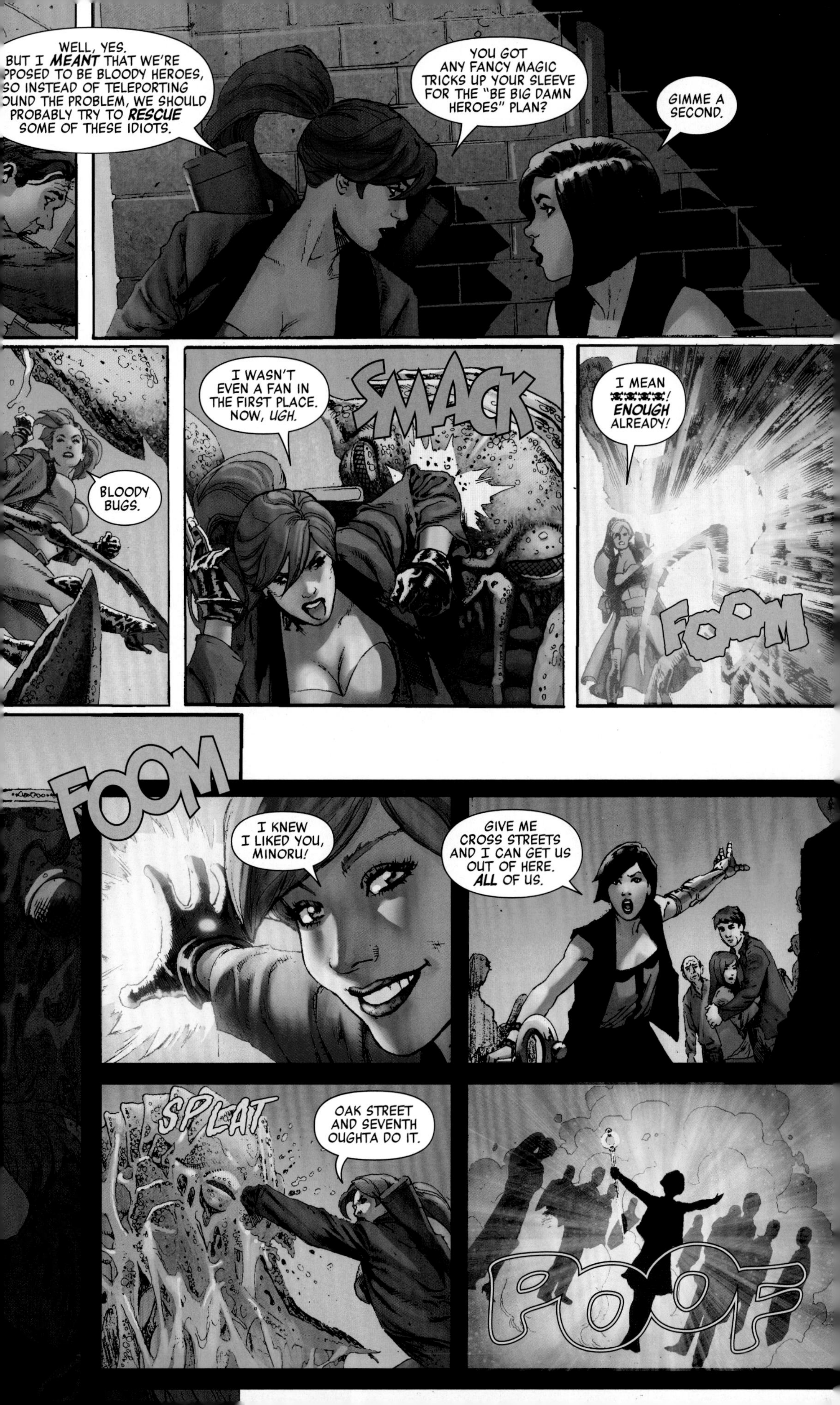
WELL, YES. BUT I MEANT THAT WE'RE SUPPOSED TO BE BLOODY HEROES, SO INSTEAD OF TELEPORTING AROUND THE PROBLEM, WE SHOULD PROBABLY TRY TO RESCUE SOME OF THESE IDIOTS.
YOU GOT ANY FANCY MAGIC TRICKS UP YOUR SLEEVE FOR THE "BE BIG DAMN HEROES" PLAN?
GIMME A SECOND.
BLOODY BUGS.
I WASN'T EVEN A FAN IN THE FIRST PLACE. NOW, UGH.
SMACK
I MEAN ☠☠☠! ENOUGH ALREADY!
FOOM
FOOM
I KNEW I LIKED YOU, MINORU!
GIVE ME CROSS STREETS AND I CAN GET US OUT OF HERE. ALL OF US.
SPLAT
OAK STREET AND SEVENTH OUGHTA DO IT.
POOF

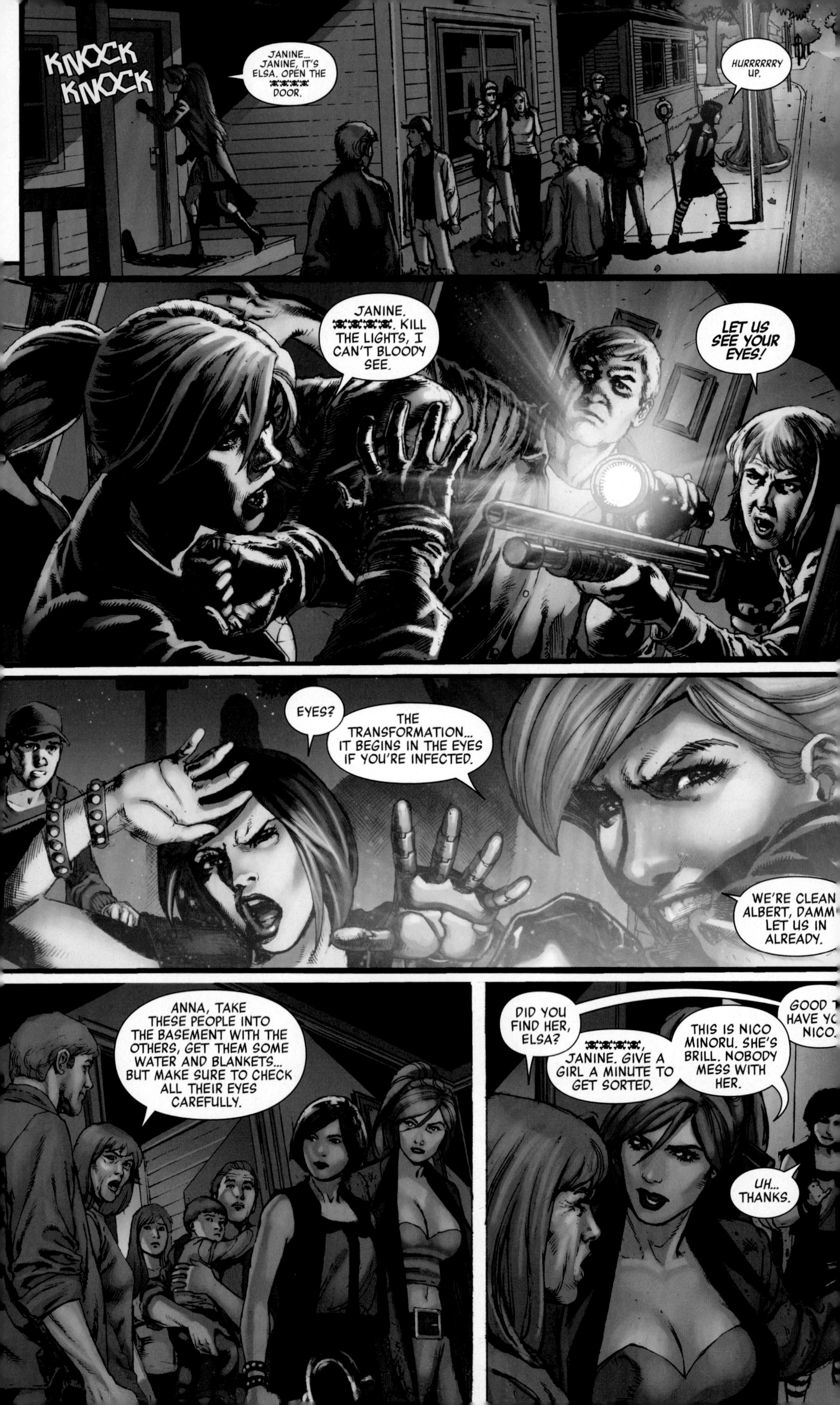
KNOCK KNOCK
JANINE... JANINE, IT'S ELSA. OPEN THE ☠☠☠☠ DOOR.
HURRRRRRY UP.
JANINE. ☠☠☠☠☠. KILL THE LIGHTS, I CAN'T BLOODY SEE.
LET US SEE YOUR EYES!
EYES?
THE TRANSFORMATION... IT BEGINS IN THE EYES IF YOU'RE INFECTED.
WE'RE CLEAN ALBERT, DAMM LET US IN ALREADY.
ANNA, TAKE THESE PEOPLE INTO THE BASEMENT WITH THE OTHERS, GET THEM SOME WATER AND BLANKETS... BUT MAKE SURE TO CHECK ALL THEIR EYES CAREFULLY.
DID YOU FIND HER, ELSA?
☠☠☠☠☠, JANINE. GIVE A GIRL A MINUTE TO GET SORTED.
THIS IS NICO MINORU. SHE'S BRILL. NOBODY MESS WITH HER.
GOOD HAVE YO NICO.
UH... THANKS.

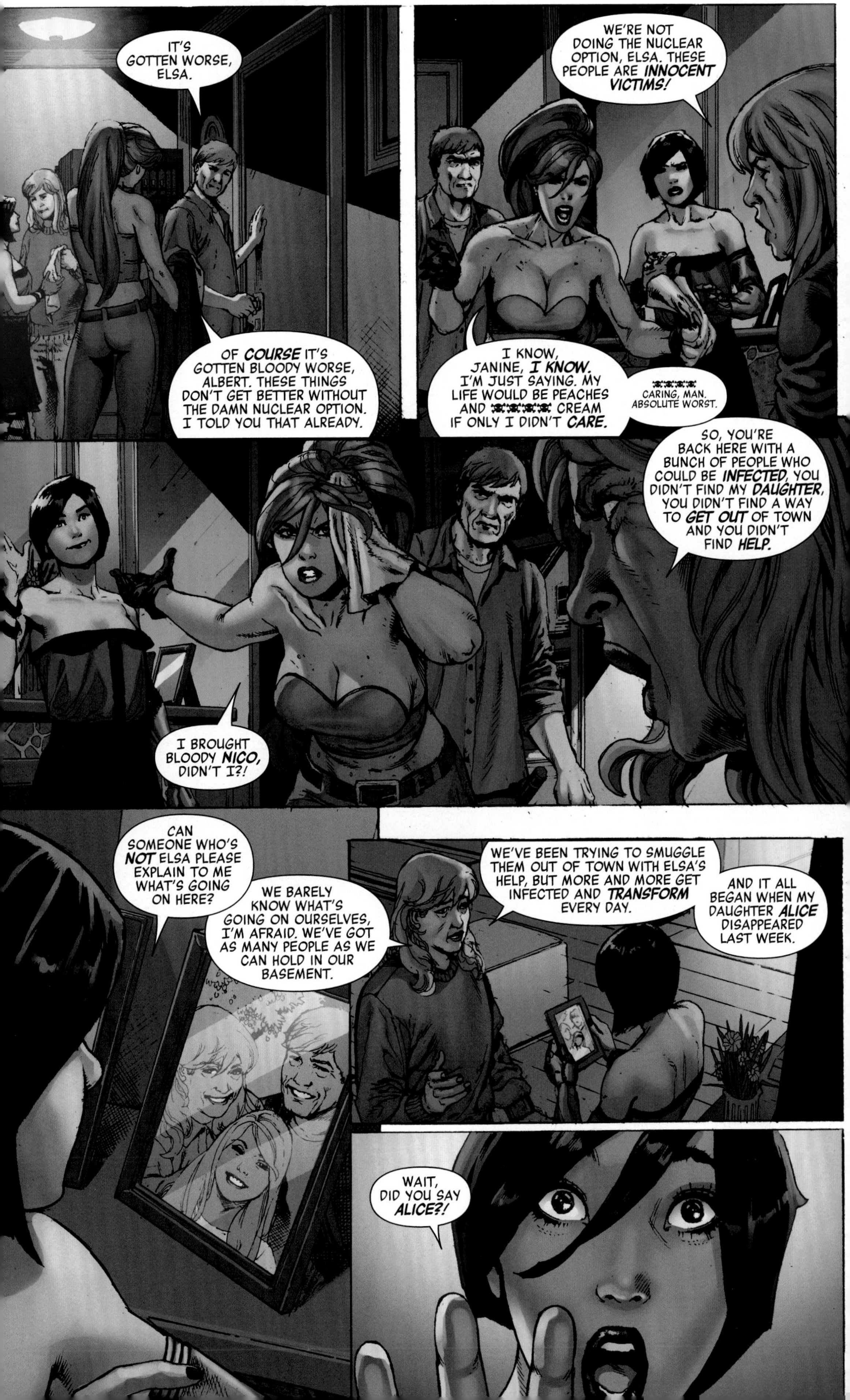
IT'S GOTTEN WORSE, ELSA.
OF COURSE IT'S GOTTEN BLOODY WORSE, ALBERT. THESE THINGS DON'T GET BETTER WITHOUT THE DAMN NUCLEAR OPTION. I TOLD YOU THAT ALREADY.
WE'RE NOT DOING THE NUCLEAR OPTION, ELSA. THESE PEOPLE ARE INNOCENT VICTIMS!
I KNOW, JANINE, I KNOW. I'M JUST SAYING. MY LIFE WOULD BE PEACHES AND CREAM IF ONLY I DIDN'T CARE.
CARING, MAN. ABSOLUTE WORST.
SO, YOU'RE BACK HERE WITH A BUNCH OF PEOPLE WHO COULD BE INFECTED, YOU DIDN'T FIND MY DAUGHTER, YOU DIDN'T FIND A WAY TO GET OUT OF TOWN AND YOU DIDN'T FIND HELP.
I BROUGHT BLOODY NICO, DIDN'T I?!
CAN SOMEONE WHO'S NOT ELSA PLEASE EXPLAIN TO ME WHAT'S GOING ON HERE?
WE BARELY KNOW WHAT'S GOING ON OURSELVES, I'M AFRAID. WE'VE GOT AS MANY PEOPLE AS WE CAN HOLD IN OUR BASEMENT.
WE'VE BEEN TRYING TO SMUGGLE THEM OUT OF TOWN WITH ELSA'S HELP, BUT MORE AND MORE GET INFECTED AND TRANSFORM EVERY DAY.
AND IT ALL BEGAN WHEN MY DAUGHTER ALICE DISAPPEARED LAST WEEK.
WAIT, DID YOU SAY ALICE?!

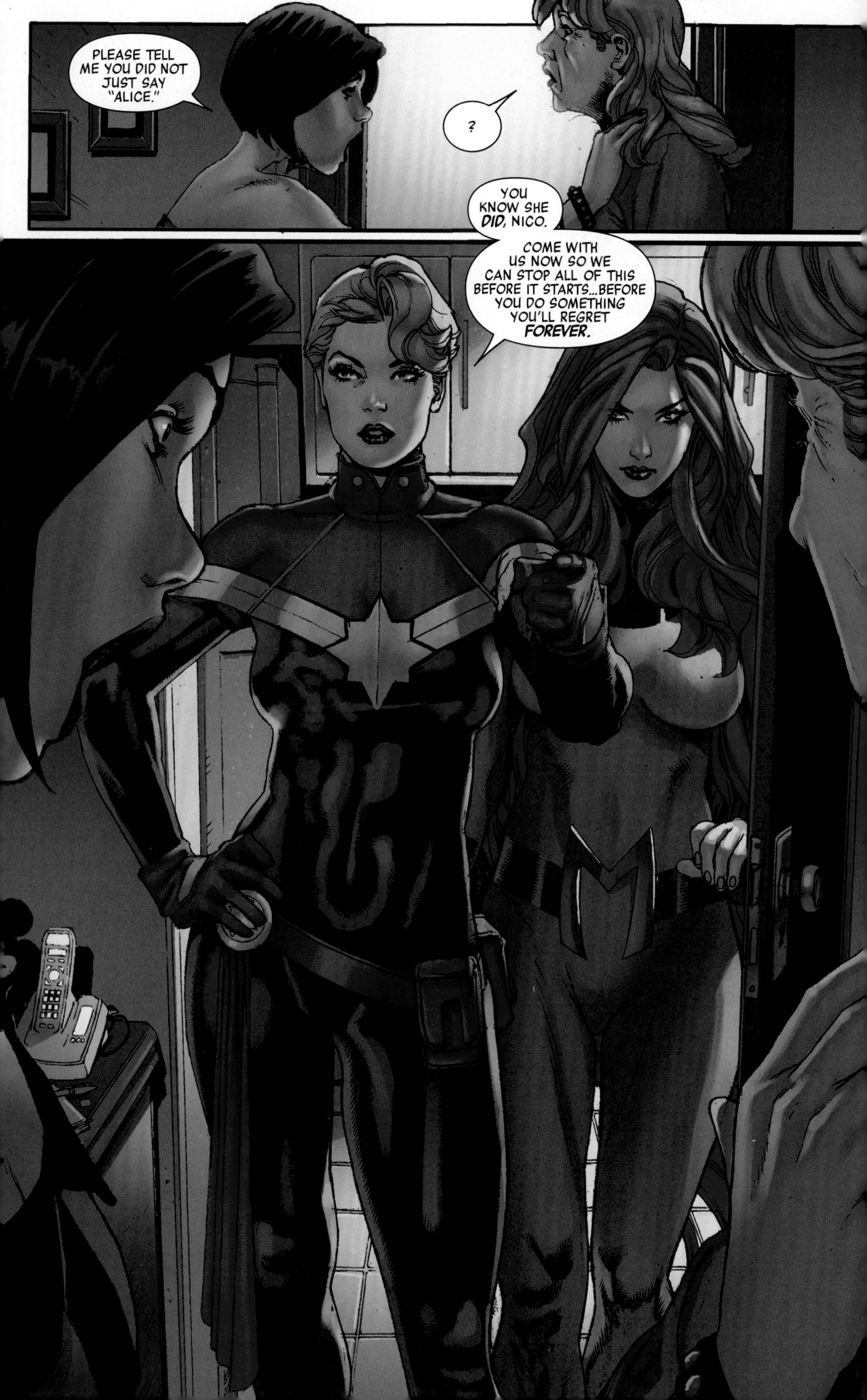
PLEASE TELL ME YOU DID NOT JUST SAY "ALICE."
?
YOU KNOW SHE DID, NICO.
COME WITH US NOW SO WE CAN STOP ALL OF THIS BEFORE IT STARTS...BEFORE YOU DO SOMETHING YOU'LL REGRET FOREVER.

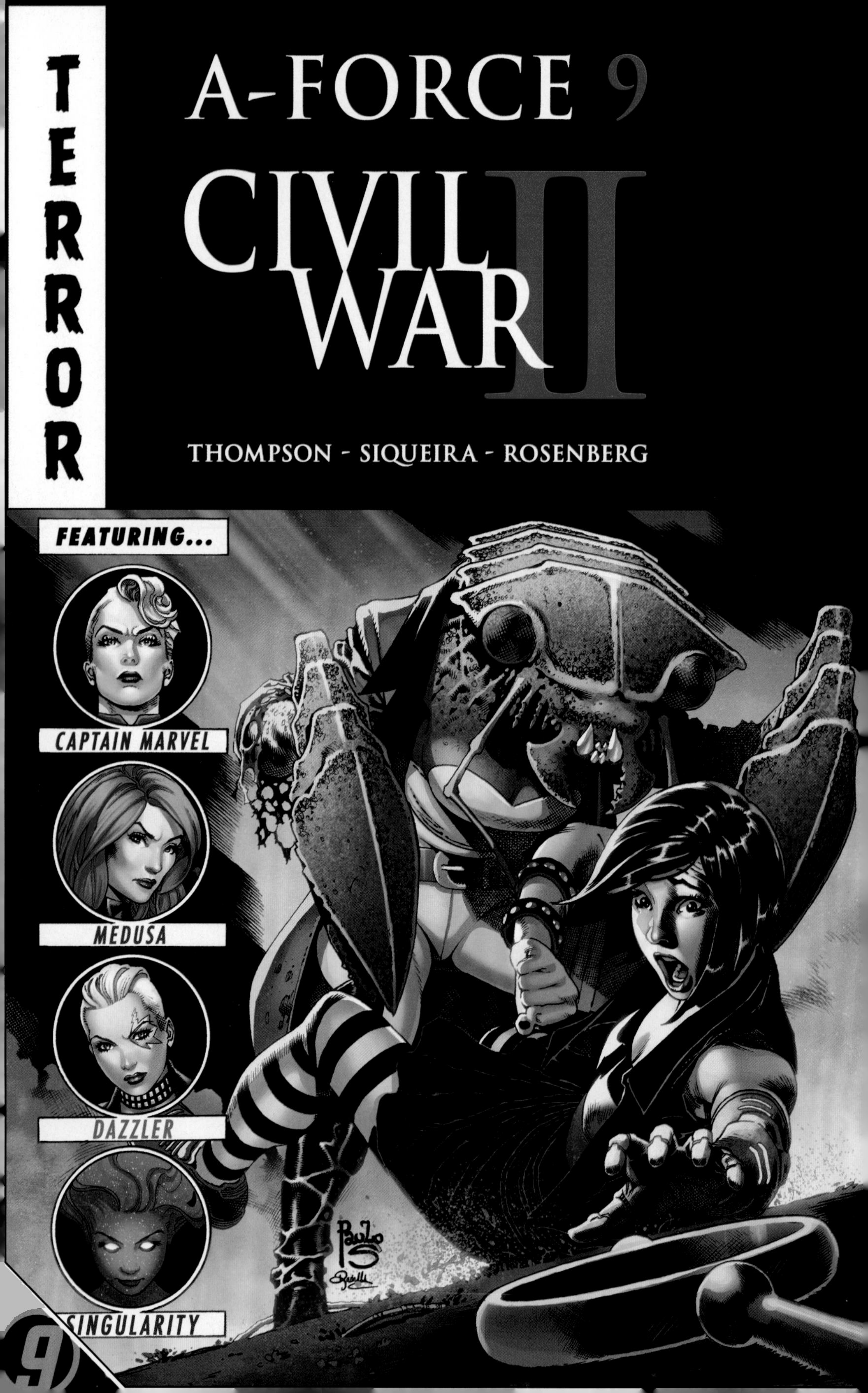
TERROR
A-FORCE 9
CIVIL WAR II
THOMPSON - SIQUEIRA - ROSENBERG
FEATURING...
CAPTAIN MARVEL
MEDUSA
DAZZLER
SINGULARITY
9

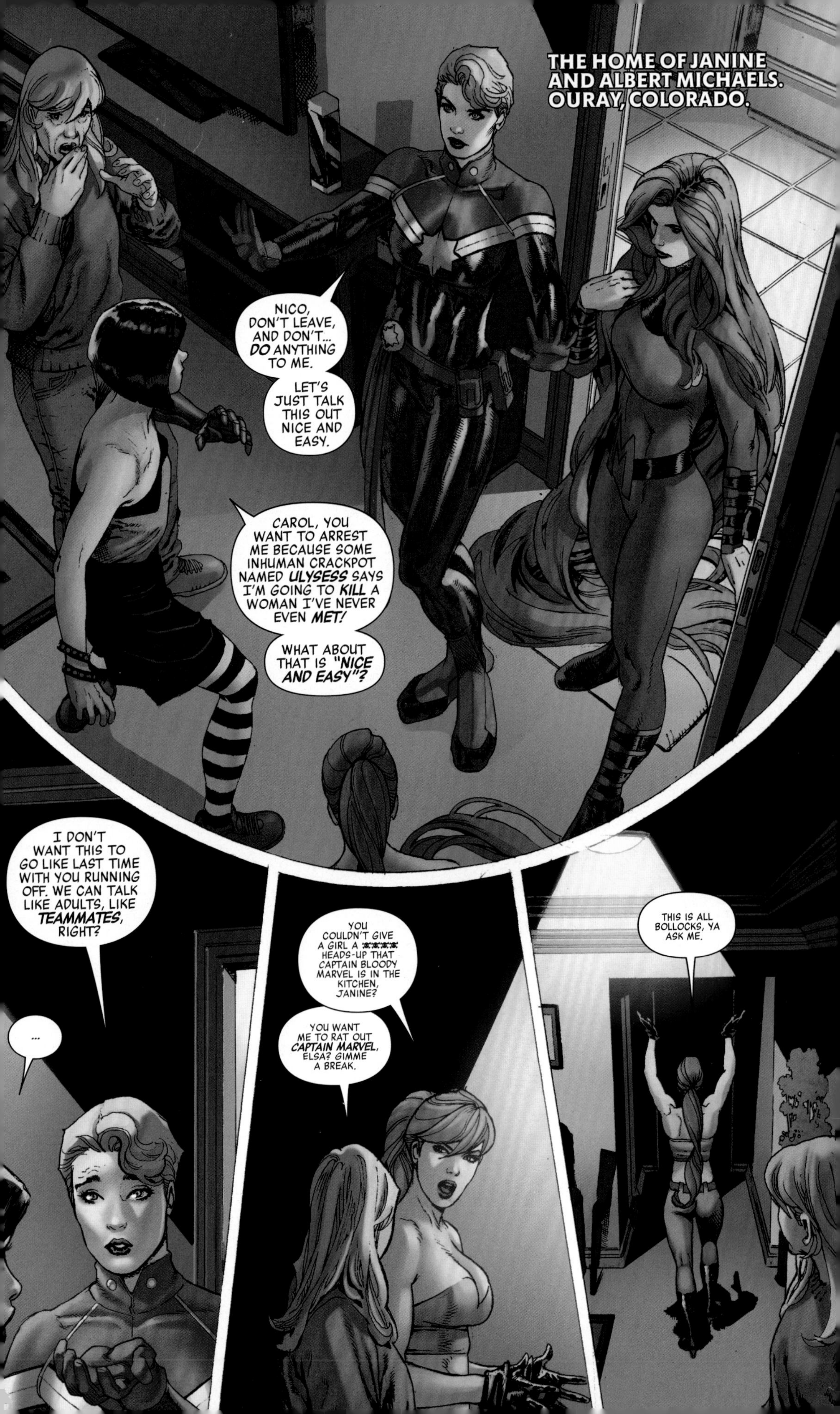
THE HOME OF JANINE AND ALBERT MICHAELS. OURAY, COLORADO.
NICO, DON'T LEAVE, AND DON'T... DO ANYTHING TO ME.
LET'S JUST TALK THIS OUT NICE AND EASY.
CAROL, YOU WANT TO ARREST ME BECAUSE SOME INHUMAN CRACKPOT NAMED ULYSESS SAYS I'M GOING TO KILL A WOMAN I'VE NEVER EVEN MET!
WHAT ABOUT THAT IS "NICE AND EASY"?
I DON'T WANT THIS TO GO LIKE LAST TIME WITH YOU RUNNING OFF. WE CAN TALK LIKE ADULTS, LIKE TEAMMATES, RIGHT?
...
YOU COULDN'T GIVE A GIRL A ※※※ HEADS-UP THAT CAPTAIN BLOODY MARVEL IS IN THE KITCHEN, JANINE?
YOU WANT ME TO RAT OUT CAPTAIN MARVEL, ELSA? GIMME A BREAK.
THIS IS ALL BOLLOCKS, YA ASK ME.

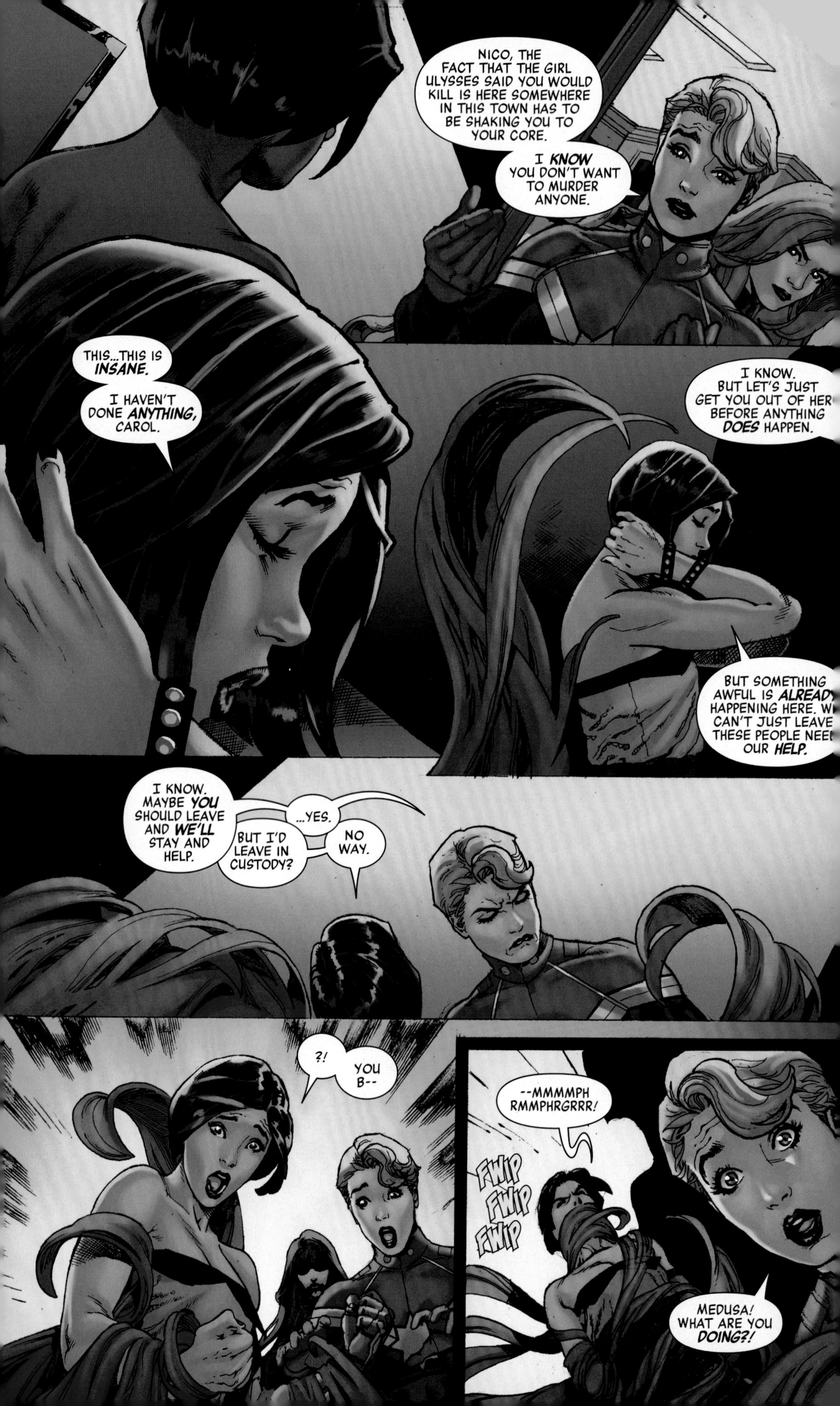
NICO, THE FACT THAT THE GIRL ULYSSES SAID YOU WOULD KILL IS HERE SOMEWHERE IN THIS TOWN HAS TO BE SHAKING YOU TO YOUR CORE.
I KNOW YOU DON'T WANT TO MURDER ANYONE.
THIS...THIS IS INSANE.
I HAVEN'T DONE ANYTHING, CAROL.
I KNOW. BUT LET'S JUST GET YOU OUT OF HER BEFORE ANYTHING DOES HAPPEN.
BUT SOMETHING AWFUL IS ALREADY HAPPENING HERE. W CAN'T JUST LEAVE THESE PEOPLE NEED OUR HELP.
I KNOW. MAYBE YOU SHOULD LEAVE AND WE'LL STAY AND HELP.
BUT I'D LEAVE IN CUSTODY?
...YES.
NO WAY.
?!
YOU B--
--MMMMPH RMMPHRGRRR!
FWIP
FWIP
FWIP
MEDUSA! WHAT ARE YOU DOING?!

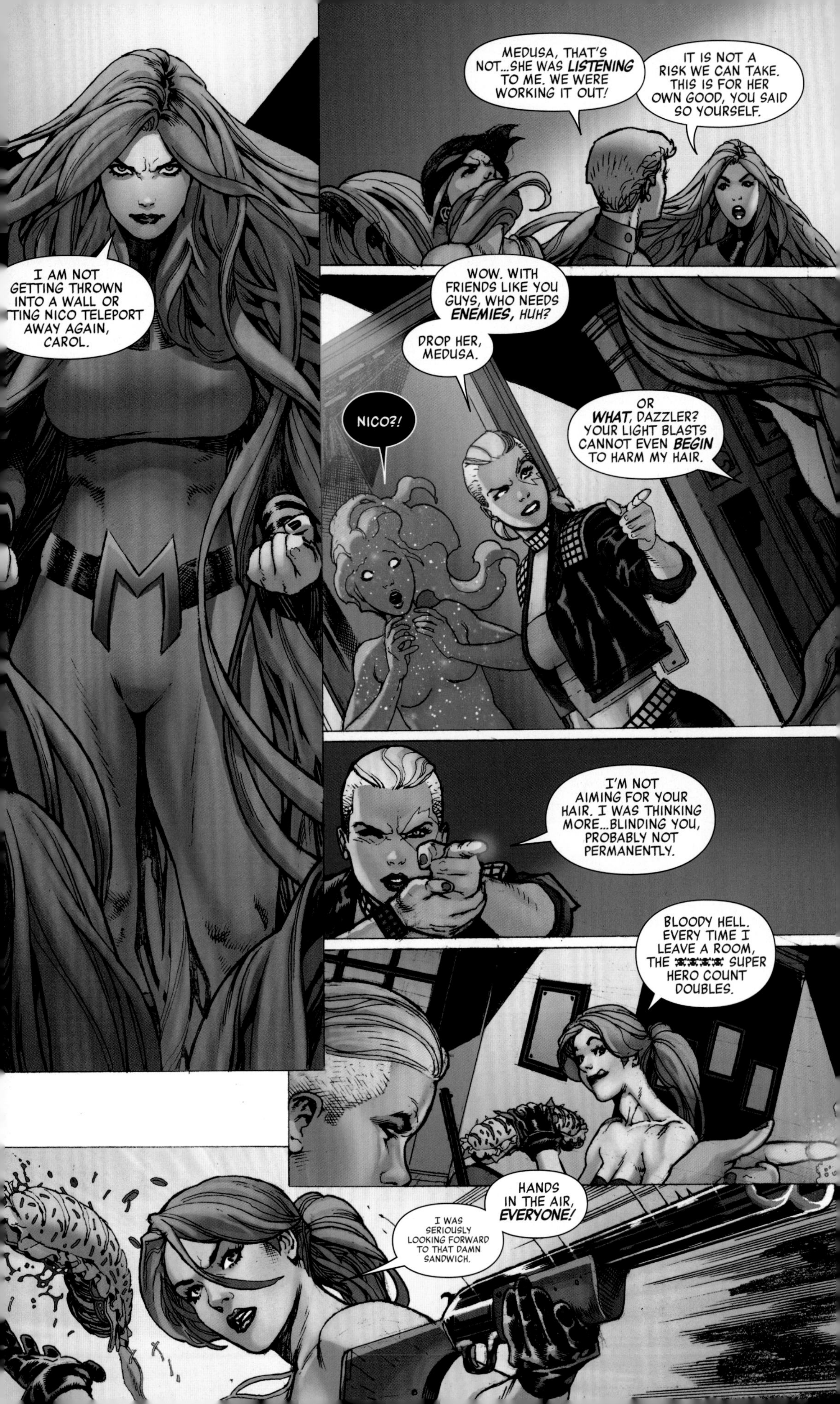

I AM NOT GETTING THROWN INTO A WALL OR TTING NICO TELEPORT AWAY AGAIN, CAROL.
MEDUSA, THAT'S NOT...SHE WAS LISTENING TO ME. WE WERE WORKING IT OUT!
IT IS NOT A RISK WE CAN TAKE. THIS IS FOR HER OWN GOOD, YOU SAID SO YOURSELF.
WOW. WITH FRIENDS LIKE YOU GUYS, WHO NEEDS ENEMIES, HUH?
DROP HER, MEDUSA.
NICO?!
OR WHAT, DAZZLER? YOUR LIGHT BLASTS CANNOT EVEN BEGIN TO HARM MY HAIR.
I'M NOT AIMING FOR YOUR HAIR. I WAS THINKING MORE...BLINDING YOU, PROBABLY NOT PERMANENTLY.
BLOODY HELL. EVERY TIME I LEAVE A ROOM, THE ☠☠☠ SUPER HERO COUNT DOUBLES.
HANDS IN THE AIR, EVERYONE!
I WAS SERIOUSLY LOOKING FORWARD TO THAT DAMN SANDWICH.

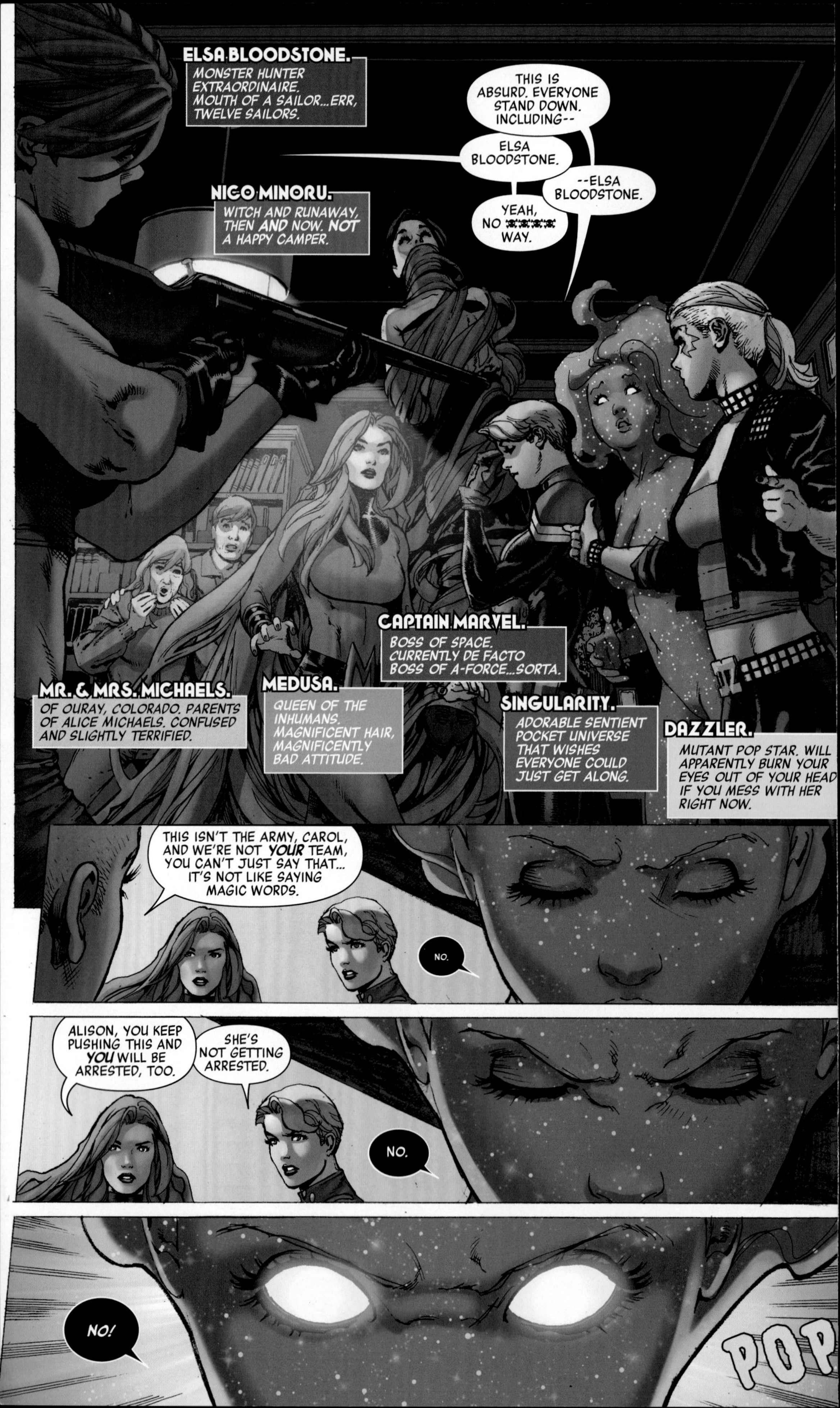
ELSA BLOODSTONE.
MONSTER HUNTER EXTRAORDINAIRE. MOUTH OF A SAILOR...ERR, TWELVE SAILORS.
THIS IS ABSURD. EVERYONE STAND DOWN. INCLUDING--
ELSA BLOODSTONE.
--ELSA BLOODSTONE.
YEAH, NO ☠☠☠☠ WAY.
NICO MINORU.
WITCH AND RUNAWAY, THEN AND NOW. NOT A HAPPY CAMPER.
CAPTAIN MARVEL.
BOSS OF SPACE. CURRENTLY DE FACTO BOSS OF A-FORCE...SORTA.
MR. & MRS. MICHAELS.
OF OURAY, COLORADO. PARENTS OF ALICE MICHAELS. CONFUSED AND SLIGHTLY TERRIFIED.
MEDUSA.
QUEEN OF THE INHUMANS. MAGNIFICENT HAIR, MAGNIFICENTLY BAD ATTITUDE.
SINGULARITY.
ADORABLE SENTIENT POCKET UNIVERSE THAT WISHES EVERYONE COULD JUST GET ALONG.
DAZZLER.
MUTANT POP STAR. WILL APPARENTLY BURN YOUR EYES OUT OF YOUR HEAD IF YOU MESS WITH HER RIGHT NOW.
THIS ISN'T THE ARMY, CAROL, AND WE'RE NOT YOUR TEAM, YOU CAN'T JUST SAY THAT... IT'S NOT LIKE SAYING MAGIC WORDS.
NO.
ALISON, YOU KEEP PUSHING THIS AND YOU WILL BE ARRESTED, TOO.
SHE'S NOT GETTING ARRESTED.
NO.
NO!
POP

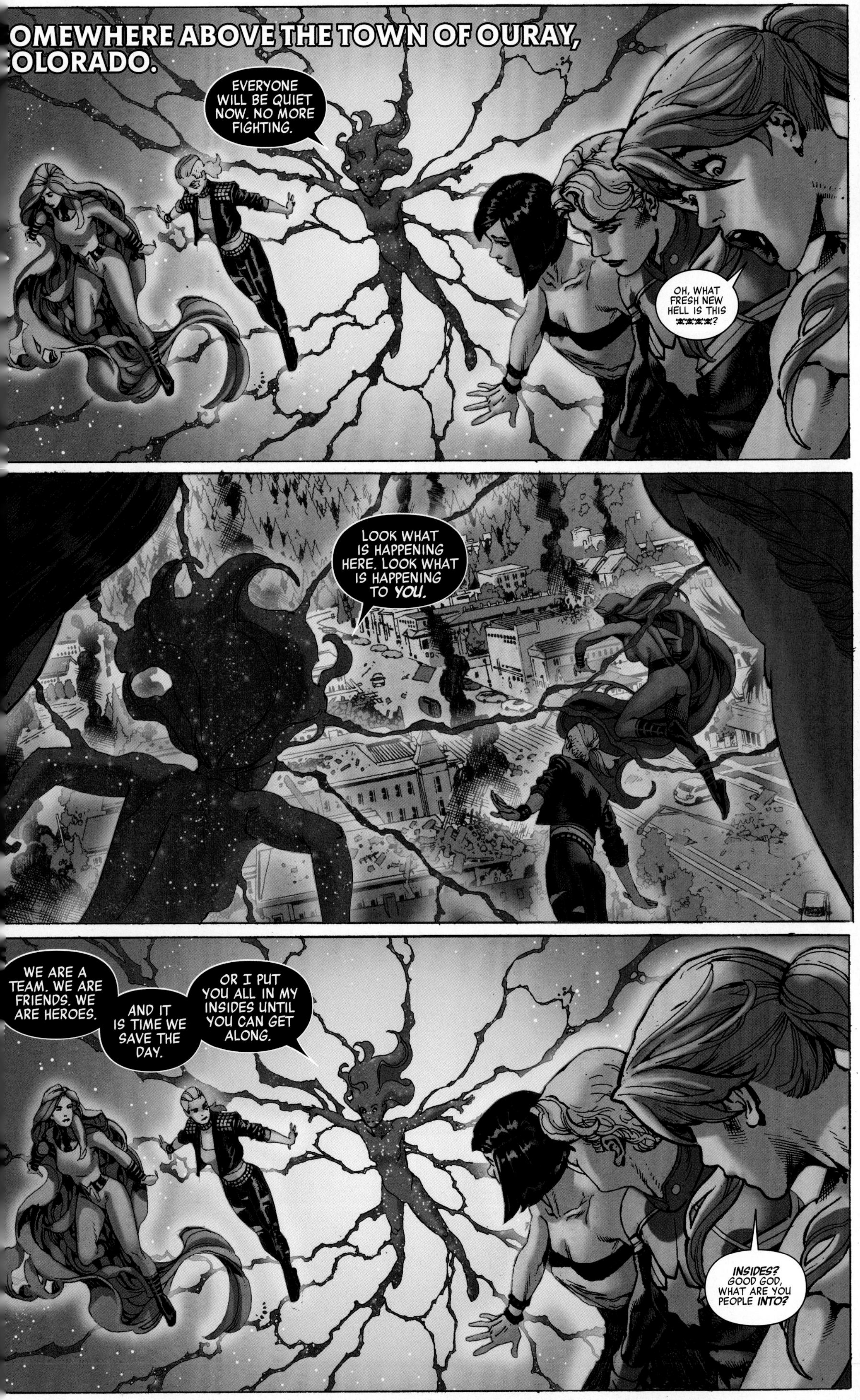
OMEWHERE ABOVE THE TOWN OF OURAY,
OLORADO.
EVERYONE WILL BE QUIET NOW. NO MORE FIGHTING.
OH, WHAT FRESH NEW HELL IS THIS ✱✱✱✱?
LOOK WHAT IS HAPPENING HERE. LOOK WHAT IS HAPPENING TO YOU.
WE ARE A TEAM. WE ARE FRIENDS. WE ARE HEROES.
AND IT IS TIME WE SAVE THE DAY.
OR I PUT YOU ALL IN MY INSIDES UNTIL YOU CAN GET ALONG.
INSIDES? GOOD GOD, WHAT ARE YOU PEOPLE INTO?

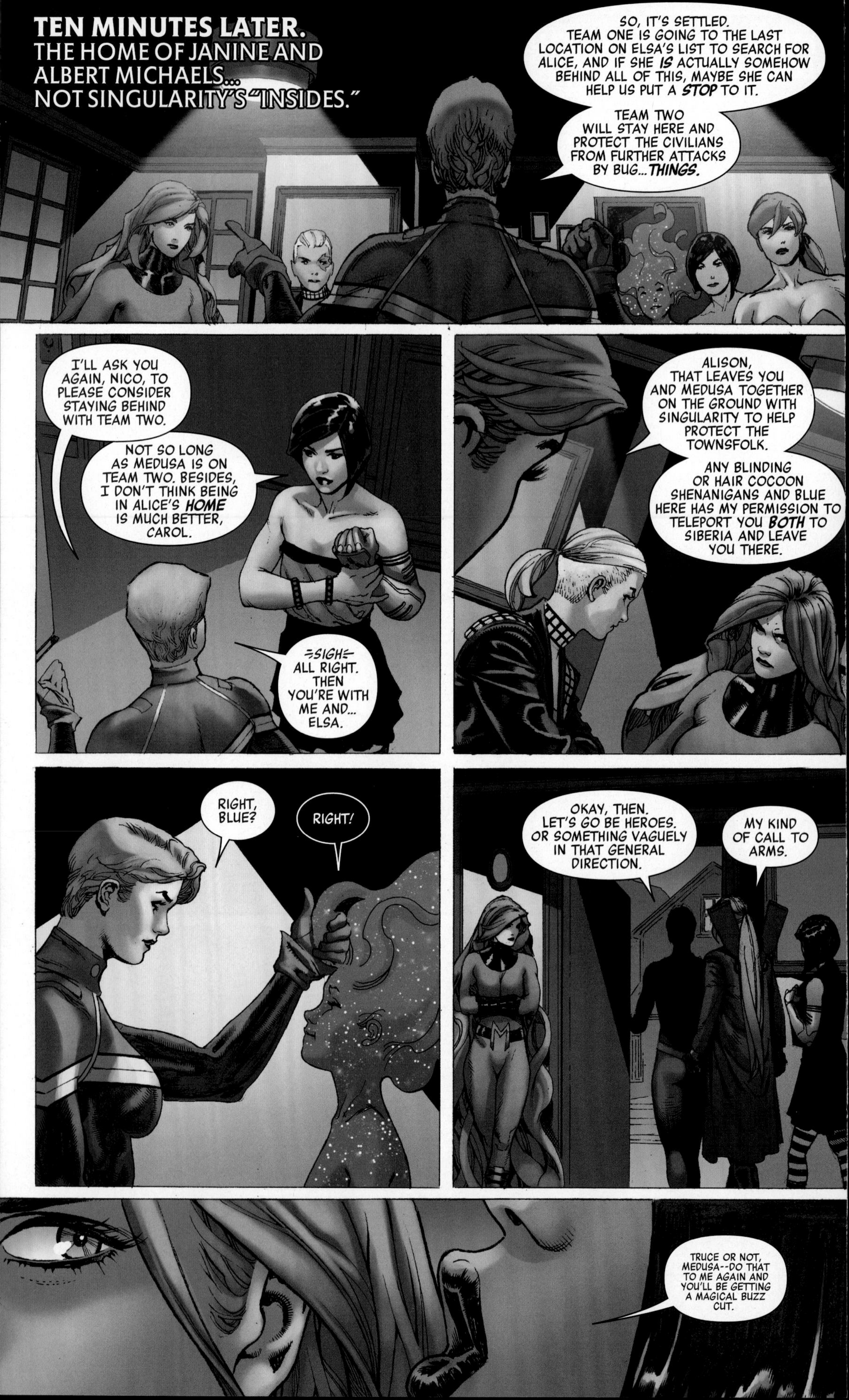
TEN MINUTES LATER.
THE HOME OF JANINE AND ALBERT MICHAELS... NOT SINGULARITY'S "INSIDES."
SO, IT'S SETTLED. TEAM ONE IS GOING TO THE LAST LOCATION ON ELSA'S LIST TO SEARCH FOR ALICE, AND IF SHE IS ACTUALLY SOMEHOW BEHIND ALL OF THIS, MAYBE SHE CAN HELP US PUT A STOP TO IT.
TEAM TWO WILL STAY HERE AND PROTECT THE CIVILIANS FROM FURTHER ATTACKS BY BUG... THINGS.
I'LL ASK YOU AGAIN, NICO, TO PLEASE CONSIDER STAYING BEHIND WITH TEAM TWO.
NOT SO LONG AS MEDUSA IS ON TEAM TWO. BESIDES, I DON'T THINK BEING IN ALICE'S HOME IS MUCH BETTER, CAROL.
=SIGH= ALL RIGHT. THEN YOU'RE WITH ME AND... ELSA.
ALISON, THAT LEAVES YOU AND MEDUSA TOGETHER ON THE GROUND WITH SINGULARITY TO HELP PROTECT THE TOWNSFOLK.
ANY BLINDING OR HAIR COCOON SHENANIGANS AND BLUE HERE HAS MY PERMISSION TO TELEPORT YOU BOTH TO SIBERIA AND LEAVE YOU THERE.
RIGHT, BLUE?
RIGHT!
OKAY, THEN. LET'S GO BE HEROES. OR SOMETHING VAGUELY IN THAT GENERAL DIRECTION.
MY KIND OF CALL TO ARMS.
TRUCE OR NOT, MEDUSA--DO THAT TO ME AGAIN AND YOU'LL BE GETTING A MAGICAL BUZZ CUT.

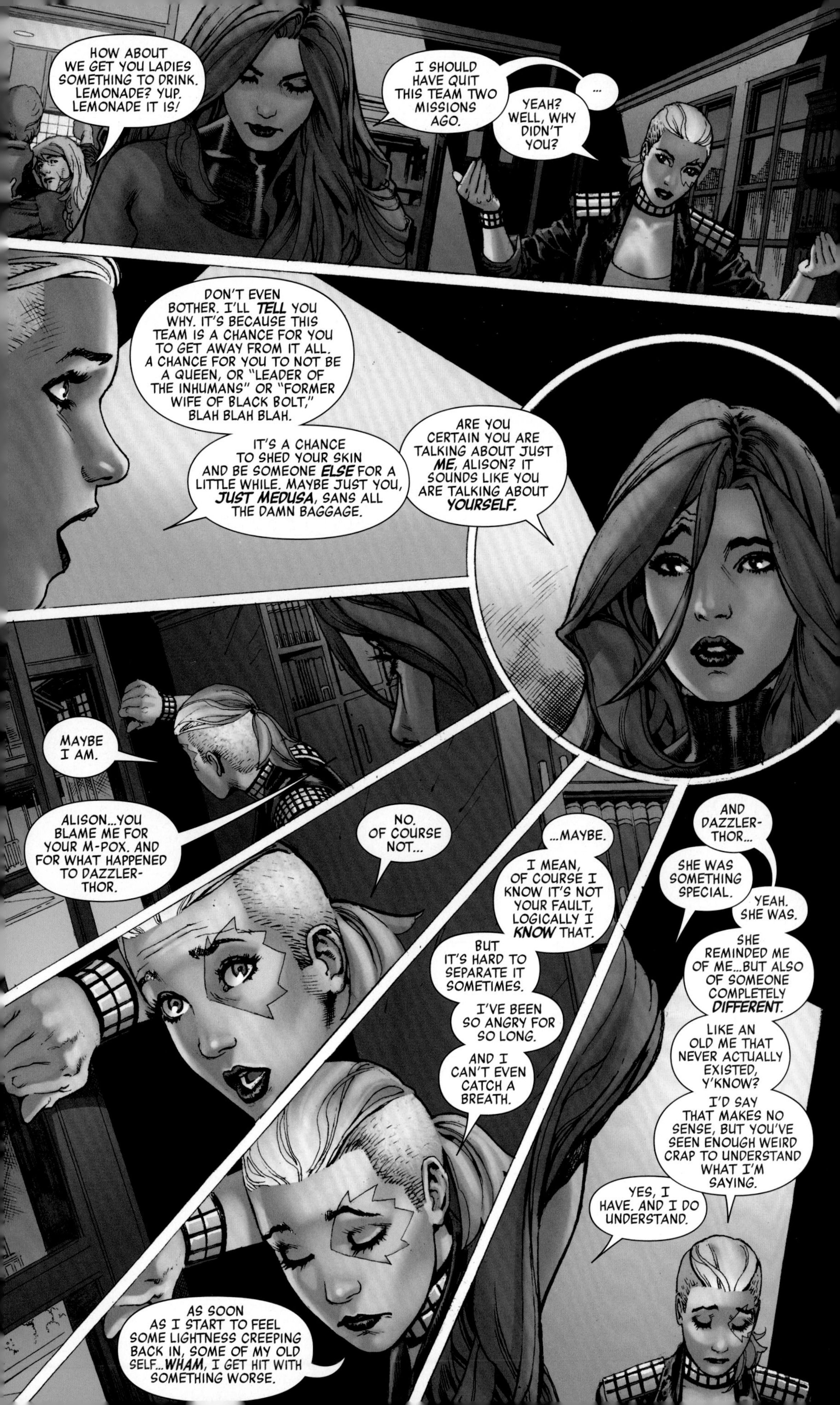

HOW ABOUT WE GET YOU LADIES SOMETHING TO DRINK. LEMONADE? YUP. LEMONADE IT IS!
I SHOULD HAVE QUIT THIS TEAM TWO MISSIONS AGO.
...
YEAH? WELL, WHY DIDN'T YOU?
DON'T EVEN BOTHER. I'LL TELL YOU WHY. IT'S BECAUSE THIS TEAM IS A CHANCE FOR YOU TO GET AWAY FROM IT ALL. A CHANCE FOR YOU TO NOT BE A QUEEN, OR "LEADER OF THE INHUMANS" OR "FORMER WIFE OF BLACK BOLT," BLAH BLAH BLAH.
IT'S A CHANCE TO SHED YOUR SKIN AND BE SOMEONE ELSE FOR A LITTLE WHILE. MAYBE JUST YOU, JUST MEDUSA, SANS ALL THE DAMN BAGGAGE.
ARE YOU CERTAIN YOU ARE TALKING ABOUT JUST ME, ALISON? IT SOUNDS LIKE YOU ARE TALKING ABOUT YOURSELF.
MAYBE I AM.
ALISON...YOU BLAME ME FOR YOUR M-POX. AND FOR WHAT HAPPENED TO DAZZLER-THOR.
NO. OF COURSE NOT...
...MAYBE.
I MEAN, OF COURSE I KNOW IT'S NOT YOUR FAULT, LOGICALLY I KNOW THAT.
BUT IT'S HARD TO SEPARATE IT SOMETIMES.
I'VE BEEN SO ANGRY FOR SO LONG.
AND I CAN'T EVEN CATCH A BREATH.
AS SOON AS I START TO FEEL SOME LIGHTNESS CREEPING BACK IN, SOME OF MY OLD SELF...WHAM, I GET HIT WITH SOMETHING WORSE.
AND DAZZLER-THOR...
SHE WAS SOMETHING SPECIAL.
YEAH. SHE WAS.
SHE REMINDED ME OF ME...BUT ALSO OF SOMEONE COMPLETELY DIFFERENT.
LIKE AN OLD ME THAT NEVER ACTUALLY EXISTED, Y'KNOW?
I'D SAY THAT MAKES NO SENSE, BUT YOU'VE SEEN ENOUGH WEIRD CRAP TO UNDERSTAND WHAT I'M SAYING.
YES, I HAVE. AND I DO UNDERSTAND.

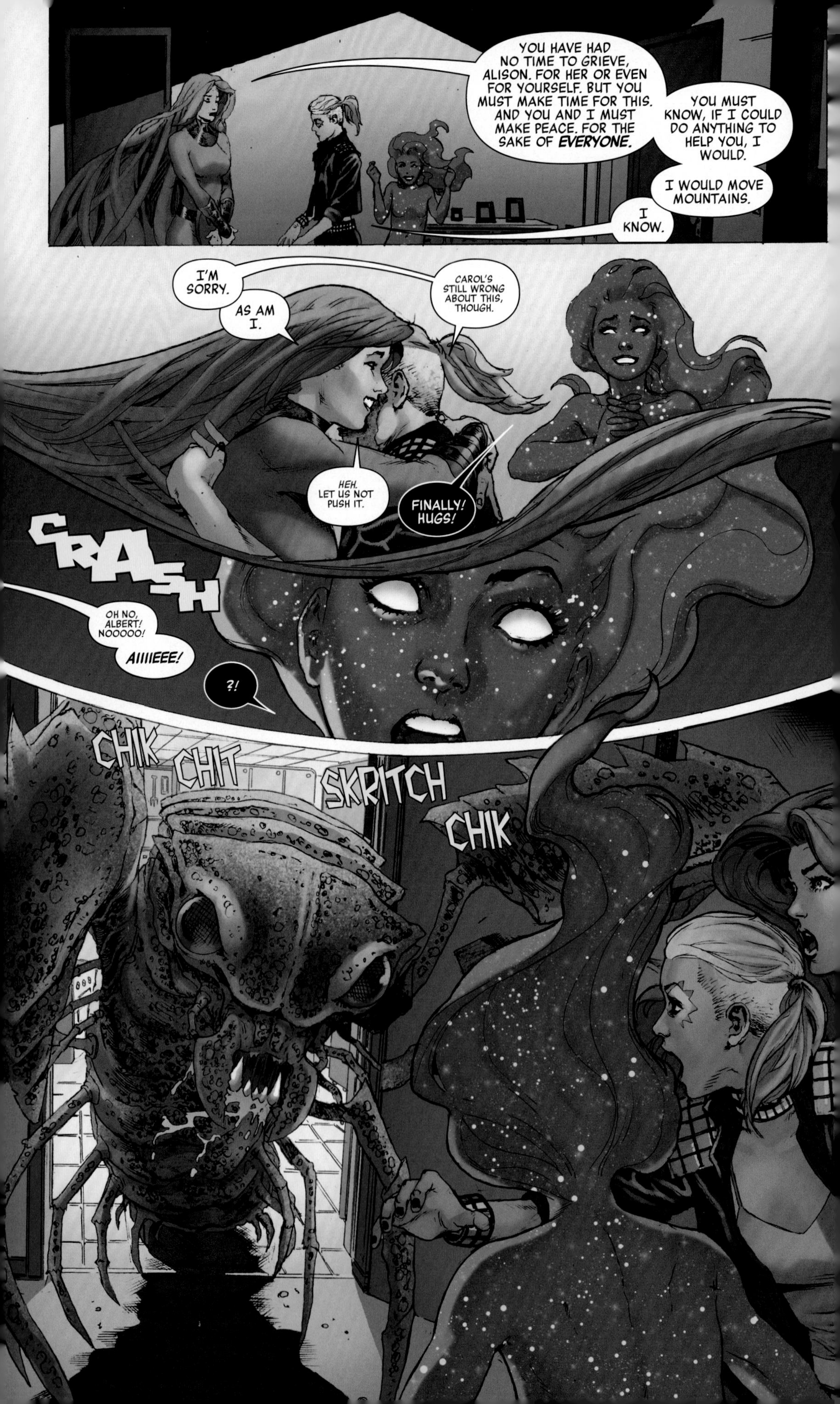
YOU HAVE HAD NO TIME TO GRIEVE, ALISON. FOR HER OR EVEN FOR YOURSELF. BUT YOU MUST MAKE TIME FOR THIS. AND YOU AND I MUST MAKE PEACE. FOR THE SAKE OF EVERYONE.
YOU MUST KNOW, IF I COULD DO ANYTHING TO HELP YOU, I WOULD.
I WOULD MOVE MOUNTAINS.
I KNOW.
I'M SORRY.
AS AM I.
CAROL'S STILL WRONG ABOUT THIS, THOUGH.
HEH. LET US NOT PUSH IT.
FINALLY! HUGS!
CRASH
OH NO, ALBERT! NOOOOO!
AIIIIEEE!
?!
CHIK
CHIT
SKRITCH
CHIK

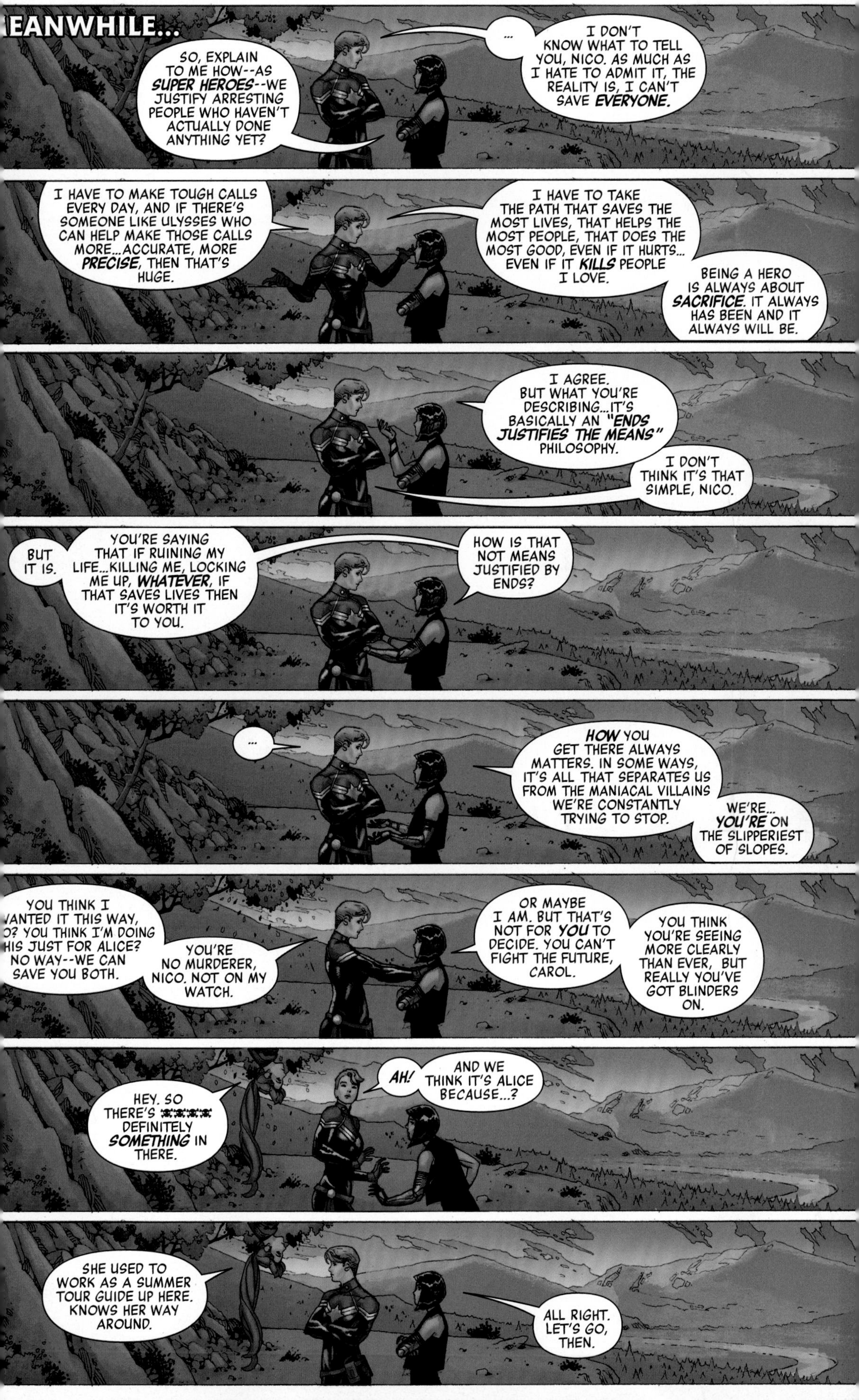
EANWHILE...
SO, EXPLAIN TO ME HOW--AS SUPER HEROES--WE JUSTIFY ARRESTING PEOPLE WHO HAVEN'T ACTUALLY DONE ANYTHING YET?
...
I DON'T KNOW WHAT TO TELL YOU, NICO. AS MUCH AS I HATE TO ADMIT IT, THE REALITY IS, I CAN'T SAVE EVERYONE.
I HAVE TO MAKE TOUGH CALLS EVERY DAY, AND IF THERE'S SOMEONE LIKE ULYSSES WHO CAN HELP MAKE THOSE CALLS MORE...ACCURATE, MORE PRECISE, THEN THAT'S HUGE.
I HAVE TO TAKE THE PATH THAT SAVES THE MOST LIVES, THAT HELPS THE MOST PEOPLE, THAT DOES THE MOST GOOD, EVEN IF IT HURTS... EVEN IF IT KILLS PEOPLE I LOVE.
BEING A HERO IS ALWAYS ABOUT SACRIFICE. IT ALWAYS HAS BEEN AND IT ALWAYS WILL BE.
I AGREE. BUT WHAT YOU'RE DESCRIBING...IT'S BASICALLY AN "ENDS JUSTIFIES THE MEANS" PHILOSOPHY.
I DON'T THINK IT'S THAT SIMPLE, NICO.
BUT IT IS.
YOU'RE SAYING THAT IF RUINING MY LIFE...KILLING ME, LOCKING ME UP, WHATEVER, IF THAT SAVES LIVES THEN IT'S WORTH IT TO YOU.
HOW IS THAT NOT MEANS JUSTIFIED BY ENDS?
...
HOW YOU GET THERE ALWAYS MATTERS. IN SOME WAYS, IT'S ALL THAT SEPARATES US FROM THE MANIACAL VILLAINS WE'RE CONSTANTLY TRYING TO STOP.
WE'RE... YOU'RE ON THE SLIPPERIEST OF SLOPES.
YOU THINK I VANTED IT THIS WAY, O? YOU THINK I'M DOING HIS JUST FOR ALICE? NO WAY--WE CAN SAVE YOU BOTH.
YOU'RE NO MURDERER, NICO. NOT ON MY WATCH.
OR MAYBE I AM. BUT THAT'S NOT FOR YOU TO DECIDE. YOU CAN'T FIGHT THE FUTURE, CAROL.
YOU THINK YOU'RE SEEING MORE CLEARLY THAN EVER, BUT REALLY YOU'VE GOT BLINDERS ON.
HEY. SO THERE'S DEFINITELY SOMETHING IN THERE.
AH!
AND WE THINK IT'S ALICE BECAUSE...?
SHE USED TO WORK AS A SUMMER TOUR GUIDE UP HERE. KNOWS HER WAY AROUND.
ALL RIGHT. LET'S GO, THEN.

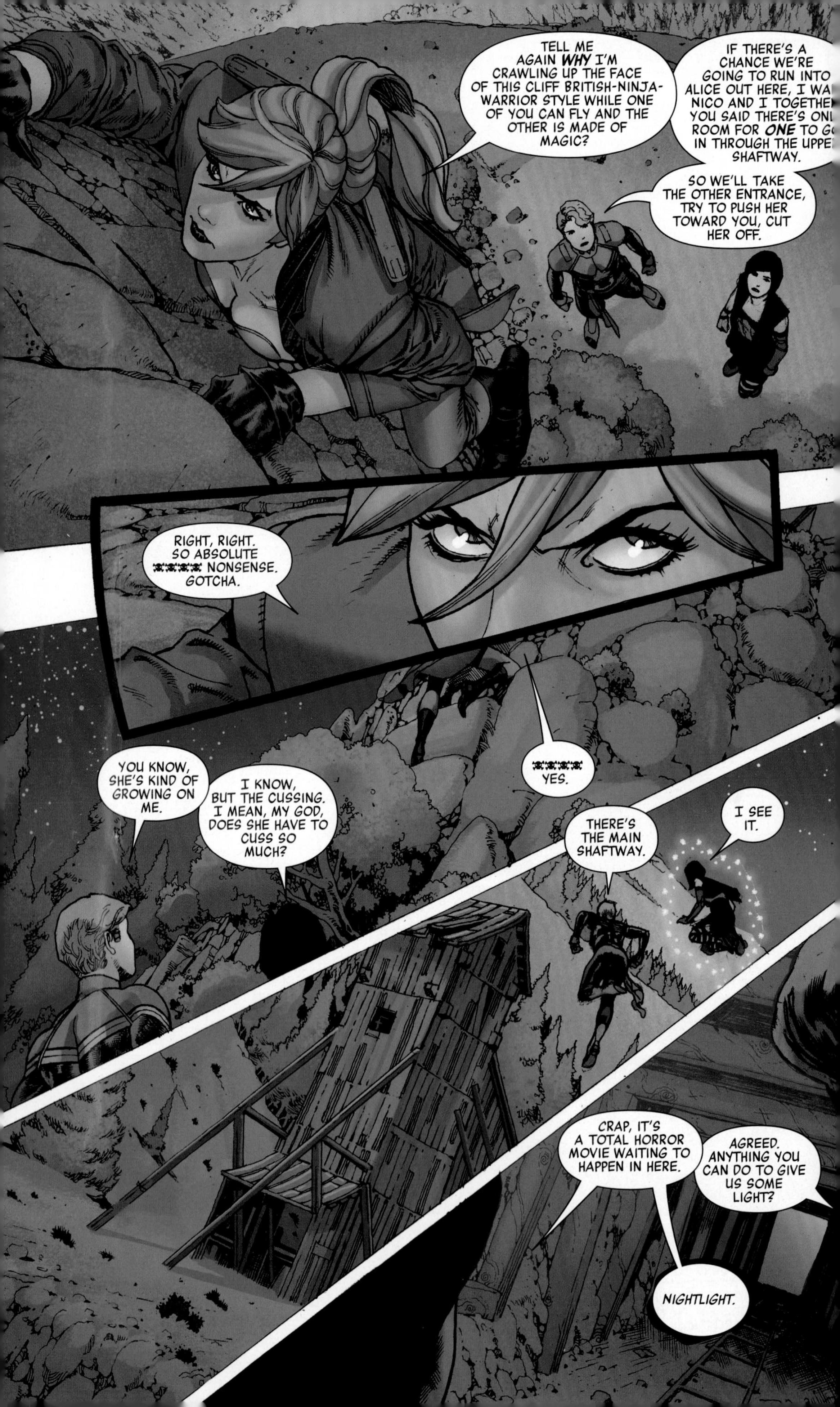
TELL ME AGAIN WHY I'M CRAWLING UP THE FACE OF THIS CLIFF BRITISH-NINJA-WARRIOR STYLE WHILE ONE OF YOU CAN FLY AND THE OTHER IS MADE OF MAGIC?
IF THERE'S A CHANCE WE'RE GOING TO RUN INTO ALICE OUT HERE, I WA NICO AND I TOGETHE YOU SAID THERE'S ONL ROOM FOR ONE TO G IN THROUGH THE UPPE SHAFTWAY.
SO WE'LL TAKE THE OTHER ENTRANCE, TRY TO PUSH HER TOWARD YOU, CUT HER OFF.
RIGHT, RIGHT. SO ABSOLUTE NONSENSE. GOTCHA.
YES.
YOU KNOW, SHE'S KIND OF GROWING ON ME.
I KNOW, BUT THE CUSSING. I MEAN, MY GOD, DOES SHE HAVE TO CUSS SO MUCH?
THERE'S THE MAIN SHAFTWAY.
I SEE IT.
CRAP, IT'S A TOTAL HORROR MOVIE WAITING TO HAPPEN IN HERE.
AGREED. ANYTHING YOU CAN DO TO GIVE US SOME LIGHT?
NIGHTLIGHT.

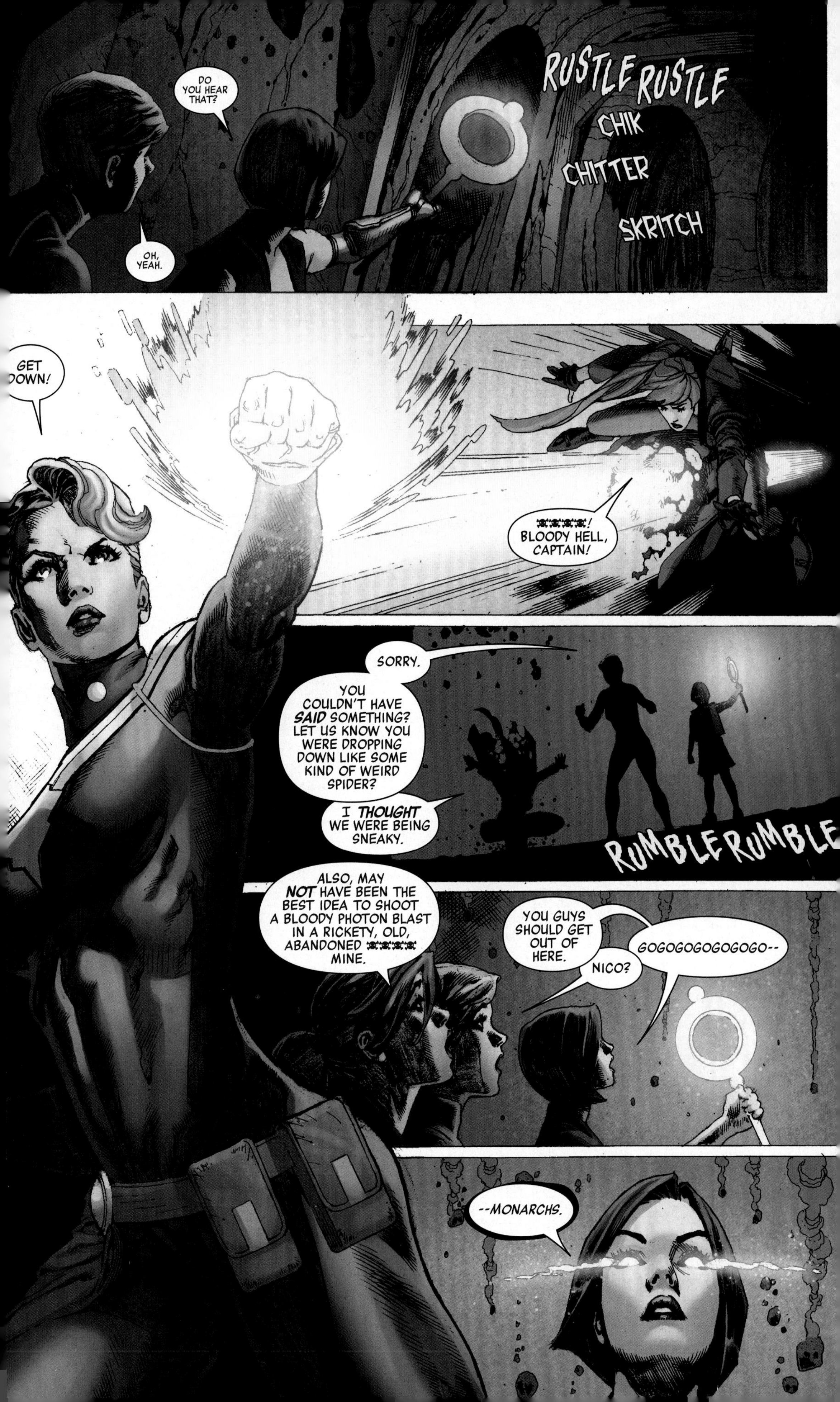
DO YOU HEAR THAT?
OH, YEAH.
RUSTLE RUSTLE
CHIK
CHITTER
SKRITCH
GET DOWN!
☠☠☠! BLOODY HELL, CAPTAIN!
SORRY.
YOU COULDN'T HAVE SAID SOMETHING? LET US KNOW YOU WERE DROPPING DOWN LIKE SOME KIND OF WEIRD SPIDER?
I THOUGHT WE WERE BEING SNEAKY.
RUMBLE RUMBLE
ALSO, MAY NOT HAVE BEEN THE BEST IDEA TO SHOOT A BLOODY PHOTON BLAST IN A RICKETY, OLD, ABANDONED ☠☠☠ MINE.
YOU GUYS SHOULD GET OUT OF HERE.
NICO?
GOGOGOGOGOGOGO--
--MONARCHS.

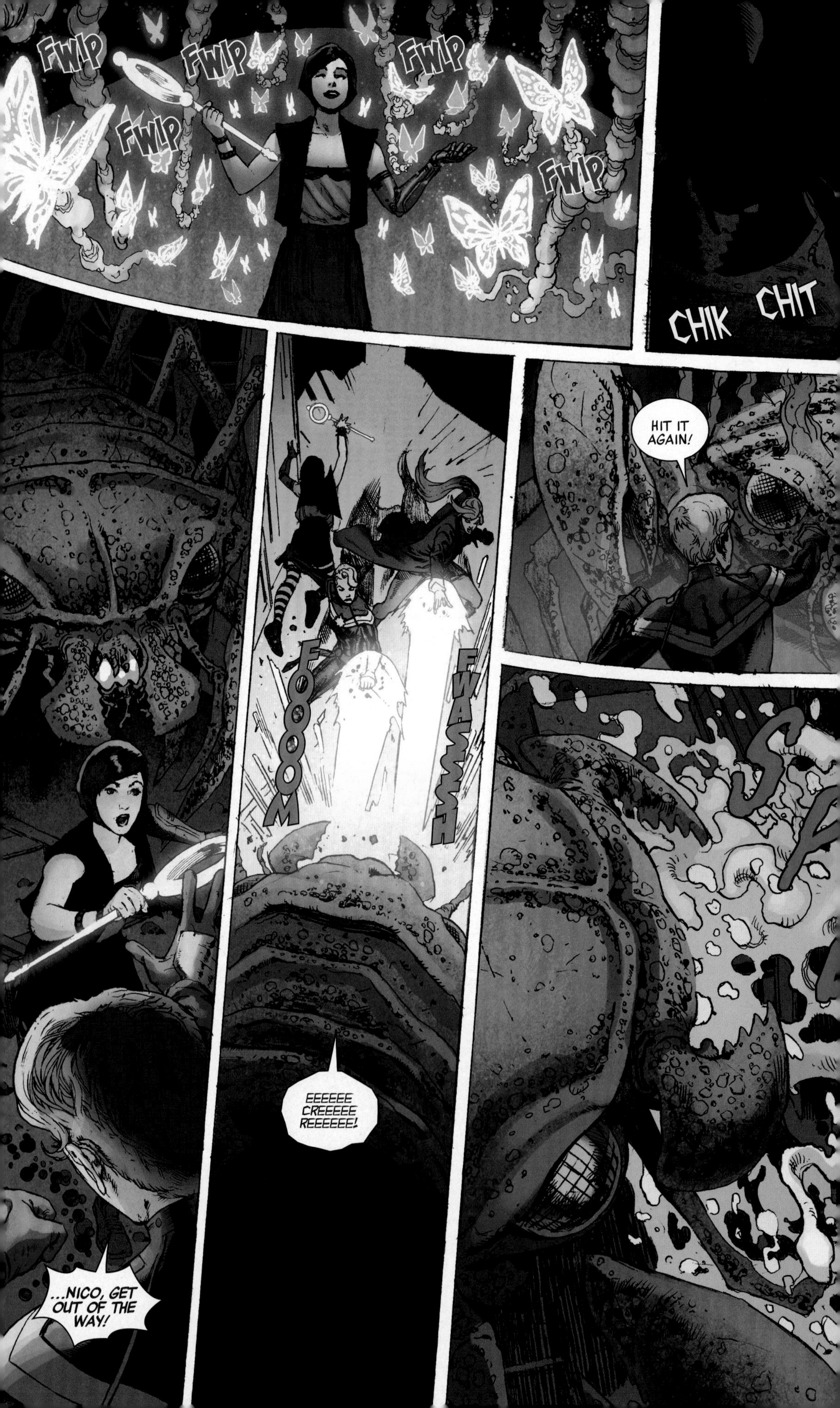
FWIP
FWIP
FWIP
FWIP
FWIP
CHIK
CHIT
HIT IT AGAIN!
FOOOOOM
FWASSSH
EEEEEE CREEEEE REEEEEE!
...NICO, GET OUT OF THE WAY!

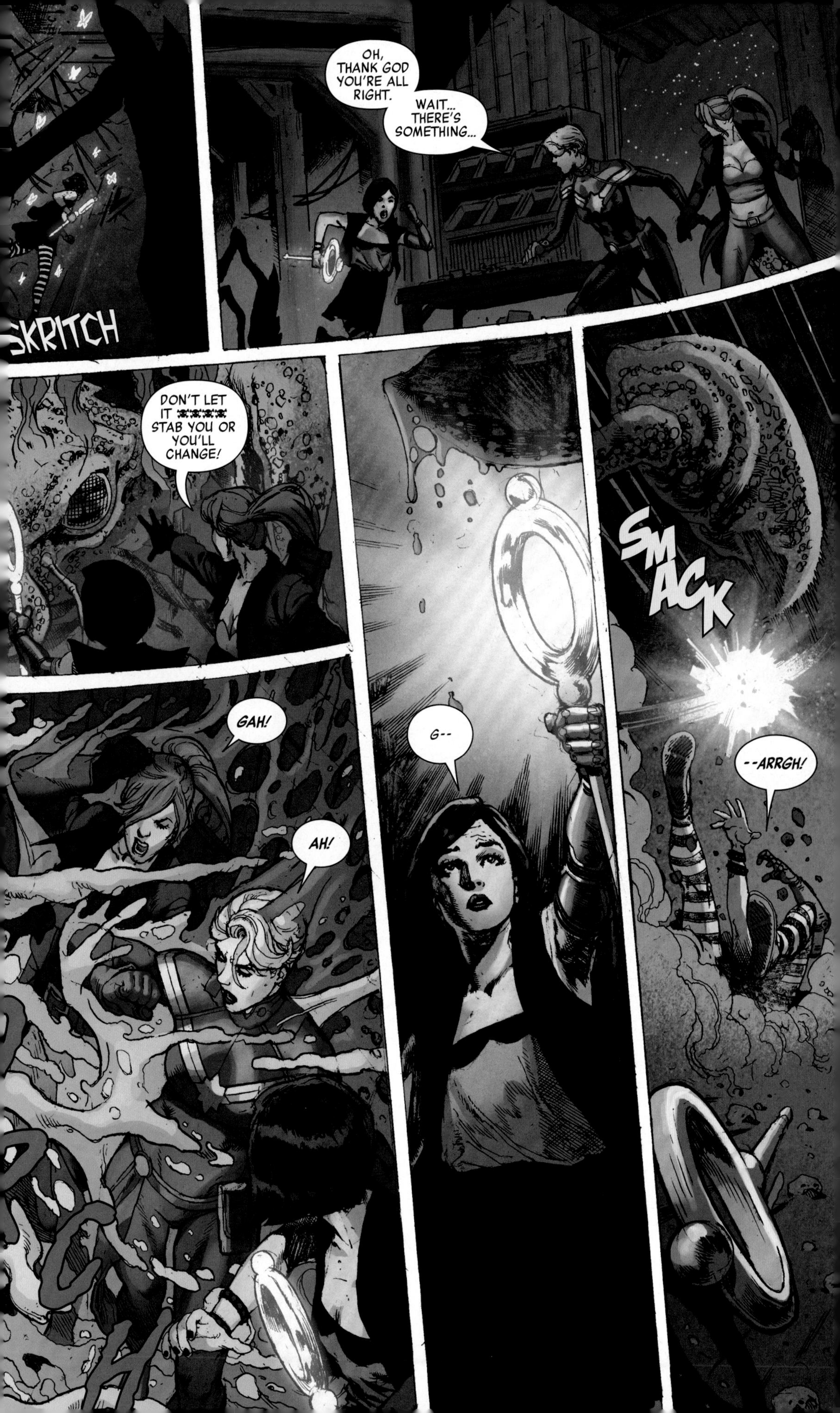
SKRITCH
OH, THANK GOD YOU'RE ALL RIGHT.
WAIT... THERE'S SOMETHING...
DON'T LET IT ☠☠☠☠ STAB YOU OR YOU'LL CHANGE!
SMACK
GAH!
AH!
G--
--ARRGH!

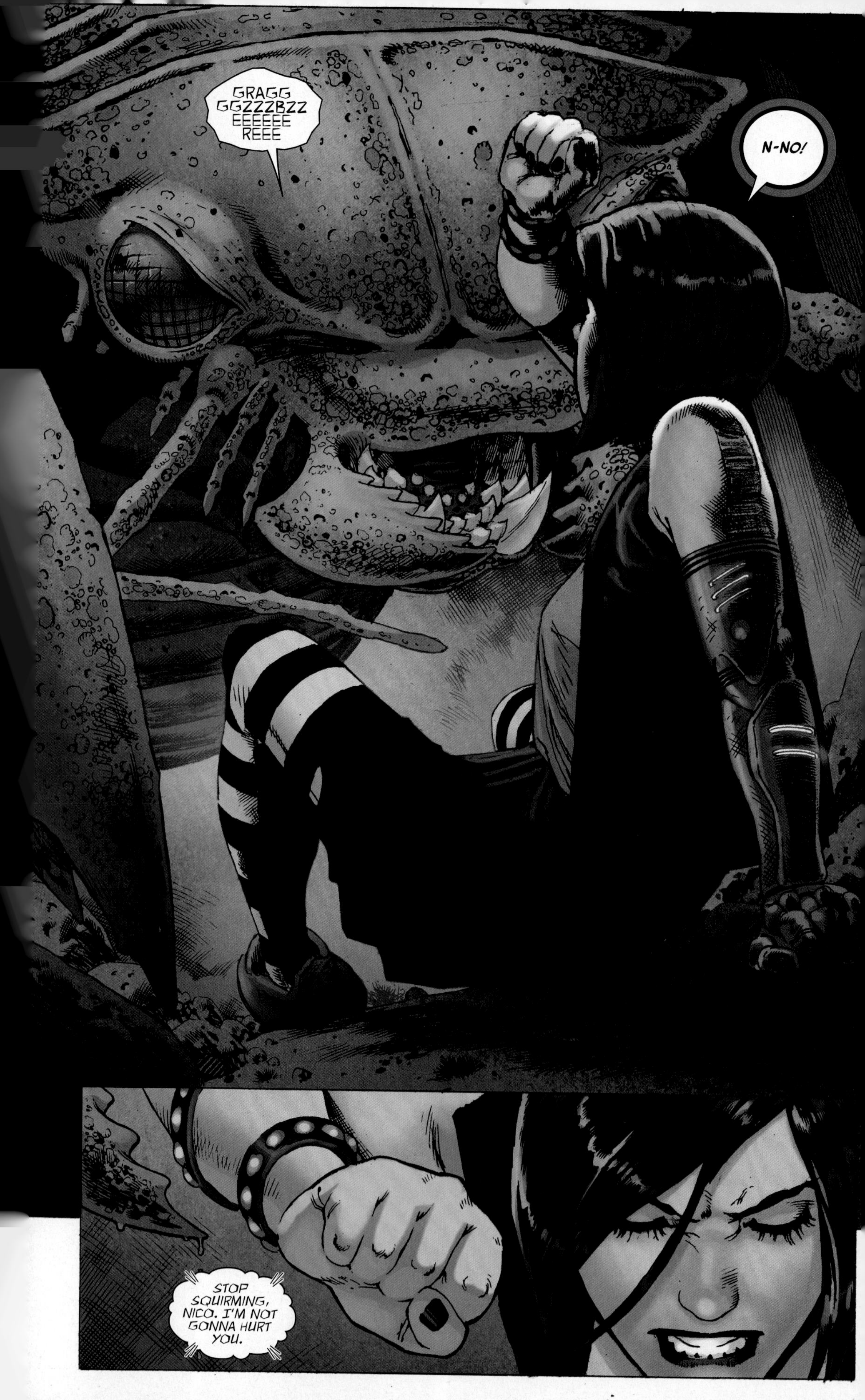
GRAGG GGZZZBZZ EEEEEE REEE
N-NO!
STOP SQUIRMING, NICO. I'M NOT GONNA HURT YOU.

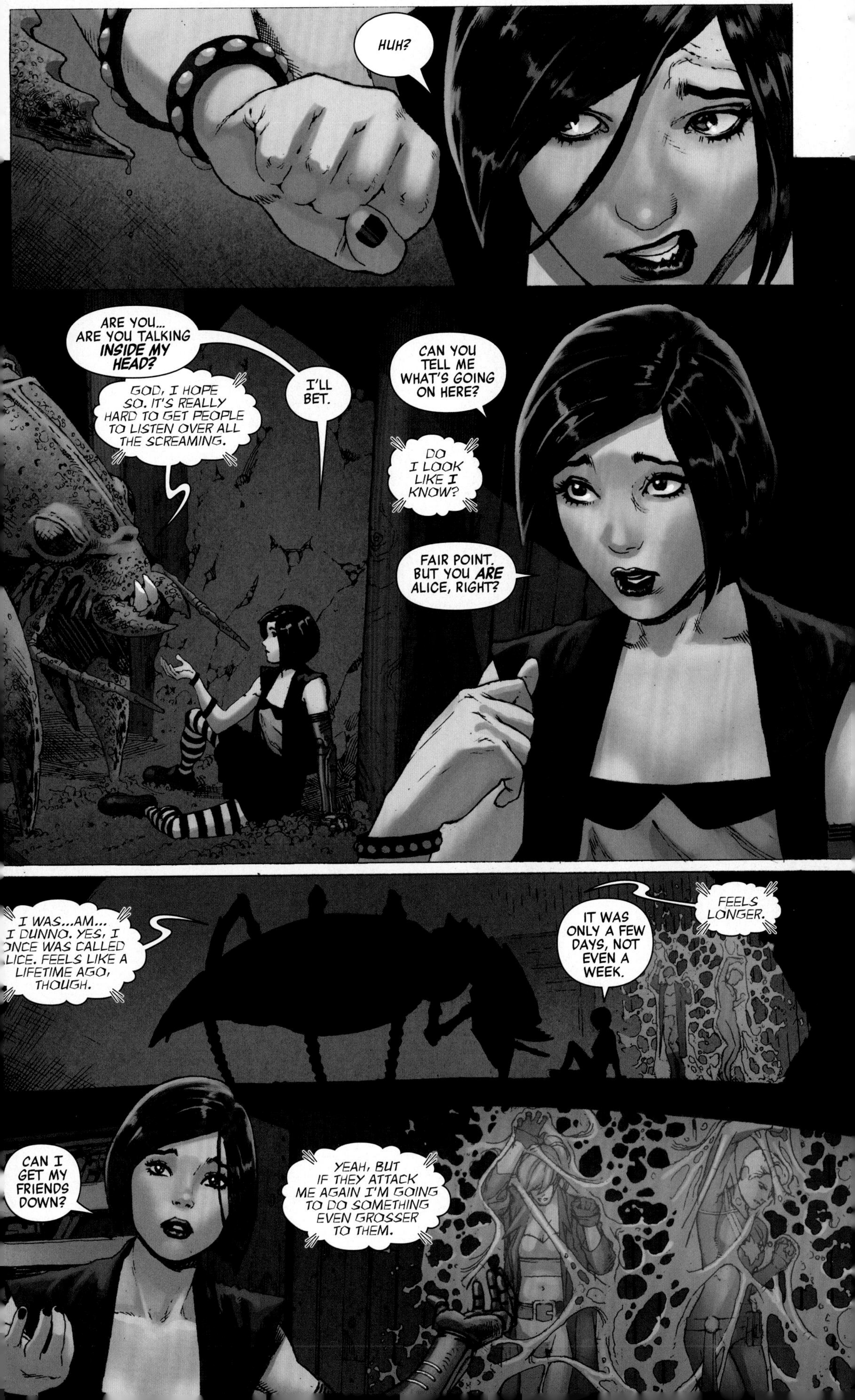
HUH?
ARE YOU... ARE YOU TALKING INSIDE MY HEAD?
GOD, I HOPE SO. IT'S REALLY HARD TO GET PEOPLE TO LISTEN OVER ALL THE SCREAMING.
I'LL BET.
CAN YOU TELL ME WHAT'S GOING ON HERE?
DO I LOOK LIKE I KNOW?
FAIR POINT. BUT YOU ARE ALICE, RIGHT?
I WAS...AM... I DUNNO. YES, I ONCE WAS CALLED ALICE. FEELS LIKE A LIFETIME AGO, THOUGH.
IT WAS ONLY A FEW DAYS, NOT EVEN A WEEK.
FEELS LONGER.
CAN I GET MY FRIENDS DOWN?
YEAH, BUT IF THEY ATTACK ME AGAIN I'M GOING TO DO SOMETHING EVEN GROSSER TO THEM.

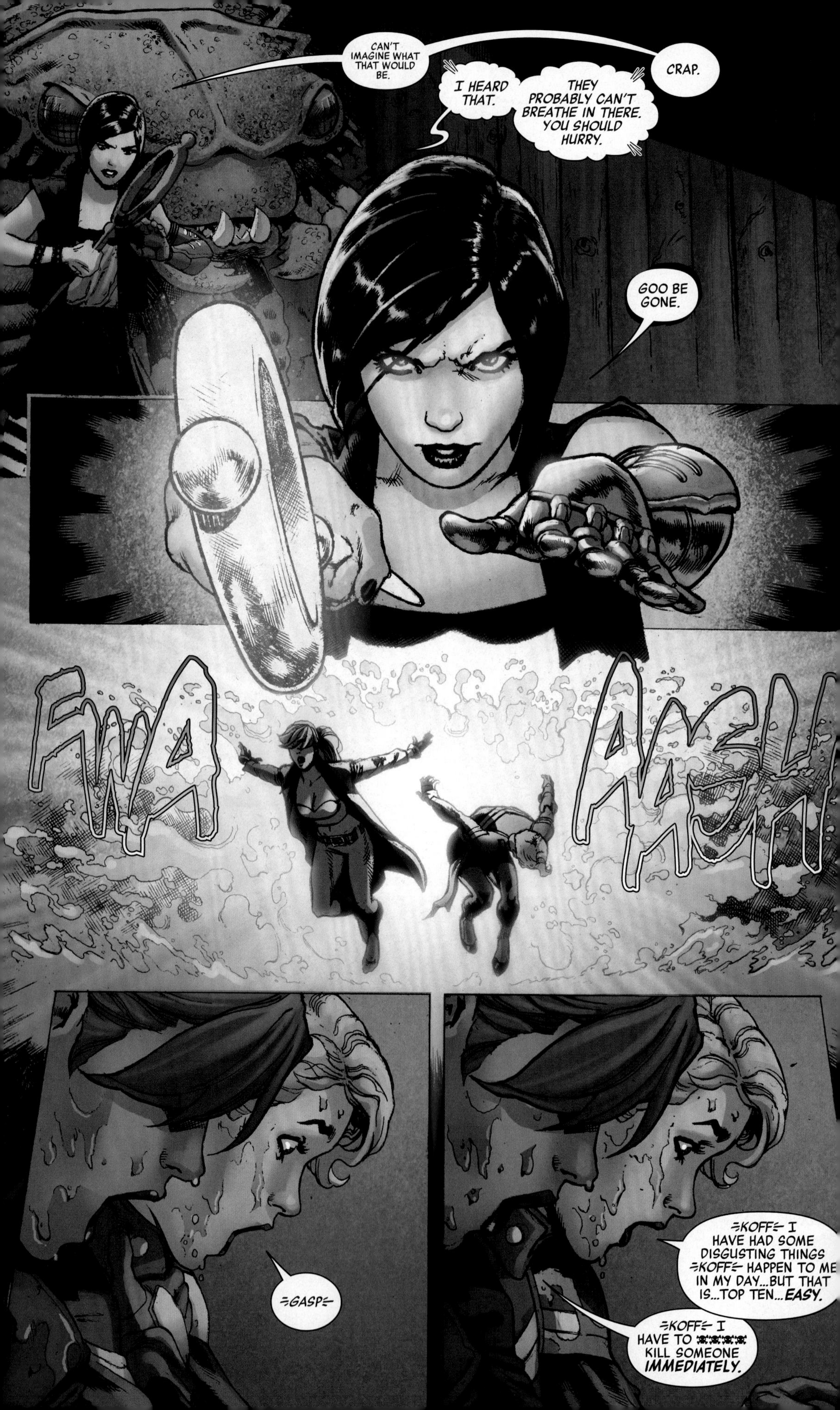

CAN'T IMAGINE WHAT THAT WOULD BE.
CRAP.
I HEARD THAT.
THEY PROBABLY CAN'T BREATHE IN THERE. YOU SHOULD HURRY.
GOO BE GONE.
FWAASH
=GASP=
=KOFF= I HAVE HAD SOME DISGUSTING THINGS =KOFF= HAPPEN TO ME IN MY DAY...BUT THAT IS...TOP TEN...EASY.
=KOFF= I HAVE TO KILL SOMEONE IMMEDIATELY.

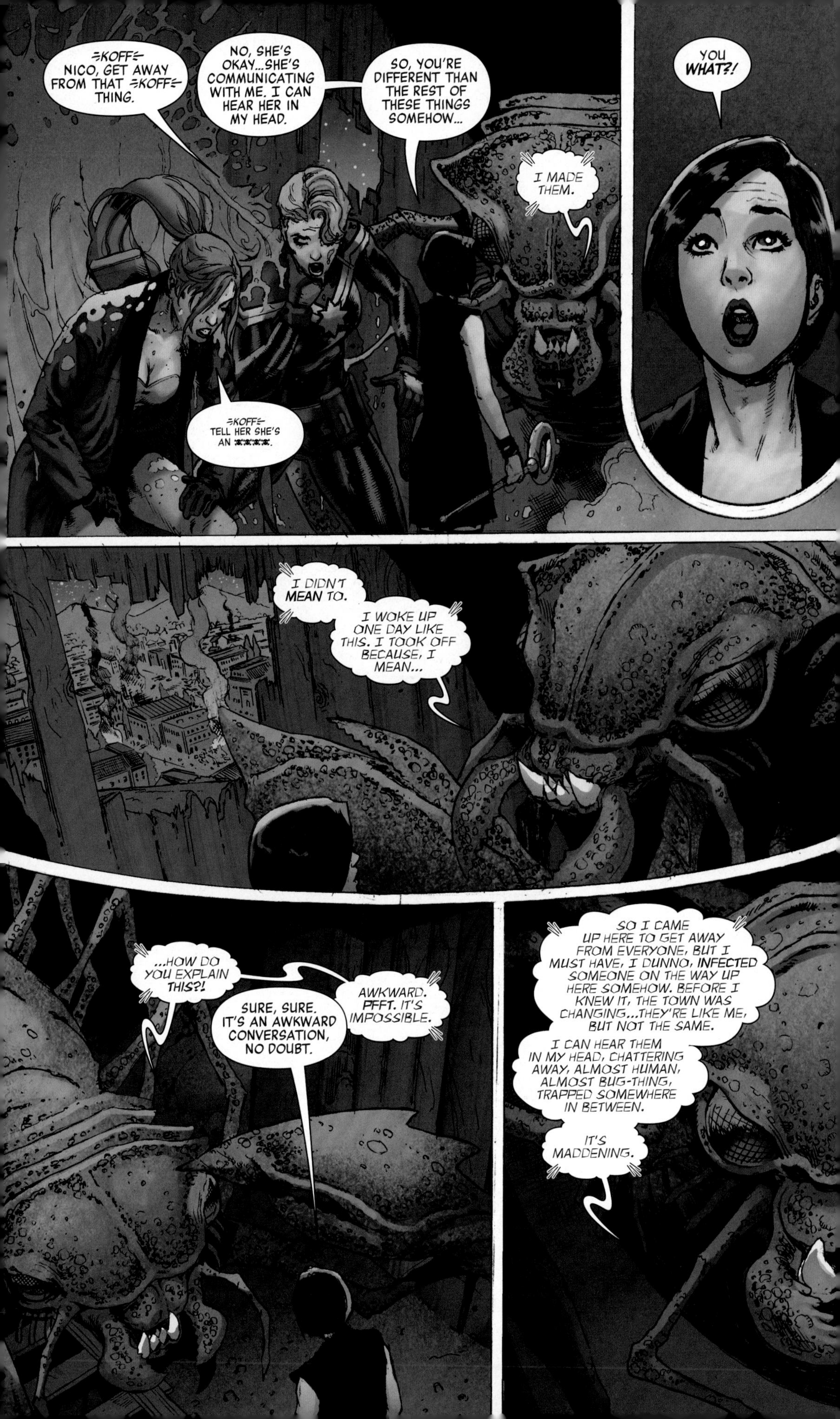
=KOFF= NICO, GET AWAY FROM THAT =KOFF= THING.
NO, SHE'S OKAY...SHE'S COMMUNICATING WITH ME. I CAN HEAR HER IN MY HEAD.
SO, YOU'RE DIFFERENT THAN THE REST OF THESE THINGS SOMEHOW...
I MADE THEM.
=KOFF= TELL HER SHE'S AN ****.
YOU WHAT?!
I DIDN'T MEAN TO.
I WOKE UP ONE DAY LIKE THIS. I TOOK OFF BECAUSE, I MEAN...
...HOW DO YOU EXPLAIN THIS?!
SURE, SURE. IT'S AN AWKWARD CONVERSATION, NO DOUBT.
AWKWARD. PFFT. IT'S IMPOSSIBLE.
SO I CAME UP HERE TO GET AWAY FROM EVERYONE, BUT I MUST HAVE, I DUNNO, INFECTED SOMEONE ON THE WAY UP HERE SOMEHOW. BEFORE I KNEW IT, THE TOWN WAS CHANGING...THEY'RE LIKE ME, BUT NOT THE SAME.
I CAN HEAR THEM IN MY HEAD, CHATTERING AWAY, ALMOST HUMAN, ALMOST BUG-THING, TRAPPED SOMEWHERE IN BETWEEN.
IT'S MADDENING.

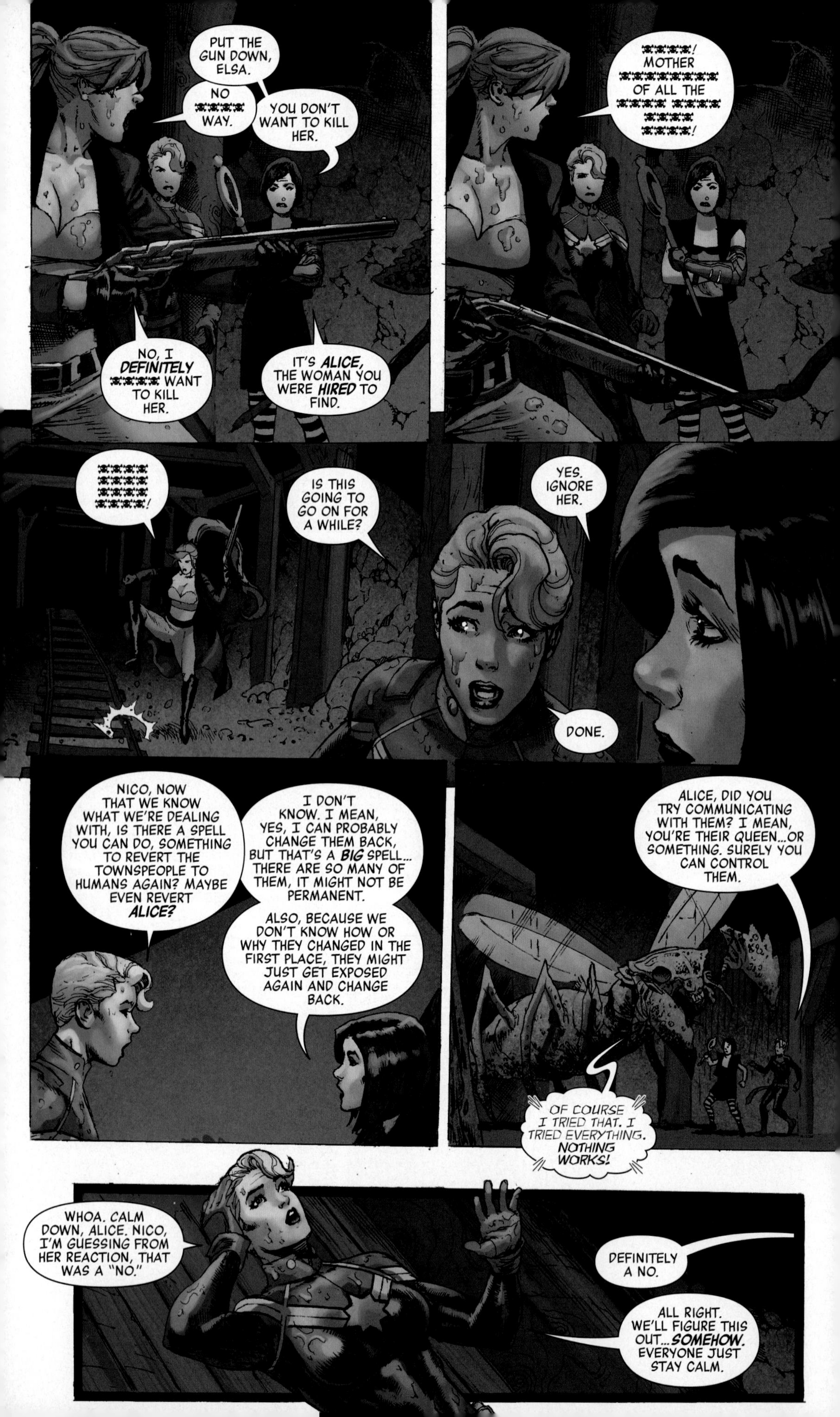
PUT THE GUN DOWN, ELSA.
NO WAY.
YOU DON'T WANT TO KILL HER.
NO, I **DEFINITELY** WANT TO KILL HER.
IT'S **ALICE**, THE WOMAN YOU WERE **HIRED** TO FIND.
! MOTHER OF ALL THE !
!
IS THIS GOING TO GO ON FOR A WHILE?
YES. IGNORE HER.
DONE.
NICO, NOW THAT WE KNOW WHAT WE'RE DEALING WITH, IS THERE A SPELL YOU CAN DO, SOMETHING TO REVERT THE TOWNSPEOPLE TO HUMANS AGAIN? MAYBE EVEN REVERT **ALICE?**
I DON'T KNOW. I MEAN, YES, I CAN PROBABLY CHANGE THEM BACK, BUT THAT'S A **BIG** SPELL... THERE ARE SO MANY OF THEM, IT MIGHT NOT BE PERMANENT.
ALSO, BECAUSE WE DON'T KNOW HOW OR WHY THEY CHANGED IN THE FIRST PLACE, THEY MIGHT JUST GET EXPOSED AGAIN AND CHANGE BACK.
ALICE, DID YOU TRY COMMUNICATING WITH THEM? I MEAN, YOU'RE THEIR QUEEN...OR SOMETHING. SURELY YOU CAN CONTROL THEM.
OF COURSE I TRIED THAT. I TRIED EVERYTHING. **NOTHING WORKS!**
WHOA. CALM DOWN, ALICE. NICO, I'M GUESSING FROM HER REACTION, THAT WAS A "NO."
DEFINITELY A NO.
ALL RIGHT. WE'LL FIGURE THIS OUT...**SOMEHOW.** EVERYONE JUST STAY CALM.

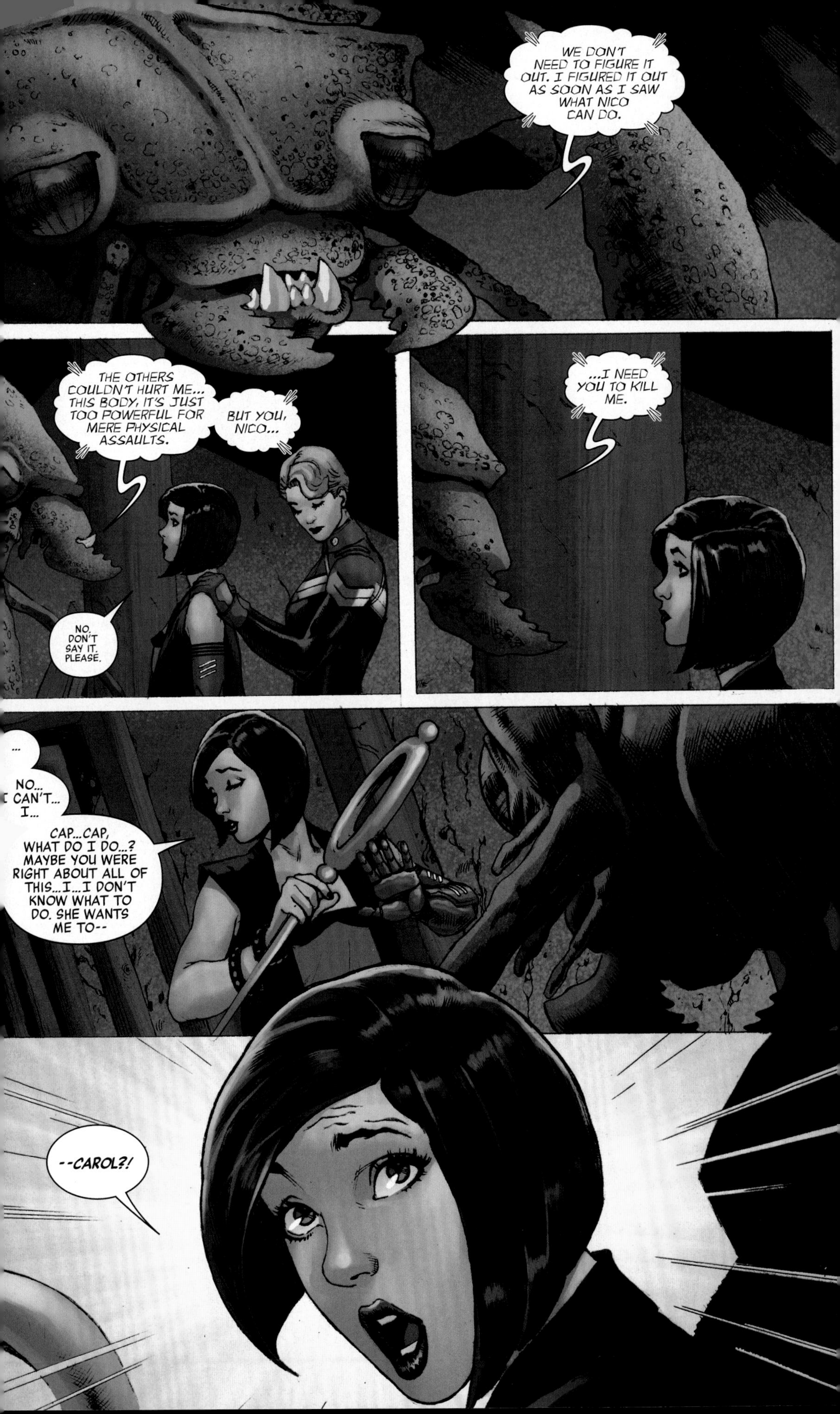
WE DON'T NEED TO FIGURE IT OUT. I FIGURED IT OUT AS SOON AS I SAW WHAT NICO CAN DO.
THE OTHERS COULDN'T HURT ME... THIS BODY, IT'S JUST TOO POWERFUL FOR MERE PHYSICAL ASSAULTS.
BUT YOU, NICO...
NO. DON'T SAY IT. PLEASE.
...I NEED YOU TO KILL ME.
...
NO... I CAN'T... I...
CAP...CAP, WHAT DO I DO...? MAYBE YOU WERE RIGHT ABOUT ALL OF THIS...I...I DON'T KNOW WHAT TO DO. SHE WANTS ME TO--
--CAROL?!

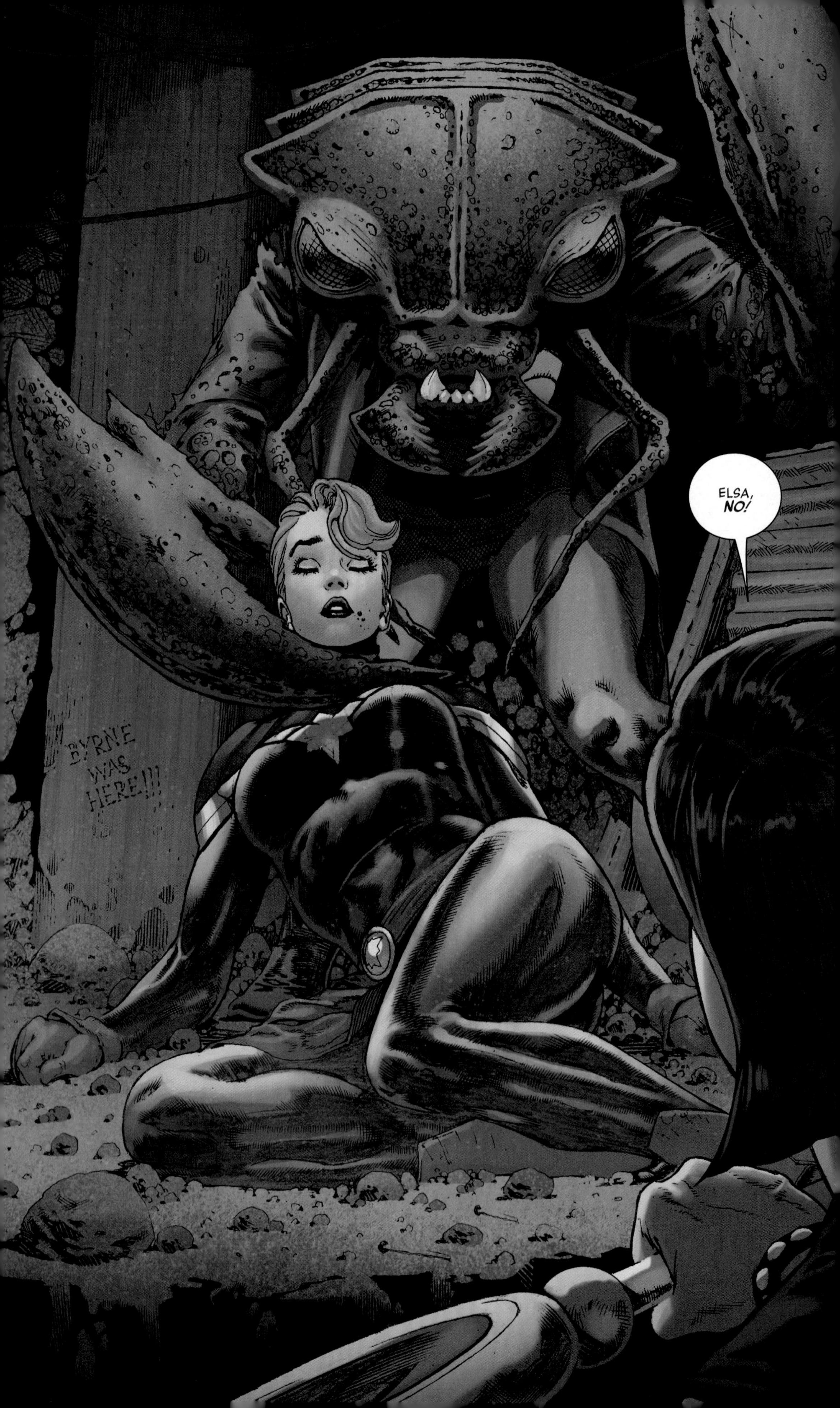
ELSA, NO!
BYRNE WAS HERE!!!

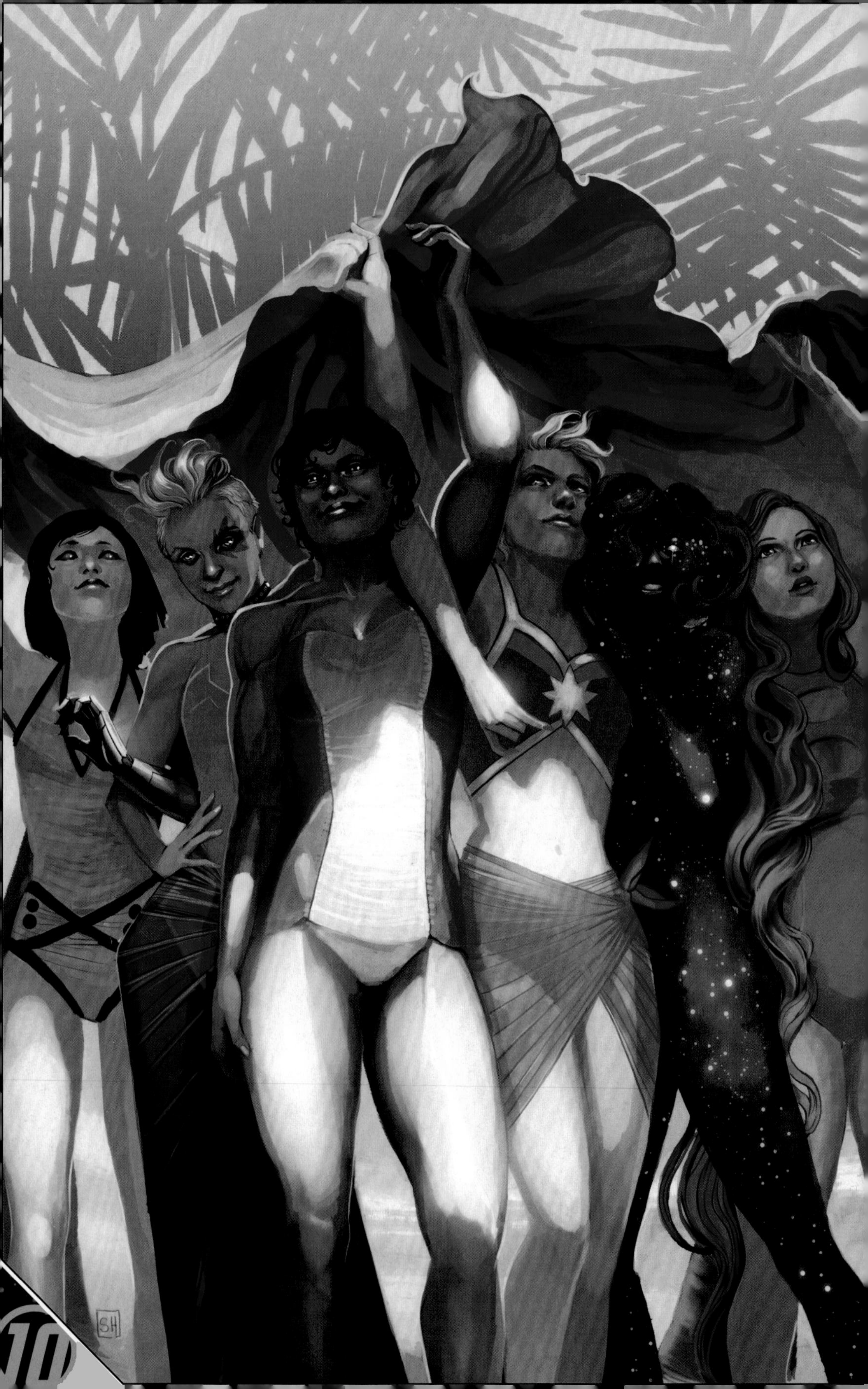
SH
10

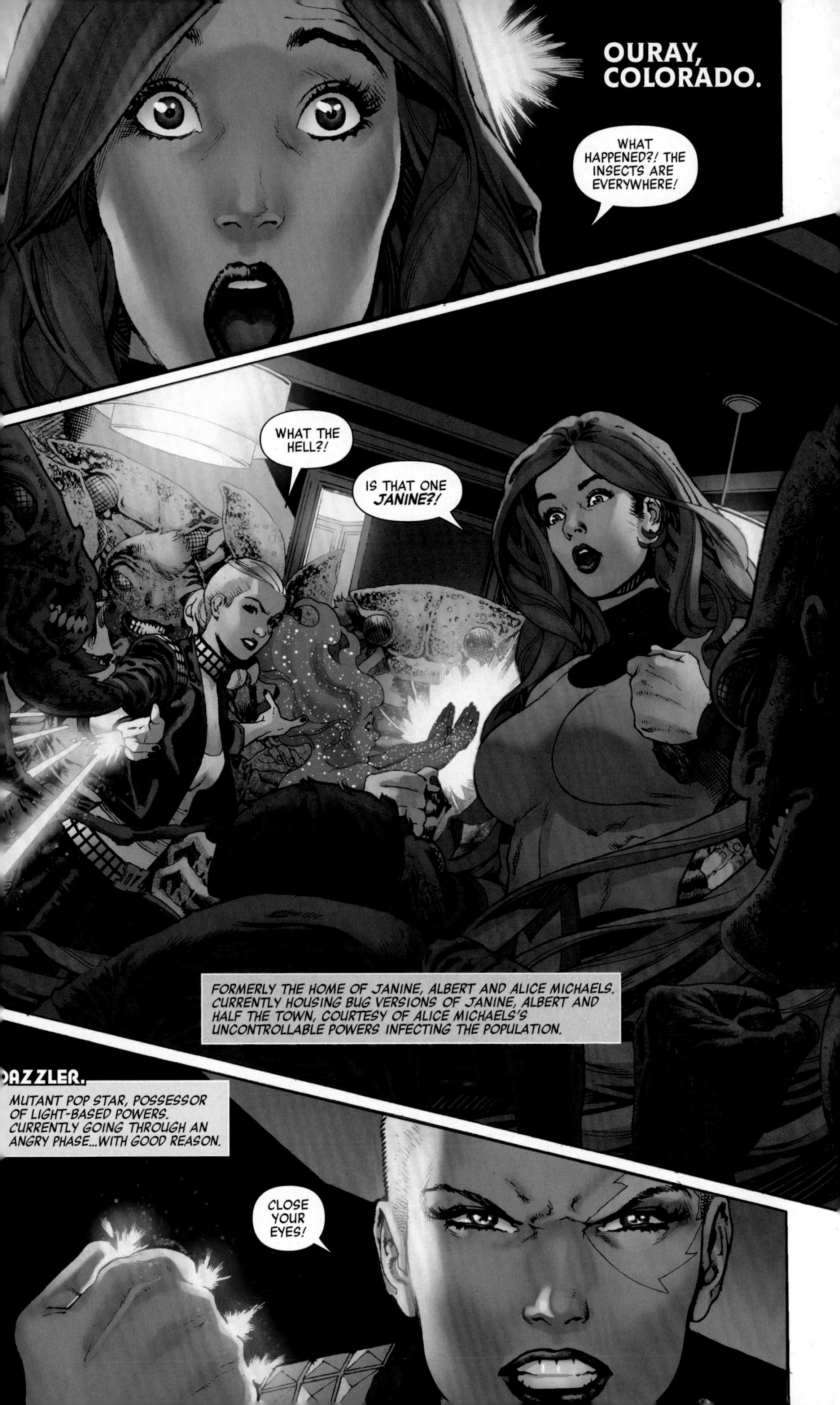

OURAY, COLORADO.
WHAT HAPPENED?! THE INSECTS ARE EVERYWHERE!
WHAT THE HELL?!
IS THAT ONE JANINE?!
FORMERLY THE HOME OF JANINE, ALBERT AND ALICE MICHAELS. CURRENTLY HOUSING BUG VERSIONS OF JANINE, ALBERT AND HALF THE TOWN, COURTESY OF ALICE MICHAELS'S UNCONTROLLABLE POWERS INFECTING THE POPULATION.
DAZZLER.
MUTANT POP STAR, POSSESSOR OF LIGHT-BASED POWERS. CURRENTLY GOING THROUGH AN ANGRY PHASE...WITH GOOD REASON.
CLOSE YOUR EYES!

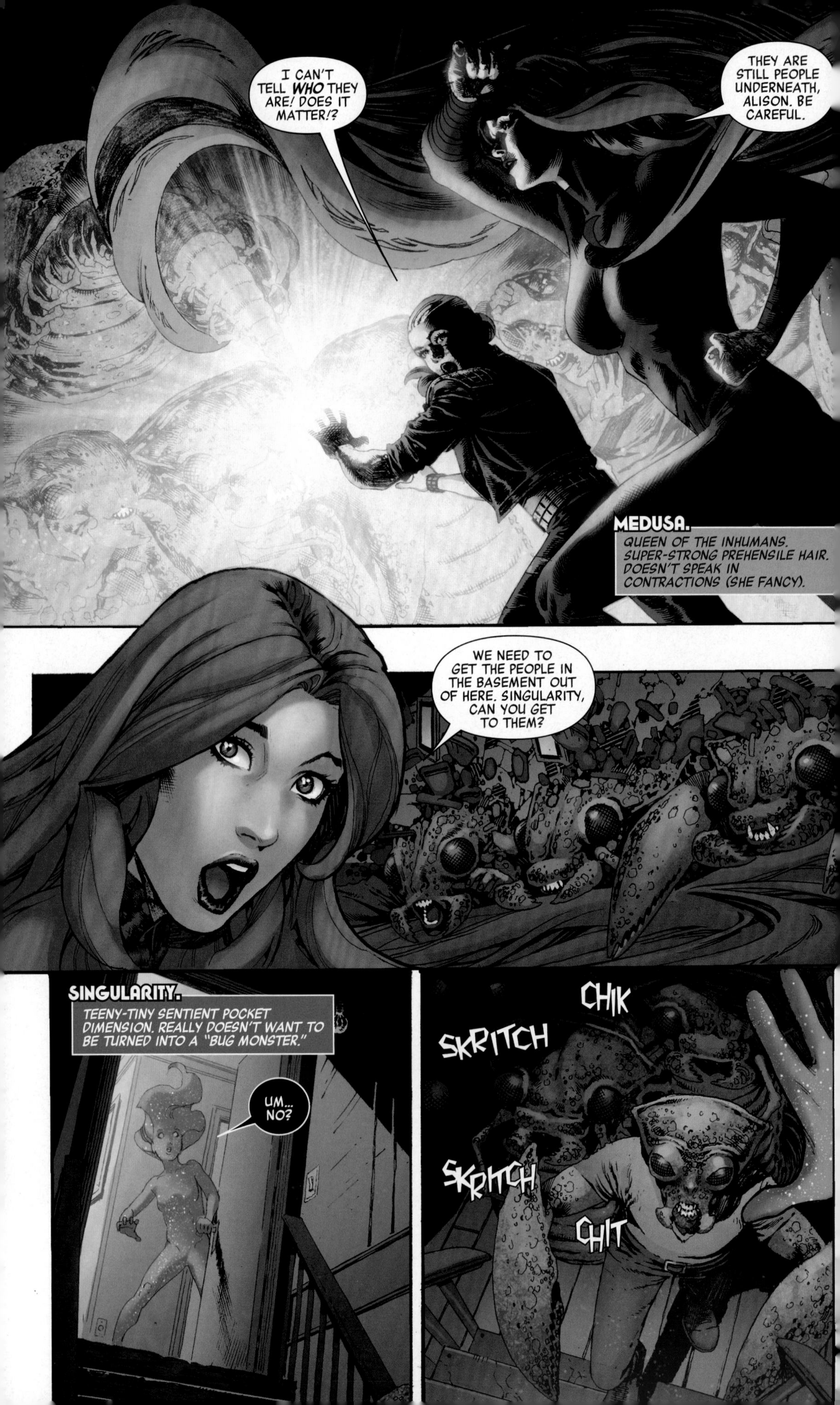
I CAN'T TELL **WHO** THEY ARE! DOES IT MATTER!?
THEY ARE STILL PEOPLE UNDERNEATH, ALISON. BE CAREFUL.
MEDUSA.
QUEEN OF THE INHUMANS. SUPER-STRONG PREHENSILE HAIR. DOESN'T SPEAK IN CONTRACTIONS (SHE FANCY).
WE NEED TO GET THE PEOPLE IN THE BASEMENT OUT OF HERE. SINGULARITY, CAN YOU GET TO THEM?
SINGULARITY.
TEENY-TINY SENTIENT POCKET DIMENSION. REALLY DOESN'T WANT TO BE TURNED INTO A "BUG MONSTER."
UM... NO?
CHIK
SKRITCH
SKRITCH
CHIT

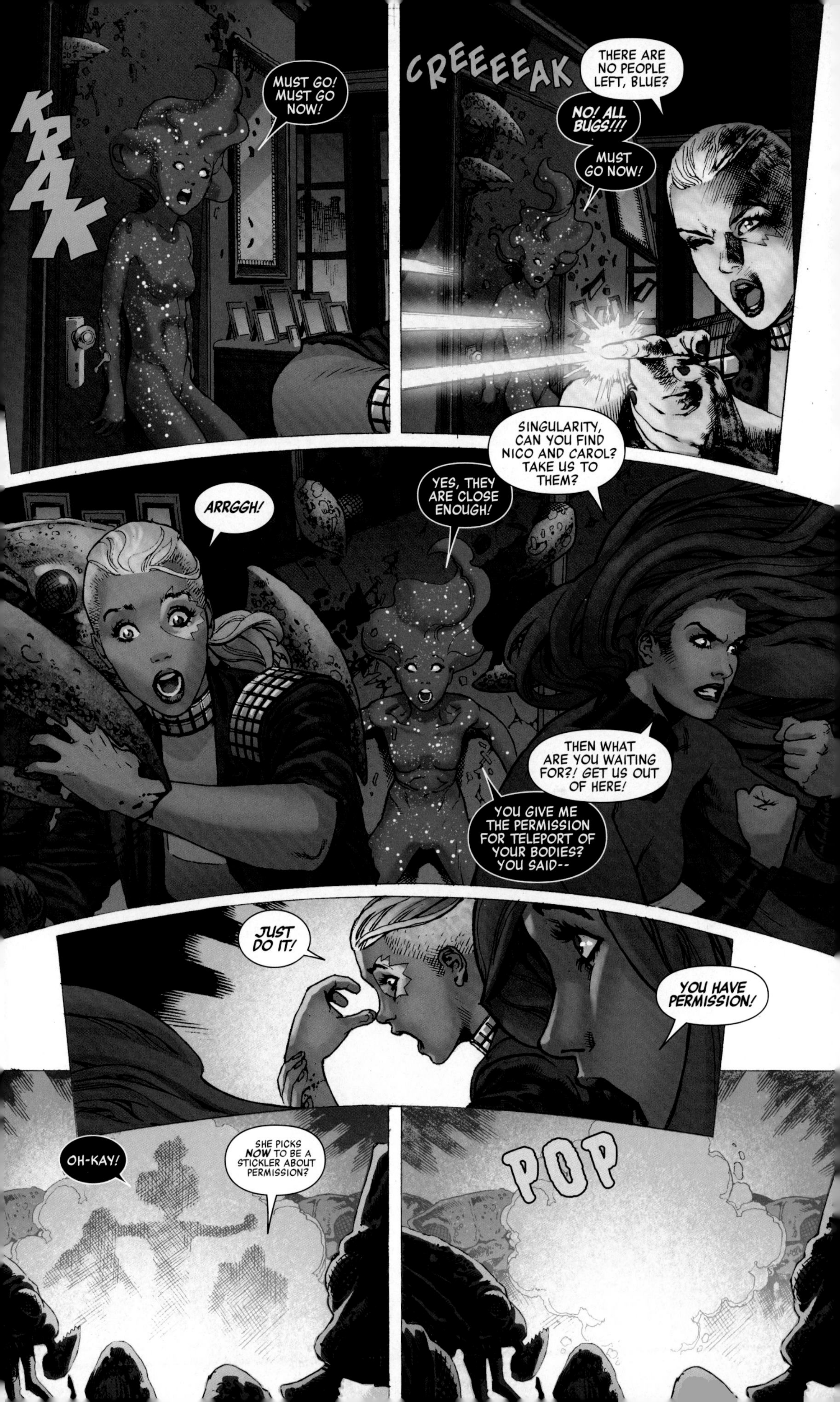
KRAK
MUST GO! MUST GO NOW!
CREEEEAK
THERE ARE NO PEOPLE LEFT, BLUE?
NO! ALL BUGS!!!
MUST GO NOW!
ARRGGH!
SINGULARITY, CAN YOU FIND NICO AND CAROL? TAKE US TO THEM?
YES, THEY ARE CLOSE ENOUGH!
THEN WHAT ARE YOU WAITING FOR?! GET US OUT OF HERE!
YOU GIVE ME THE PERMISSION FOR TELEPORT OF YOUR BODIES? YOU SAID--
JUST DO IT!
YOU HAVE PERMISSION!
OH-KAY!
SHE PICKS NOW TO BE A STICKLER ABOUT PERMISSION?
POP

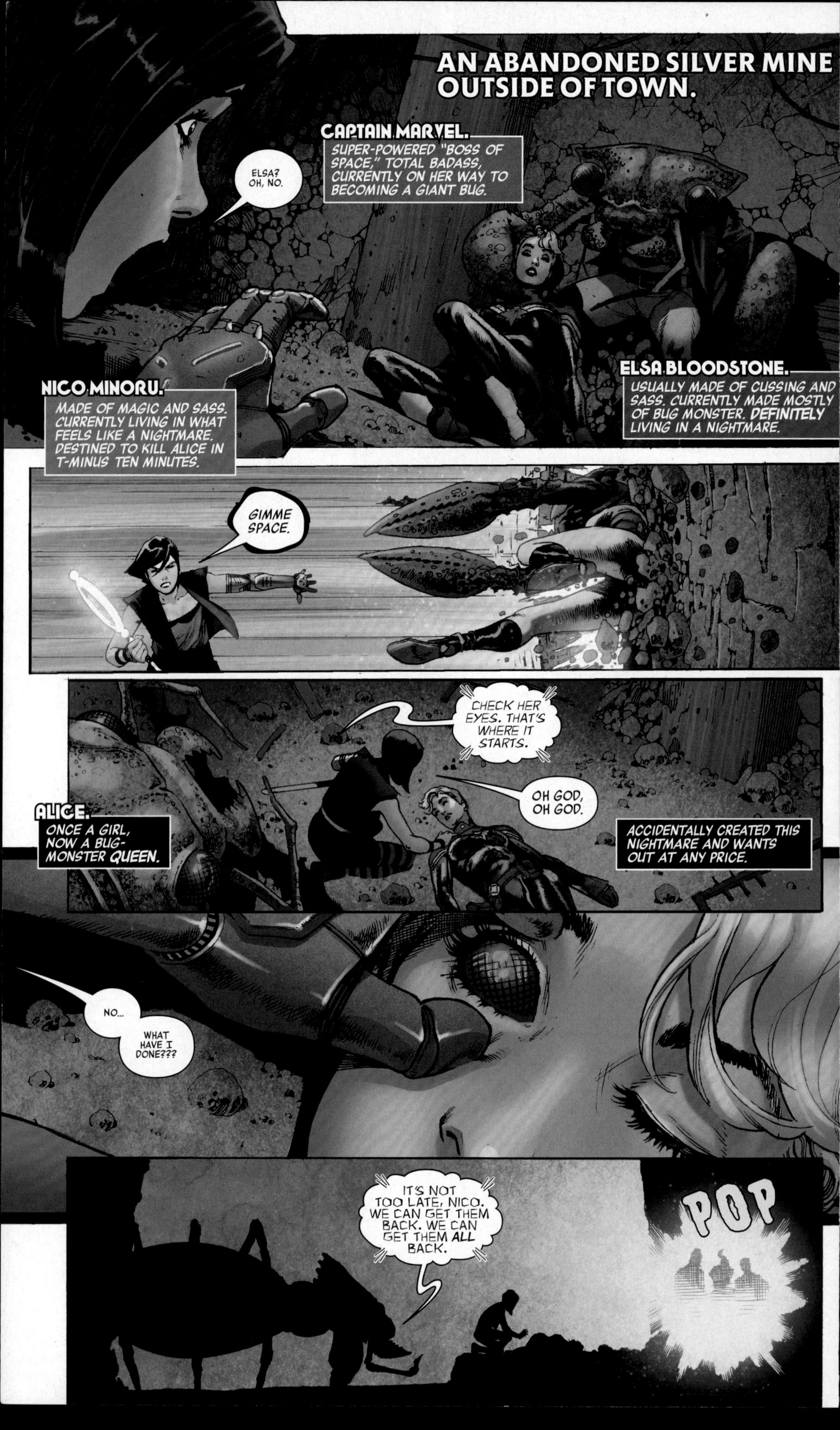
AN ABANDONED SILVER MINE OUTSIDE OF TOWN.
CAPTAIN MARVEL.
SUPER-POWERED "BOSS OF SPACE," TOTAL BADASS, CURRENTLY ON HER WAY TO BECOMING A GIANT BUG.
ELSA? OH, NO.
NICO MINORU.
MADE OF MAGIC AND SASS. CURRENTLY LIVING IN WHAT FEELS LIKE A NIGHTMARE. DESTINED TO KILL ALICE IN T-MINUS TEN MINUTES.
ELSA BLOODSTONE.
USUALLY MADE OF CUSSING AND SASS. CURRENTLY MADE MOSTLY OF BUG MONSTER. DEFINITELY LIVING IN A NIGHTMARE.
GIMME SPACE.
CHECK HER EYES. THAT'S WHERE IT STARTS.
OH GOD, OH GOD.
ALICE.
ONCE A GIRL, NOW A BUG-MONSTER QUEEN.
ACCIDENTALLY CREATED THIS NIGHTMARE AND WANTS OUT AT ANY PRICE.
NO...
WHAT HAVE I DONE???
IT'S NOT TOO LATE, NICO. WE CAN GET THEM BACK. WE CAN GET THEM ALL BACK.
POP

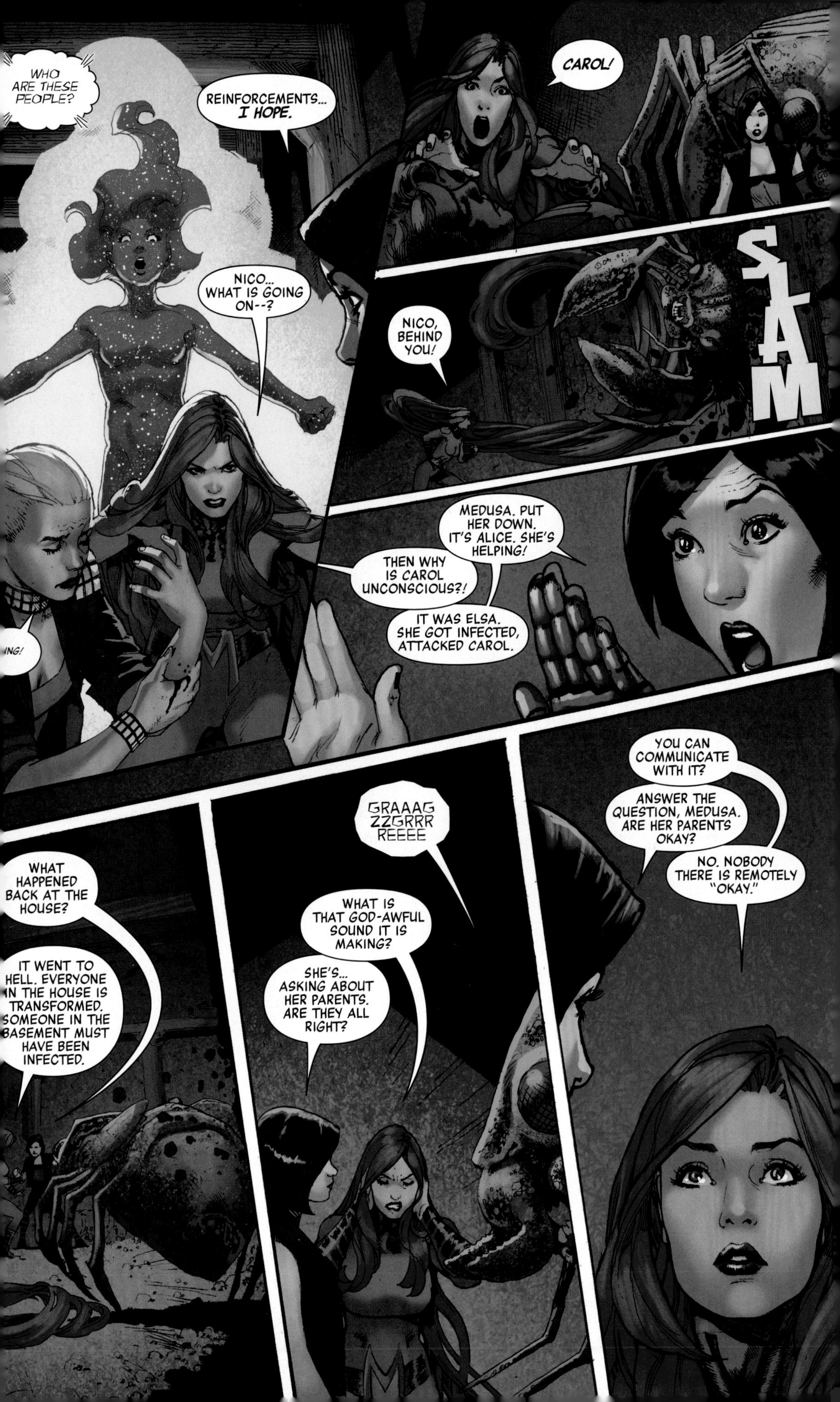

WHO ARE THESE PEOPLE?
REINFORCEMENTS... I HOPE.
CAROL!
NICO... WHAT IS GOING ON--?
NICO, BEHIND YOU!
SLAM
ING!
MEDUSA. PUT HER DOWN. IT'S ALICE. SHE'S HELPING!
THEN WHY IS CAROL UNCONSCIOUS?!
IT WAS ELSA. SHE GOT INFECTED, ATTACKED CAROL.
WHAT HAPPENED BACK AT THE HOUSE?
IT WENT TO HELL. EVERYONE IN THE HOUSE IS TRANSFORMED. SOMEONE IN THE BASEMENT MUST HAVE BEEN INFECTED.
GRAAAG ZZGRRR REEEE
WHAT IS THAT GOD-AWFUL SOUND IT IS MAKING?
SHE'S... ASKING ABOUT HER PARENTS. ARE THEY ALL RIGHT?
YOU CAN COMMUNICATE WITH IT?
ANSWER THE QUESTION, MEDUSA. ARE HER PARENTS OKAY?
NO. NOBODY THERE IS REMOTELY "OKAY."

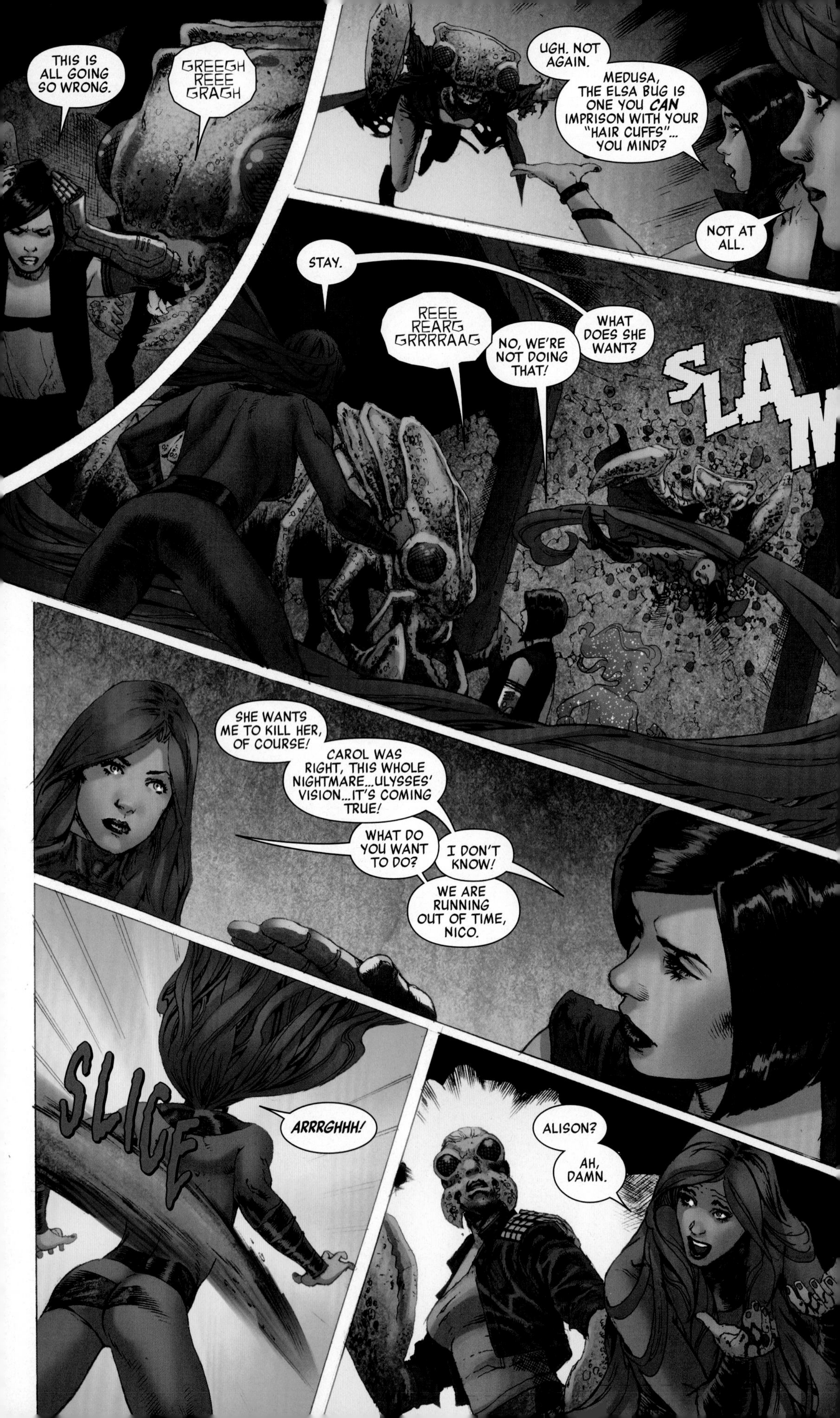
THIS IS ALL GOING SO WRONG.
GREEGH REEE GRAGH
UGH. NOT AGAIN.
MEDUSA, THE ELSA BUG IS ONE YOU CAN IMPRISON WITH YOUR "HAIR CUFFS"... YOU MIND?
NOT AT ALL.
STAY.
REEE REARG GRRRRAAG
WHAT DOES SHE WANT?
NO, WE'RE NOT DOING THAT!
SLAM
SHE WANTS ME TO KILL HER, OF COURSE!
CAROL WAS RIGHT, THIS WHOLE NIGHTMARE...ULYSSES' VISION...IT'S COMING TRUE!
WHAT DO YOU WANT TO DO?
I DON'T KNOW!
WE ARE RUNNING OUT OF TIME, NICO.
SLICE
ARRRGHHH!
ALISON?
AH, DAMN.

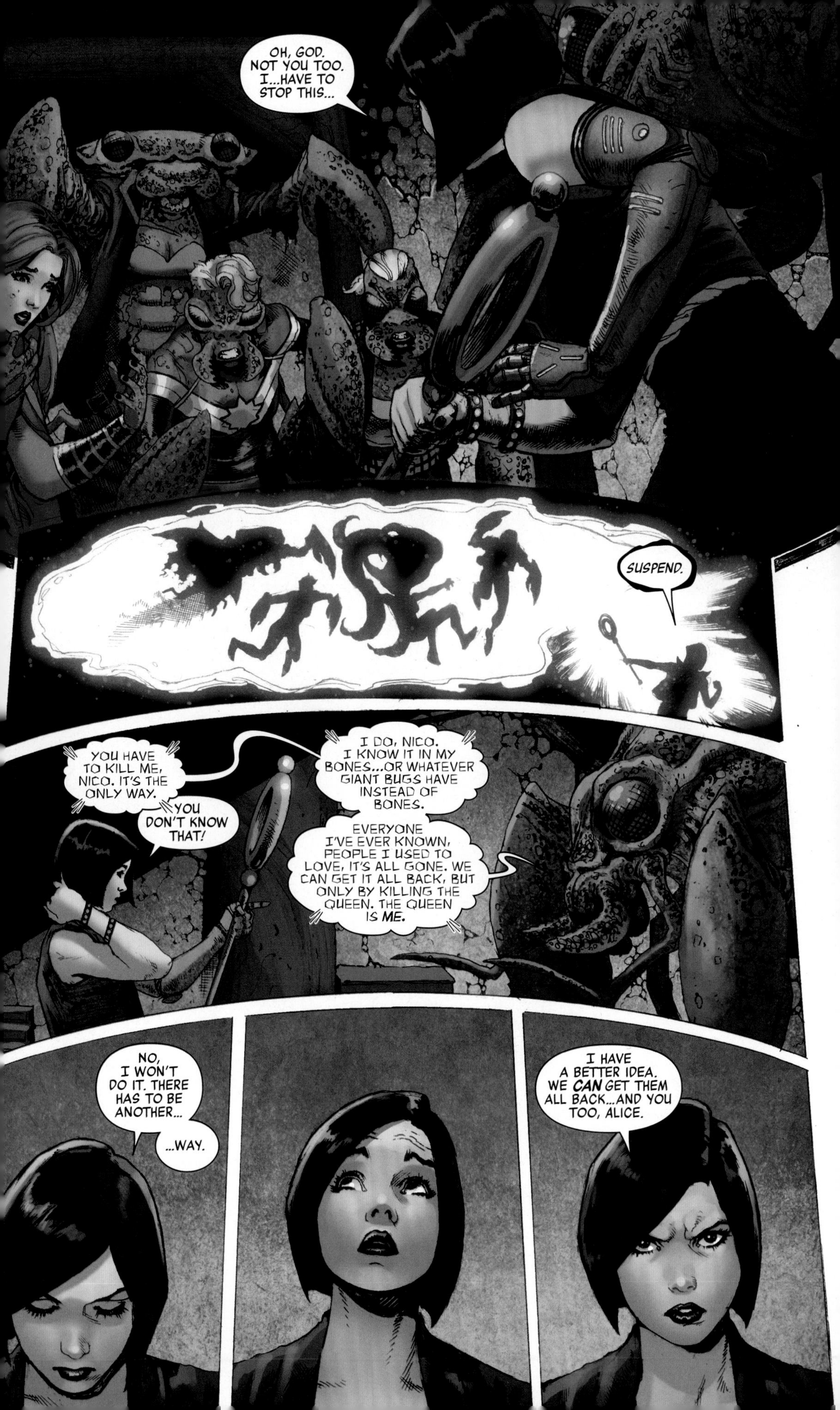
OH, GOD. NOT YOU TOO. I...HAVE TO STOP THIS...
SUSPEND.
YOU HAVE TO KILL ME, NICO. IT'S THE ONLY WAY.
YOU DON'T KNOW THAT!
I DO, NICO. I KNOW IT IN MY BONES...OR WHATEVER GIANT BUGS HAVE INSTEAD OF BONES.
EVERYONE I'VE EVER KNOWN, PEOPLE I USED TO LOVE, IT'S ALL GONE. WE CAN GET IT ALL BACK, BUT ONLY BY KILLING THE QUEEN. THE QUEEN IS ME.
NO, I WON'T DO IT. THERE HAS TO BE ANOTHER...
...WAY.
I HAVE A BETTER IDEA. WE CAN GET THEM ALL BACK...AND YOU TOO, ALICE.

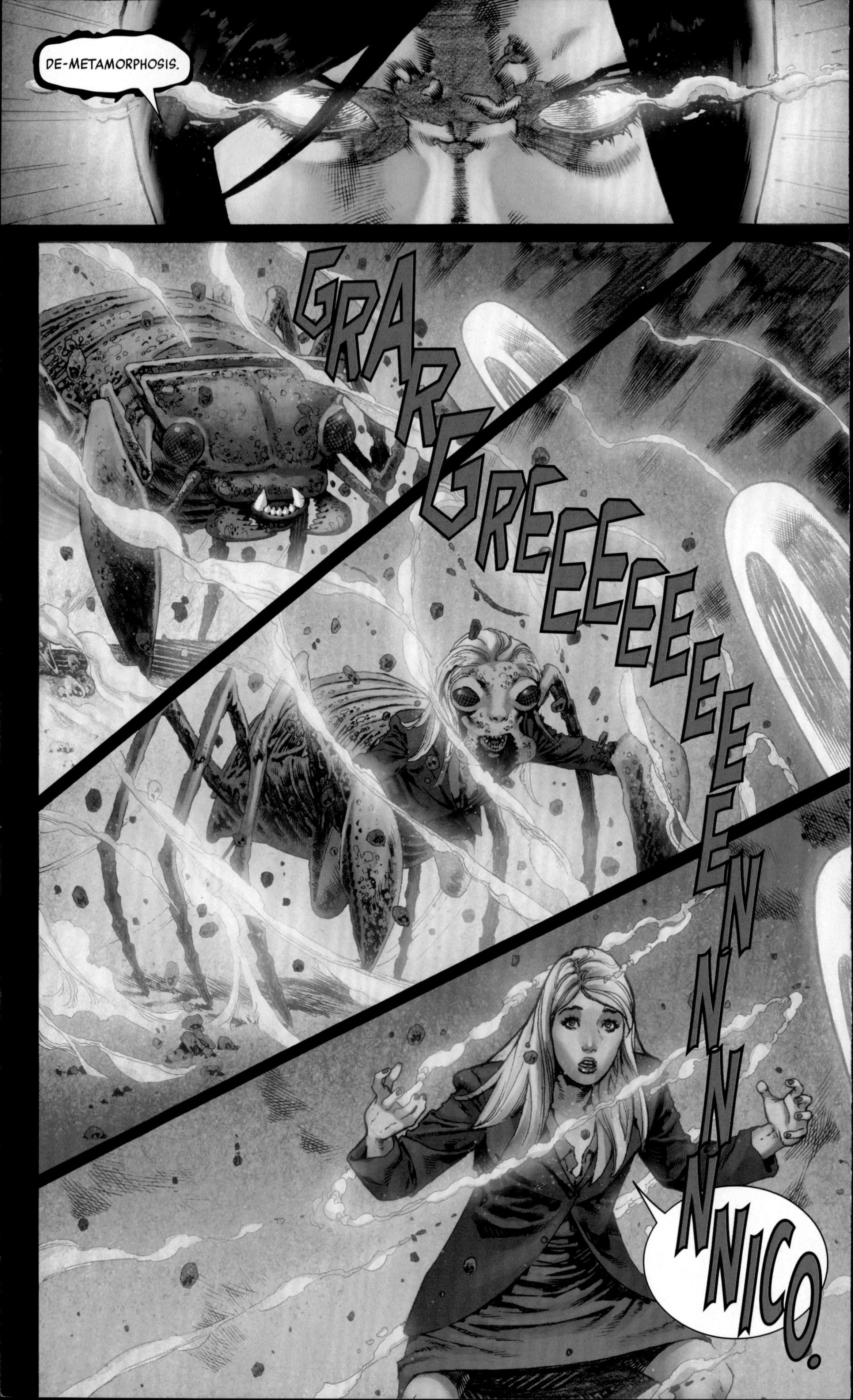
DE-METAMORPHOSIS.
GRARGREEEEEEEEEENNNNNNNICO.

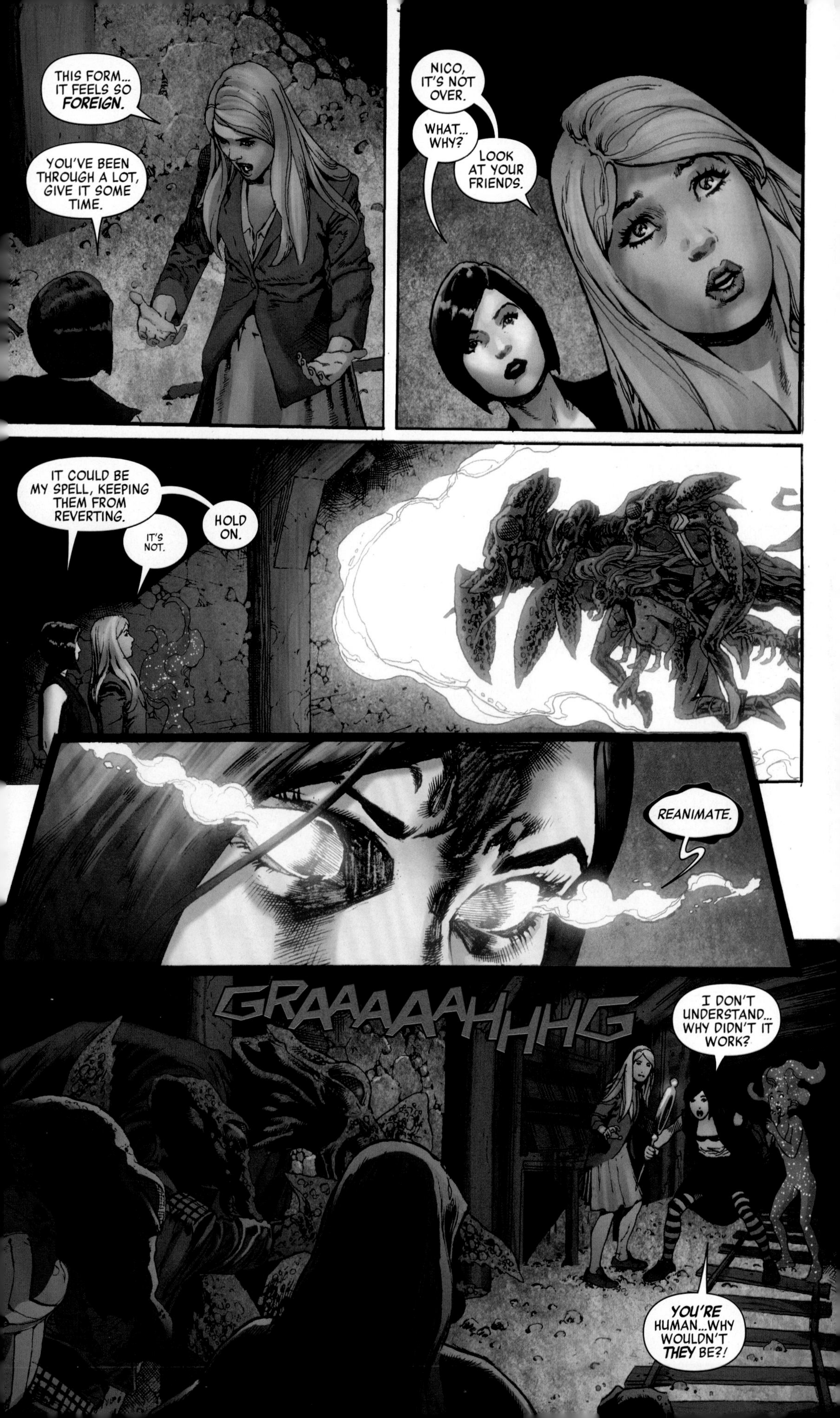
THIS FORM... IT FEELS SO FOREIGN.
YOU'VE BEEN THROUGH A LOT, GIVE IT SOME TIME.
NICO, IT'S NOT OVER.
WHAT... WHY?
LOOK AT YOUR FRIENDS.
IT COULD BE MY SPELL, KEEPING THEM FROM REVERTING.
IT'S NOT.
HOLD ON.
REANIMATE.
GRAAAAAHHHG
I DON'T UNDERSTAND... WHY DIDN'T IT WORK?
YOU'RE HUMAN...WHY WOULDN'T THEY BE?!

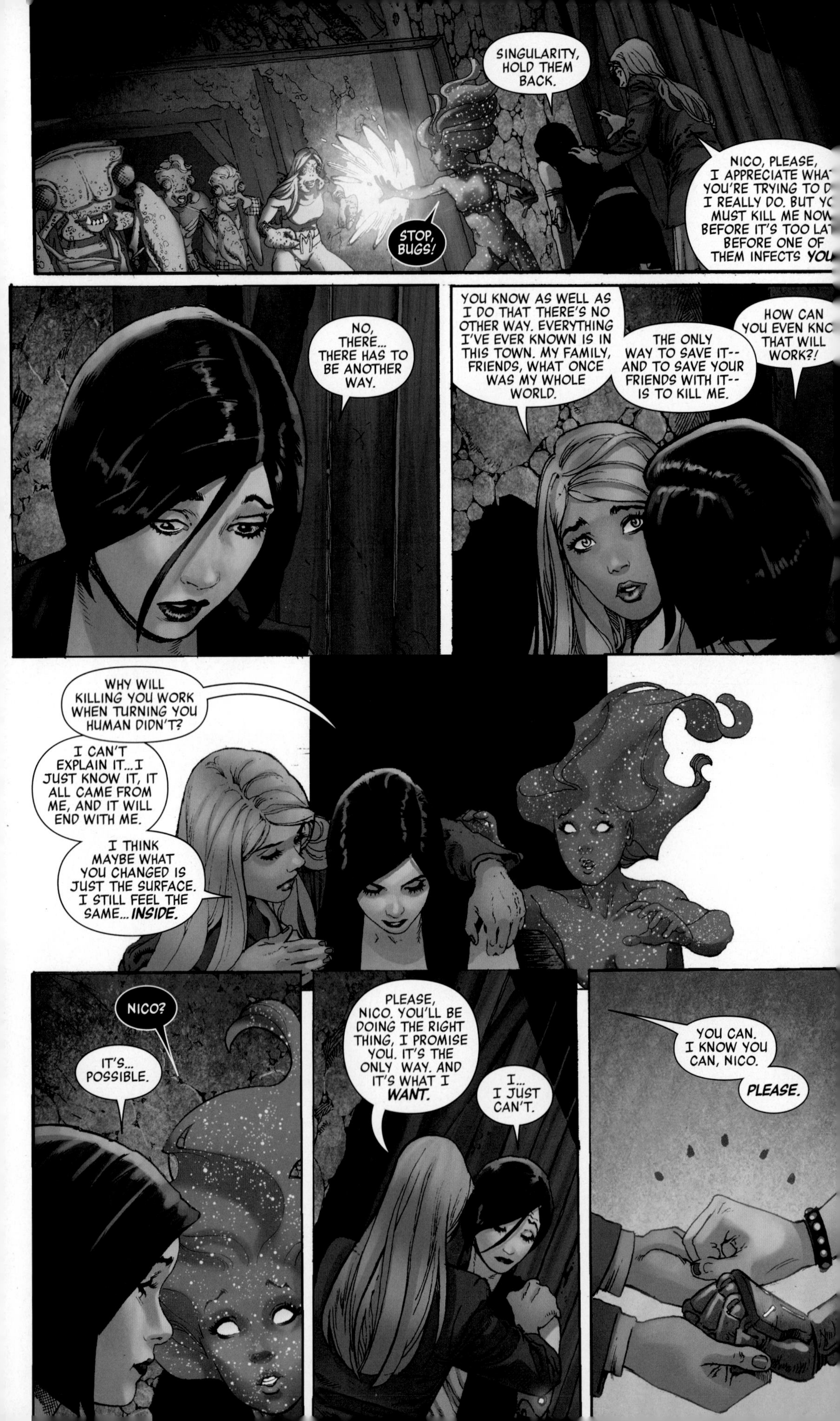
SINGULARITY, HOLD THEM BACK.
STOP, BUGS!
NICO, PLEASE, I APPRECIATE WHAT YOU'RE TRYING TO D I REALLY DO. BUT YO MUST KILL ME NOW BEFORE IT'S TOO LAT BEFORE ONE OF THEM INFECTS YOU
NO, THERE... THERE HAS TO BE ANOTHER WAY.
YOU KNOW AS WELL AS I DO THAT THERE'S NO OTHER WAY. EVERYTHING I'VE EVER KNOWN IS IN THIS TOWN. MY FAMILY, FRIENDS, WHAT ONCE WAS MY WHOLE WORLD.
THE ONLY WAY TO SAVE IT-- AND TO SAVE YOUR FRIENDS WITH IT-- IS TO KILL ME.
HOW CAN YOU EVEN KNO THAT WILL WORK?!
WHY WILL KILLING YOU WORK WHEN TURNING YOU HUMAN DIDN'T?
I CAN'T EXPLAIN IT... I JUST KNOW IT, IT ALL CAME FROM ME, AND IT WILL END WITH ME.
I THINK MAYBE WHAT YOU CHANGED IS JUST THE SURFACE. I STILL FEEL THE SAME... INSIDE.
NICO?
IT'S... POSSIBLE.
PLEASE, NICO. YOU'LL BE DOING THE RIGHT THING, I PROMISE YOU. IT'S THE ONLY WAY. AND IT'S WHAT I WANT.
I... I JUST CAN'T.
YOU CAN. I KNOW YOU CAN, NICO.
PLEASE.

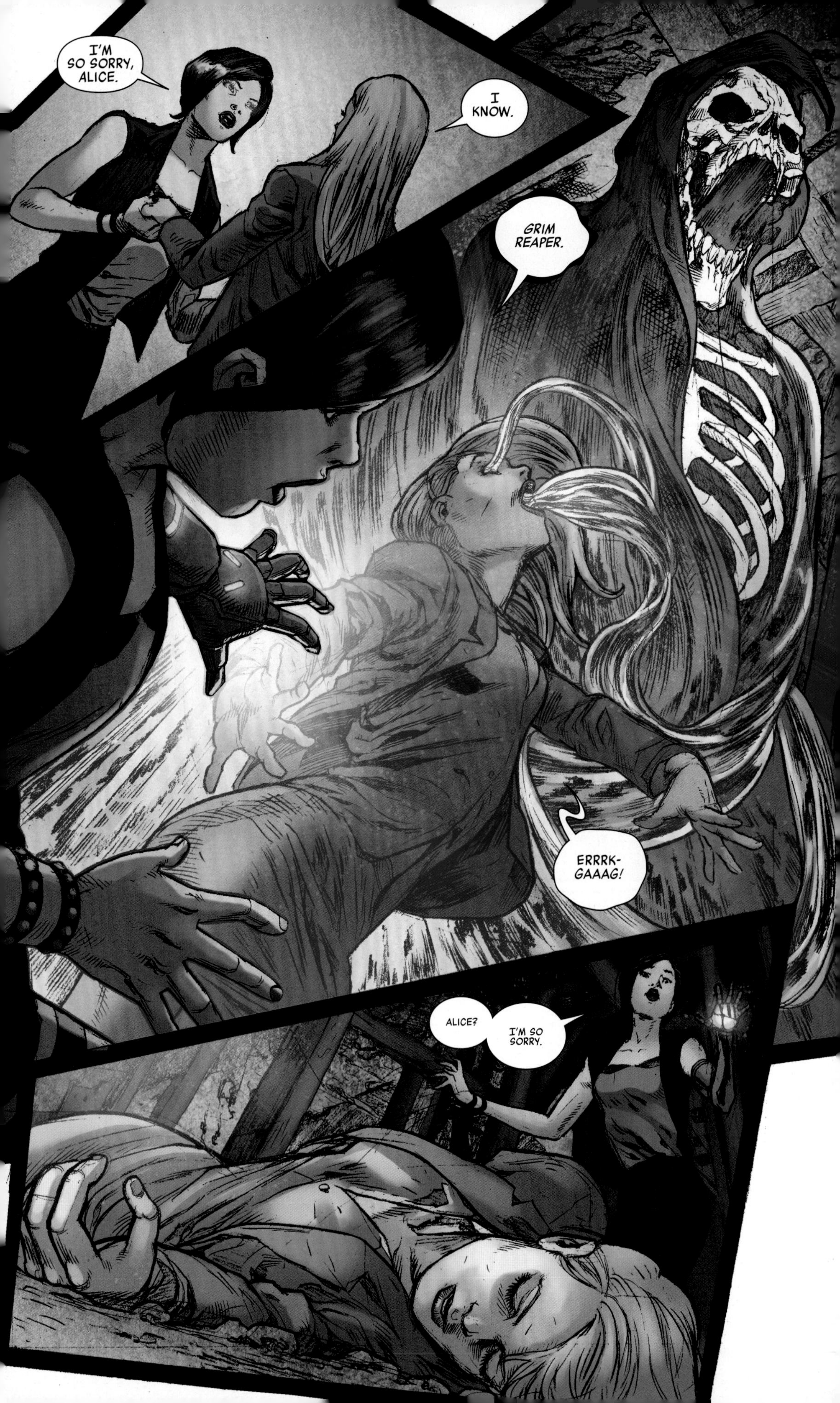
I'M SO SORRY, ALICE.
I KNOW.
GRIM REAPER.
ERRRK-GAAAG!
ALICE?
I'M SO SORRY.

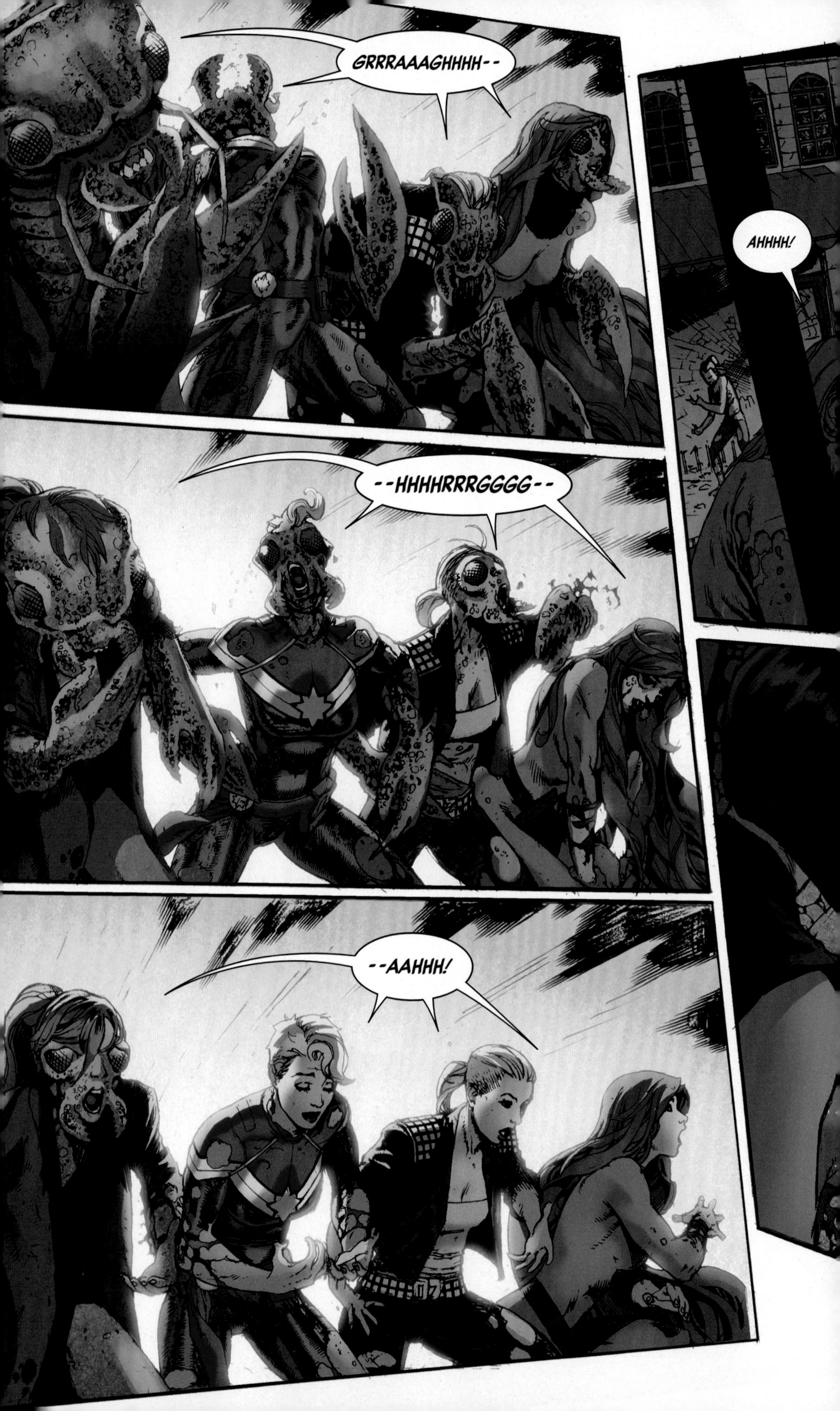
GRRRAAAGHHHH--
AHHHH!
--HHHHRRRGGGG--
--AAHHH!

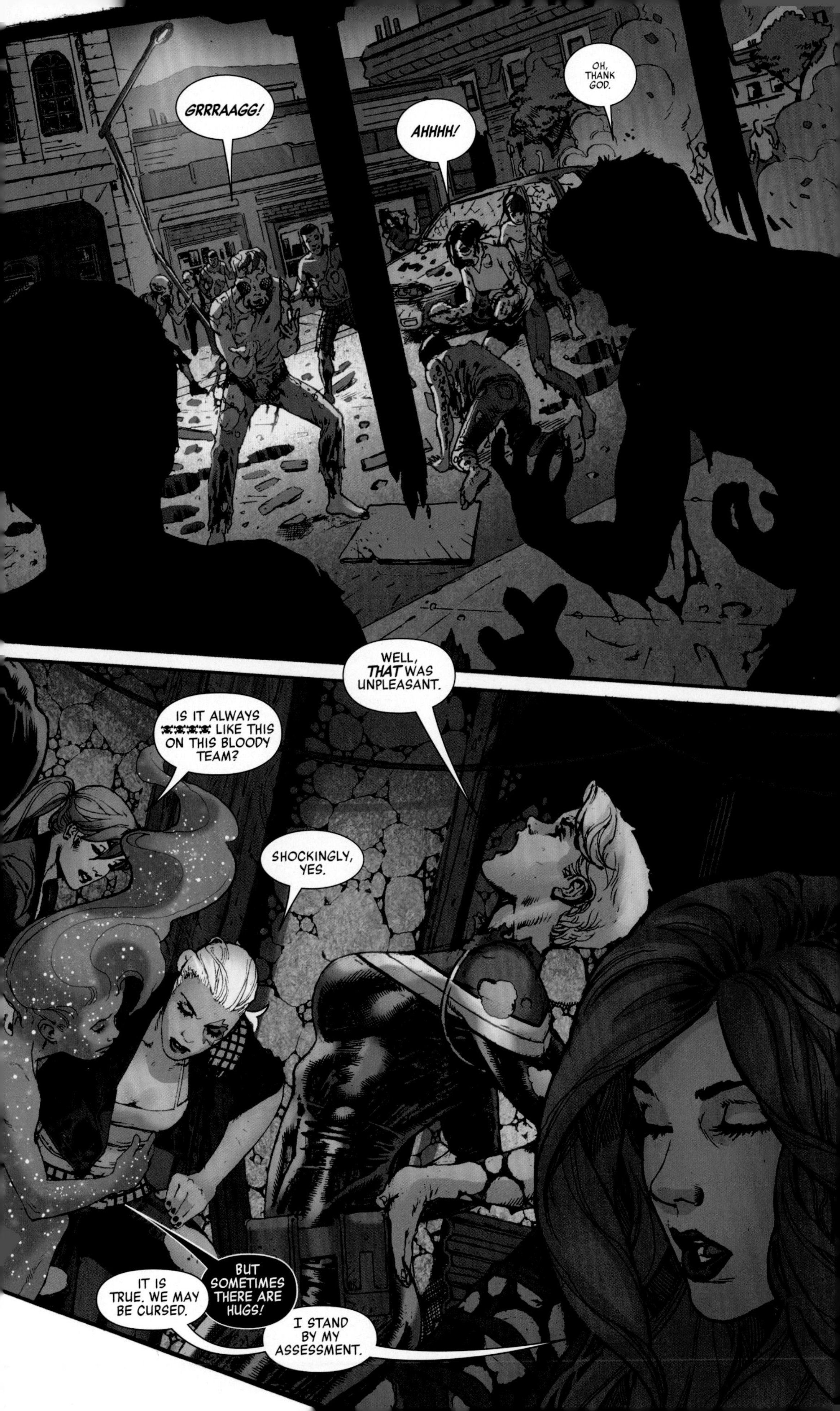
GRRRAAGG!
AHHHH!
OH, THANK GOD.
WELL, THAT WAS UNPLEASANT.
IS IT ALWAYS ☠☠☠☠ LIKE THIS ON THIS BLOODY TEAM?
SHOCKINGLY, YES.
IT IS TRUE. WE MAY BE CURSED.
BUT SOMETIMES THERE ARE HUGS!
I STAND BY MY ASSESSMENT.

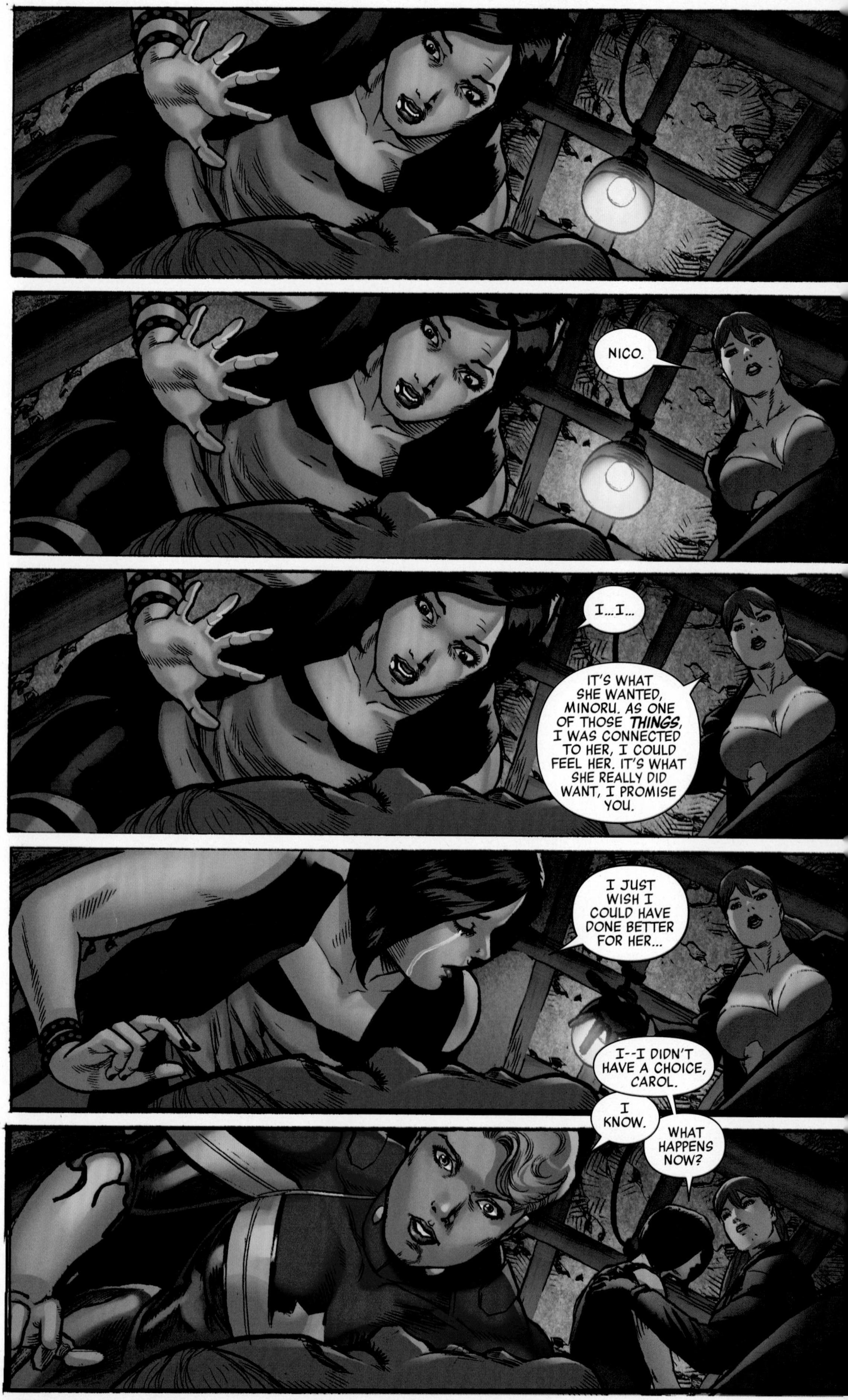
NICO.
I...I...
IT'S WHAT SHE WANTED, MINORU. AS ONE OF THOSE THINGS, I WAS CONNECTED TO HER, I COULD FEEL HER. IT'S WHAT SHE REALLY DID WANT, I PROMISE YOU.
I JUST WISH I COULD HAVE DONE BETTER FOR HER...
I--I DIDN'T HAVE A CHOICE, CAROL.
I KNOW.
WHAT HAPPENS NOW?

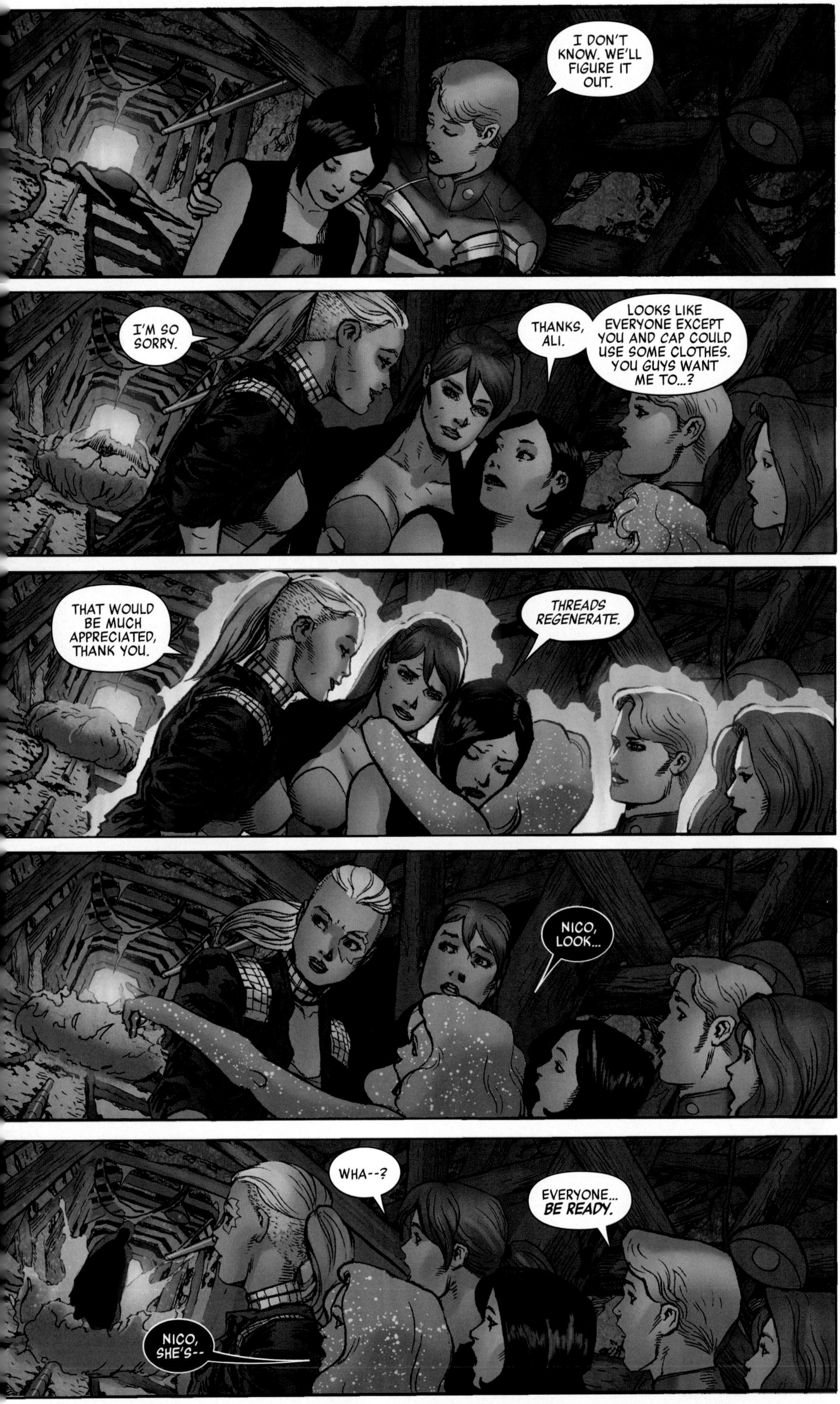
I DON'T KNOW. WE'LL FIGURE IT OUT.
I'M SO SORRY.
THANKS, ALI.
LOOKS LIKE EVERYONE EXCEPT YOU AND CAP COULD USE SOME CLOTHES. YOU GUYS WANT ME TO...?
THAT WOULD BE MUCH APPRECIATED, THANK YOU.
THREADS REGENERATE.
NICO, LOOK...
WHA--?
EVERYONE... BE READY.
NICO, SHE'S--

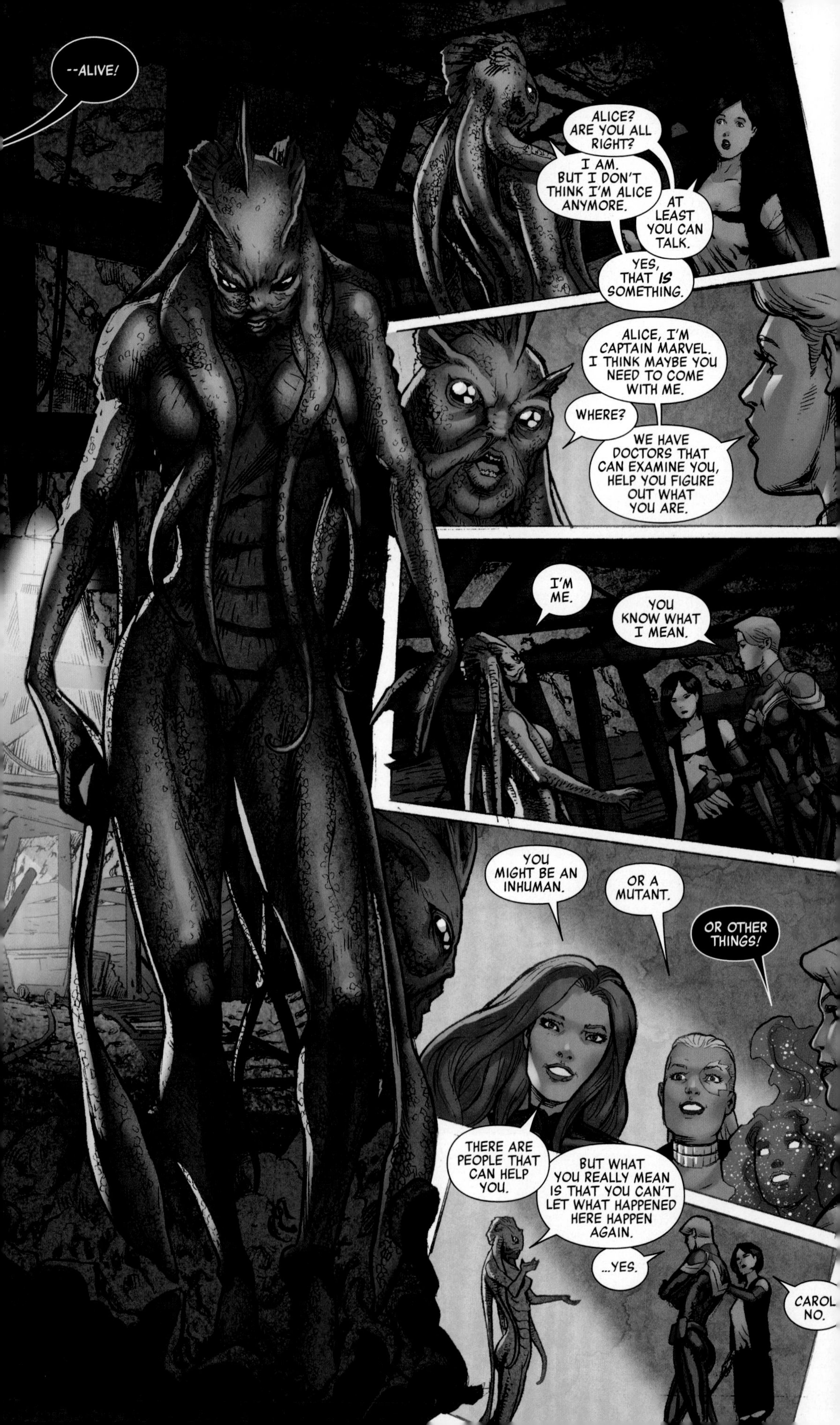

--ALIVE!
ALICE? ARE YOU ALL RIGHT?
I AM. BUT I DON'T THINK I'M ALICE ANYMORE.
AT LEAST YOU CAN TALK.
YES, THAT *IS* SOMETHING.
ALICE, I'M CAPTAIN MARVEL. I THINK MAYBE YOU NEED TO COME WITH ME.
WHERE?
WE HAVE DOCTORS THAT CAN EXAMINE YOU, HELP YOU FIGURE OUT WHAT YOU ARE.
I'M ME.
YOU KNOW WHAT I MEAN.
YOU MIGHT BE AN INHUMAN.
OR A MUTANT.
OR OTHER THINGS!
THERE ARE PEOPLE THAT CAN HELP YOU.
BUT WHAT YOU REALLY MEAN IS THAT YOU CAN'T LET WHAT HAPPENED HERE HAPPEN AGAIN.
...YES.
CAROL NO.

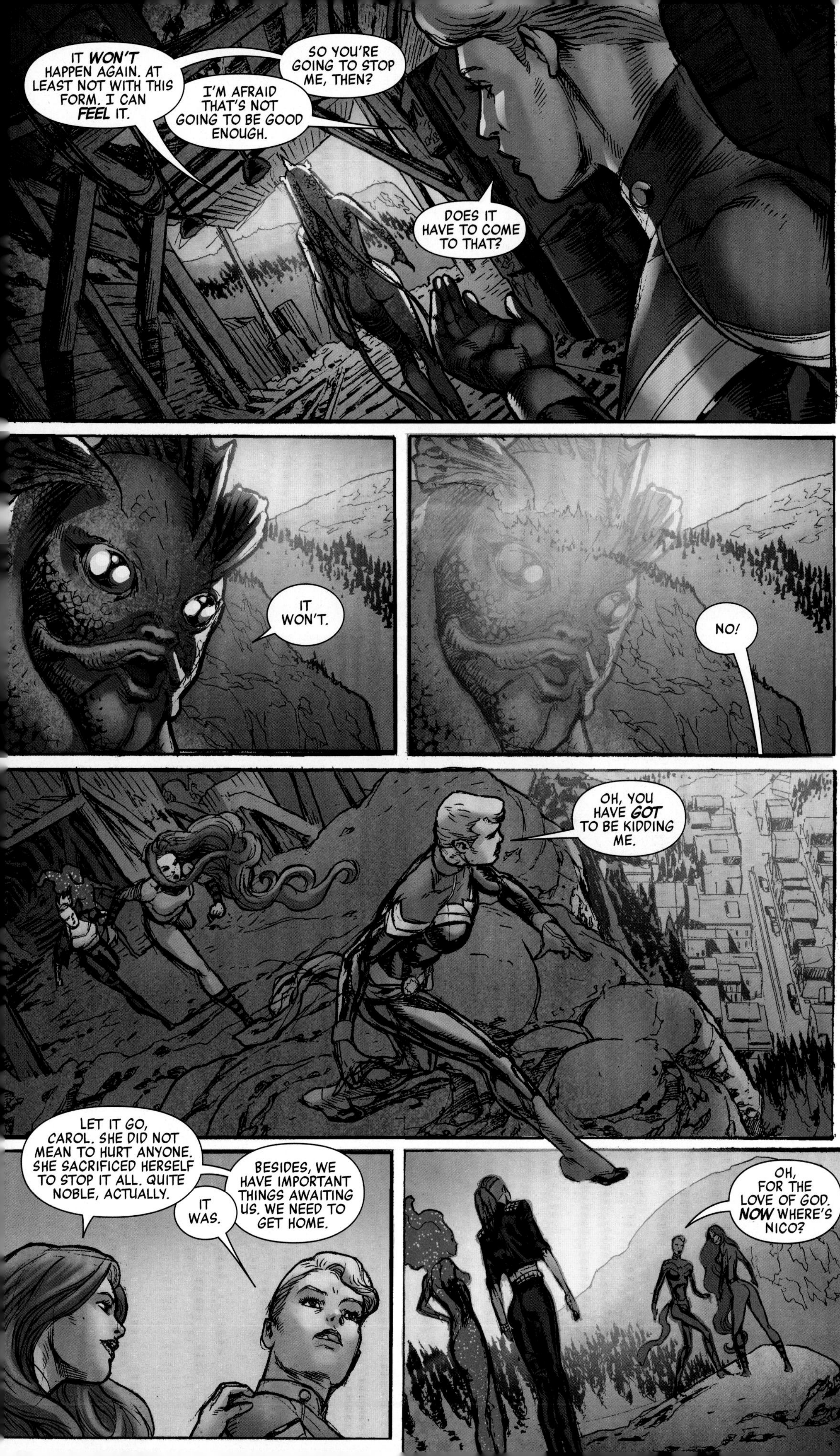

IT WON'T HAPPEN AGAIN. AT LEAST NOT WITH THIS FORM. I CAN FEEL IT.
SO YOU'RE GOING TO STOP ME, THEN?
I'M AFRAID THAT'S NOT GOING TO BE GOOD ENOUGH.
DOES IT HAVE TO COME TO THAT?
IT WON'T.
NO!
OH, YOU HAVE GOT TO BE KIDDING ME.
LET IT GO, CAROL. SHE DID NOT MEAN TO HURT ANYONE. SHE SACRIFICED HERSELF TO STOP IT ALL. QUITE NOBLE, ACTUALLY.
IT WAS.
BESIDES, WE HAVE IMPORTANT THINGS AWAITING US. WE NEED TO GET HOME.
OH, FOR THE LOVE OF GOD. NOW WHERE'S NICO?

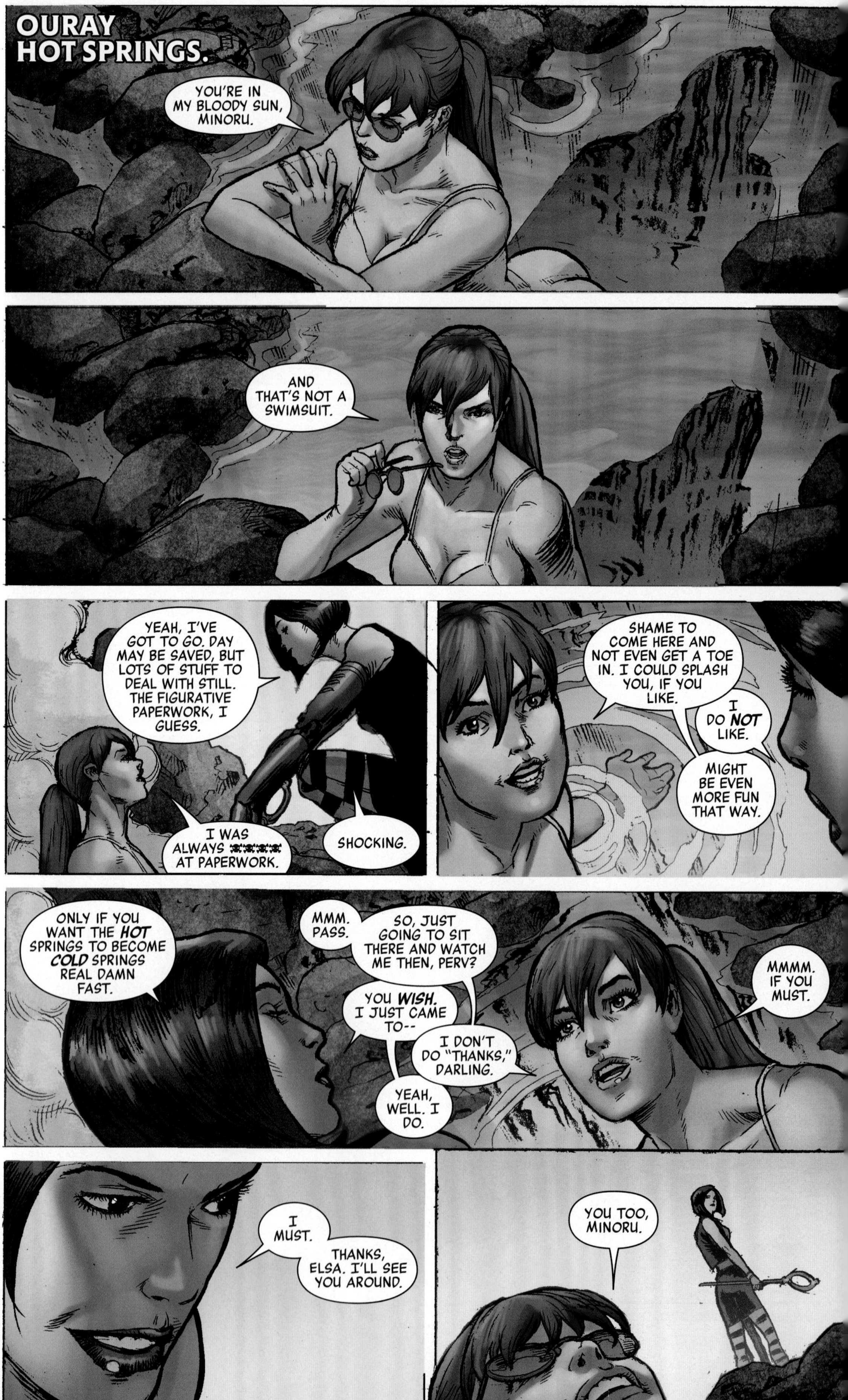
OURAY HOT SPRINGS.
YOU'RE IN MY BLOODY SUN, MINORU.
AND THAT'S NOT A SWIMSUIT.
YEAH, I'VE GOT TO GO. DAY MAY BE SAVED, BUT LOTS OF STUFF TO DEAL WITH STILL. THE FIGURATIVE PAPERWORK, I GUESS.
I WAS ALWAYS ☠☠☠☠ AT PAPERWORK.
SHOCKING.
SHAME TO COME HERE AND NOT EVEN GET A TOE IN. I COULD SPLASH YOU, IF YOU LIKE.
I DO NOT LIKE.
MIGHT BE EVEN MORE FUN THAT WAY.
ONLY IF YOU WANT THE HOT SPRINGS TO BECOME COLD SPRINGS REAL DAMN FAST.
MMM. PASS.
SO, JUST GOING TO SIT THERE AND WATCH ME THEN, PERV?
YOU WISH. I JUST CAME TO--
I DON'T DO "THANKS," DARLING.
YEAH, WELL. I DO.
MMMM. IF YOU MUST.
I MUST.
THANKS, ELSA. I'LL SEE YOU AROUND.
YOU TOO, MINORU.

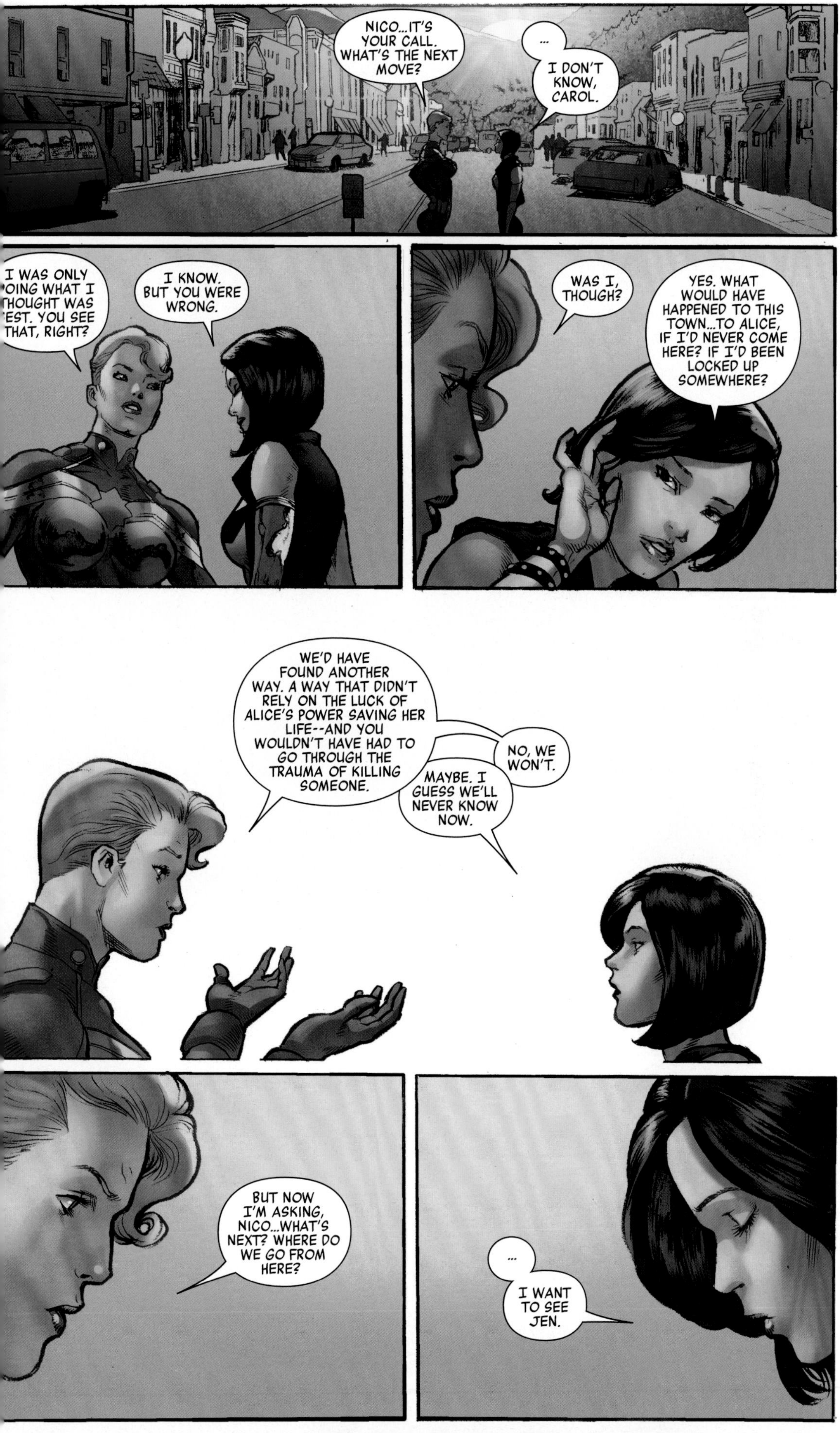
NICO...IT'S YOUR CALL. WHAT'S THE NEXT MOVE?
...
I DON'T KNOW, CAROL.
I WAS ONLY OING WHAT I THOUGHT WAS EST. YOU SEE THAT, RIGHT?
I KNOW. BUT YOU WERE WRONG.
WAS I, THOUGH?
YES. WHAT WOULD HAVE HAPPENED TO THIS TOWN...TO ALICE, IF I'D NEVER COME HERE? IF I'D BEEN LOCKED UP SOMEWHERE?
WE'D HAVE FOUND ANOTHER WAY. A WAY THAT DIDN'T RELY ON THE LUCK OF ALICE'S POWER SAVING HER LIFE--AND YOU WOULDN'T HAVE HAD TO GO THROUGH THE TRAUMA OF KILLING SOMEONE.
MAYBE. I GUESS WE'LL NEVER KNOW NOW.
NO, WE WON'T.
BUT NOW I'M ASKING, NICO...WHAT'S NEXT? WHERE DO WE GO FROM HERE?
...
I WANT TO SEE JEN.

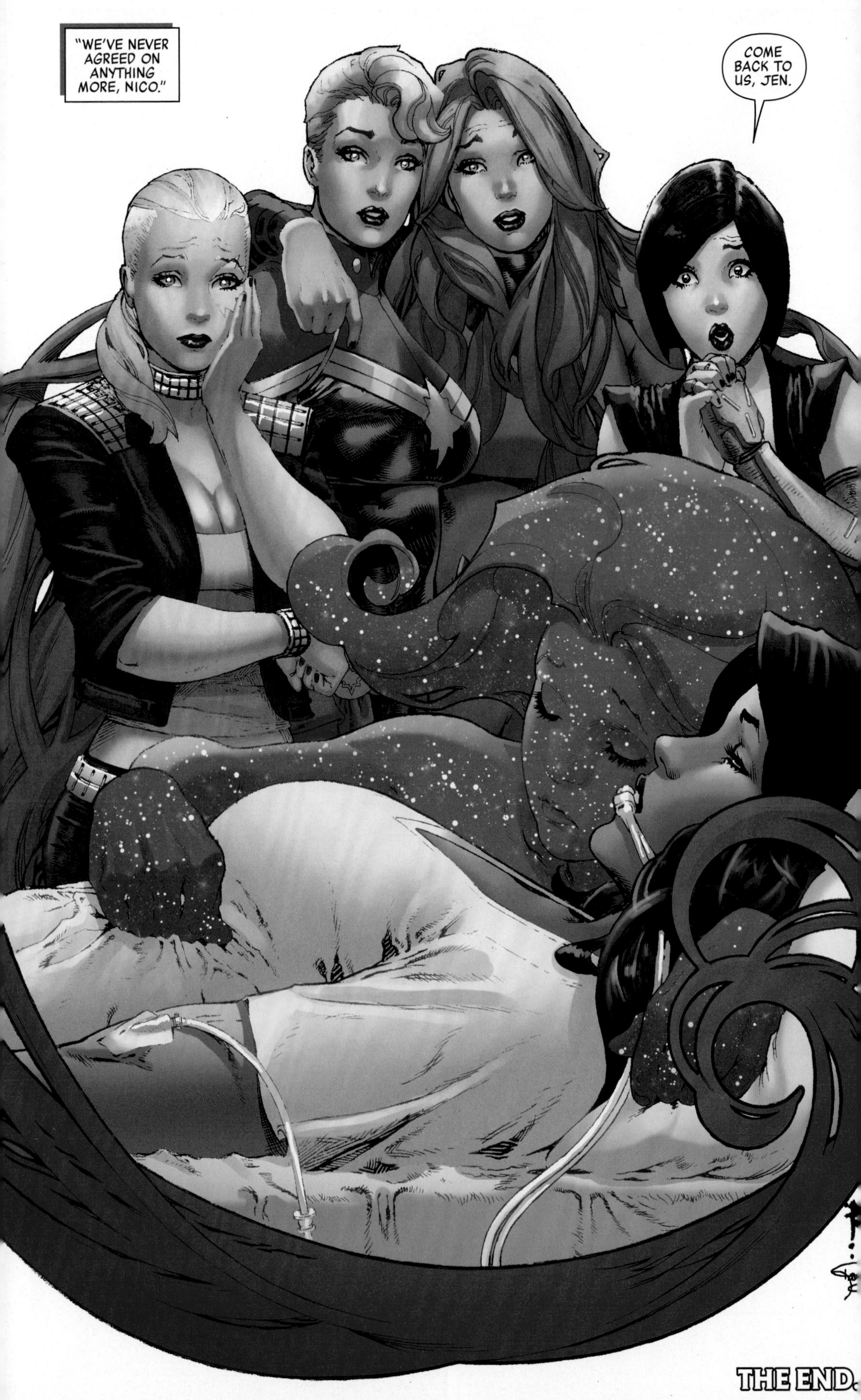
"WE'VE NEVER AGREED ON ANYTHING MORE, NICO."
COME BACK TO US, JEN.
THE END.

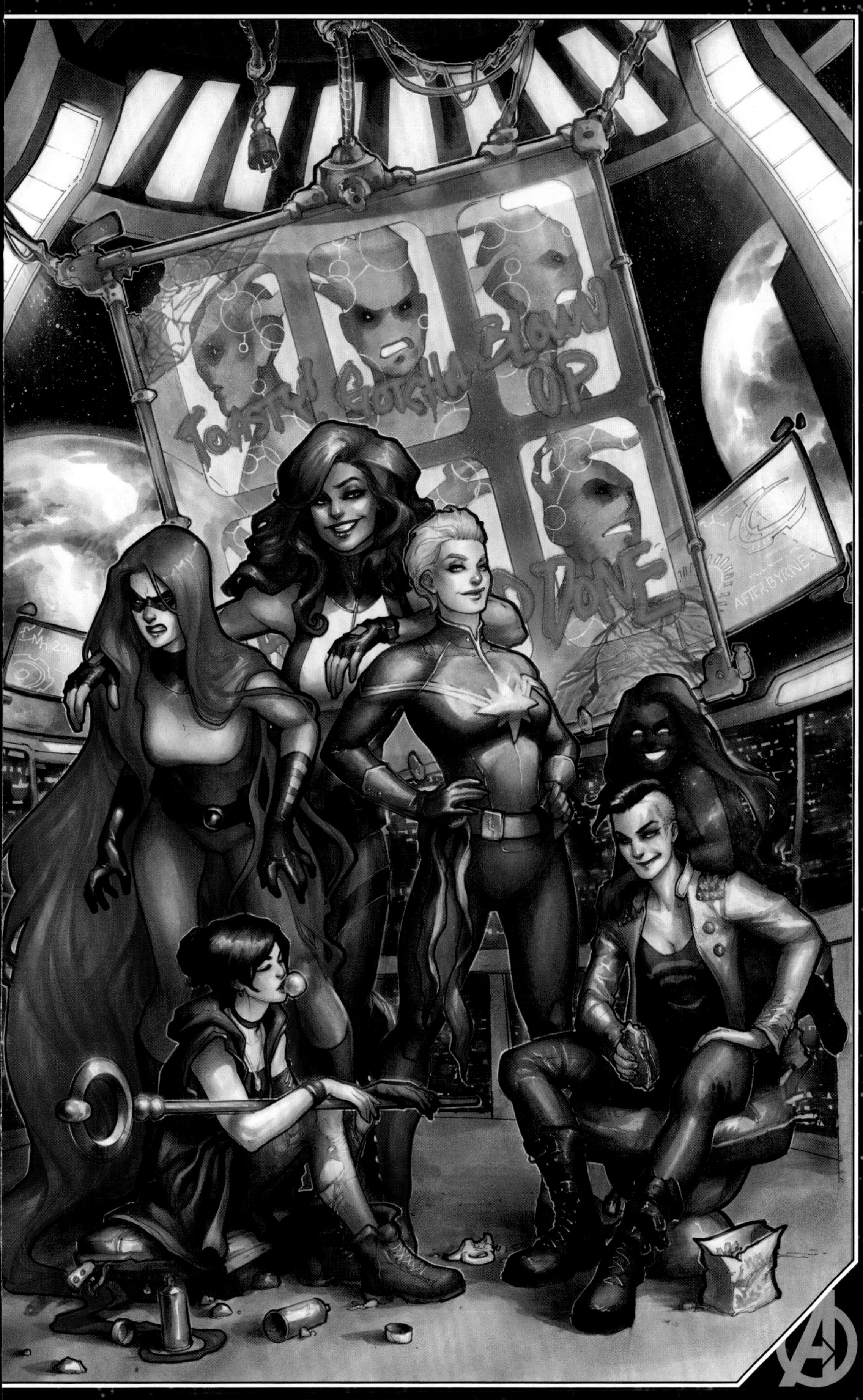
TOASTY!
GOTCHA
BLOWN UP
DONE
AFTER BYRNE

#5 STORY THUS FAR VARIANT BY **MEGHAN HETRICK**

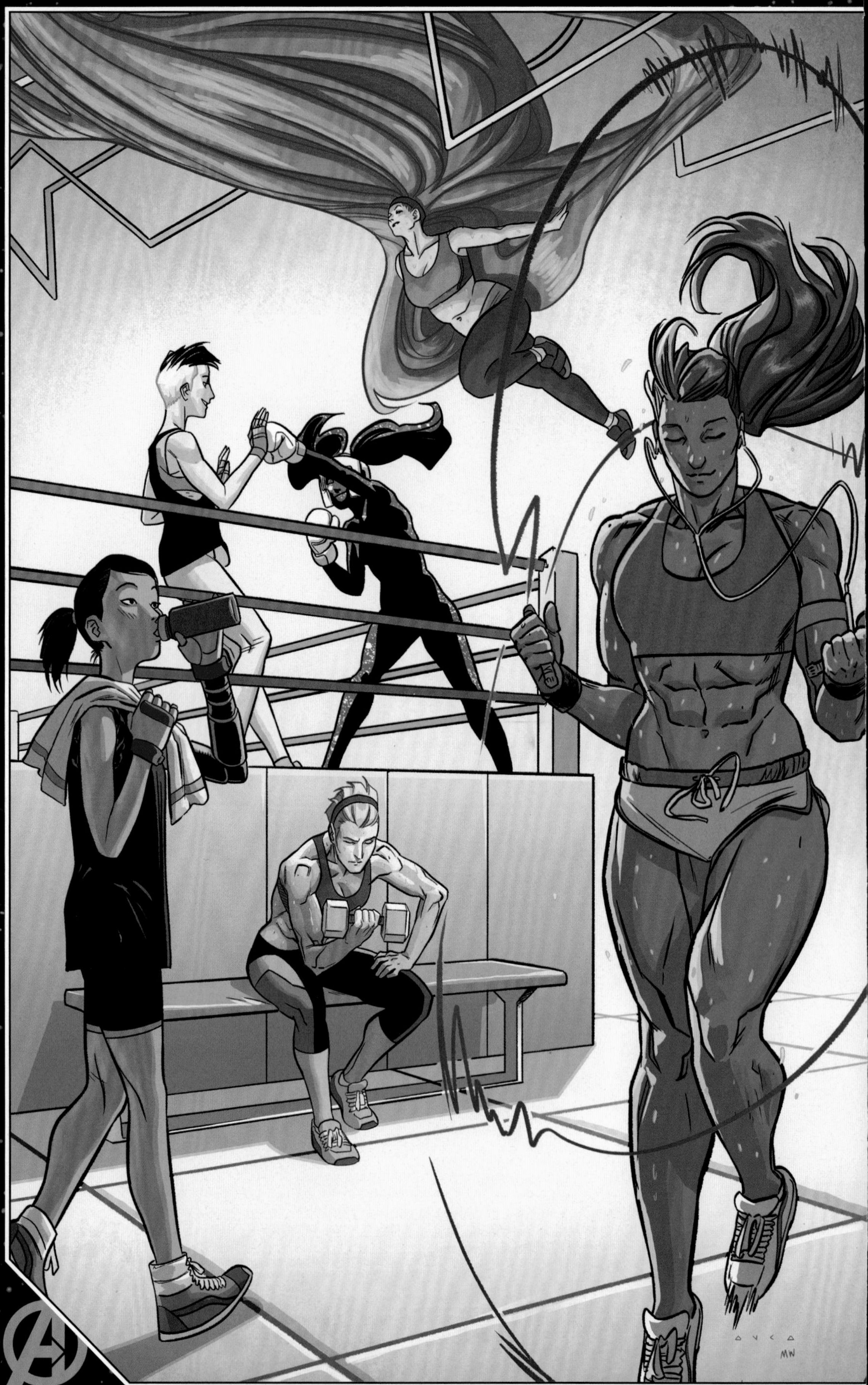
ANKA
MW

#5 VARIANT BY **KRIS ANKA**

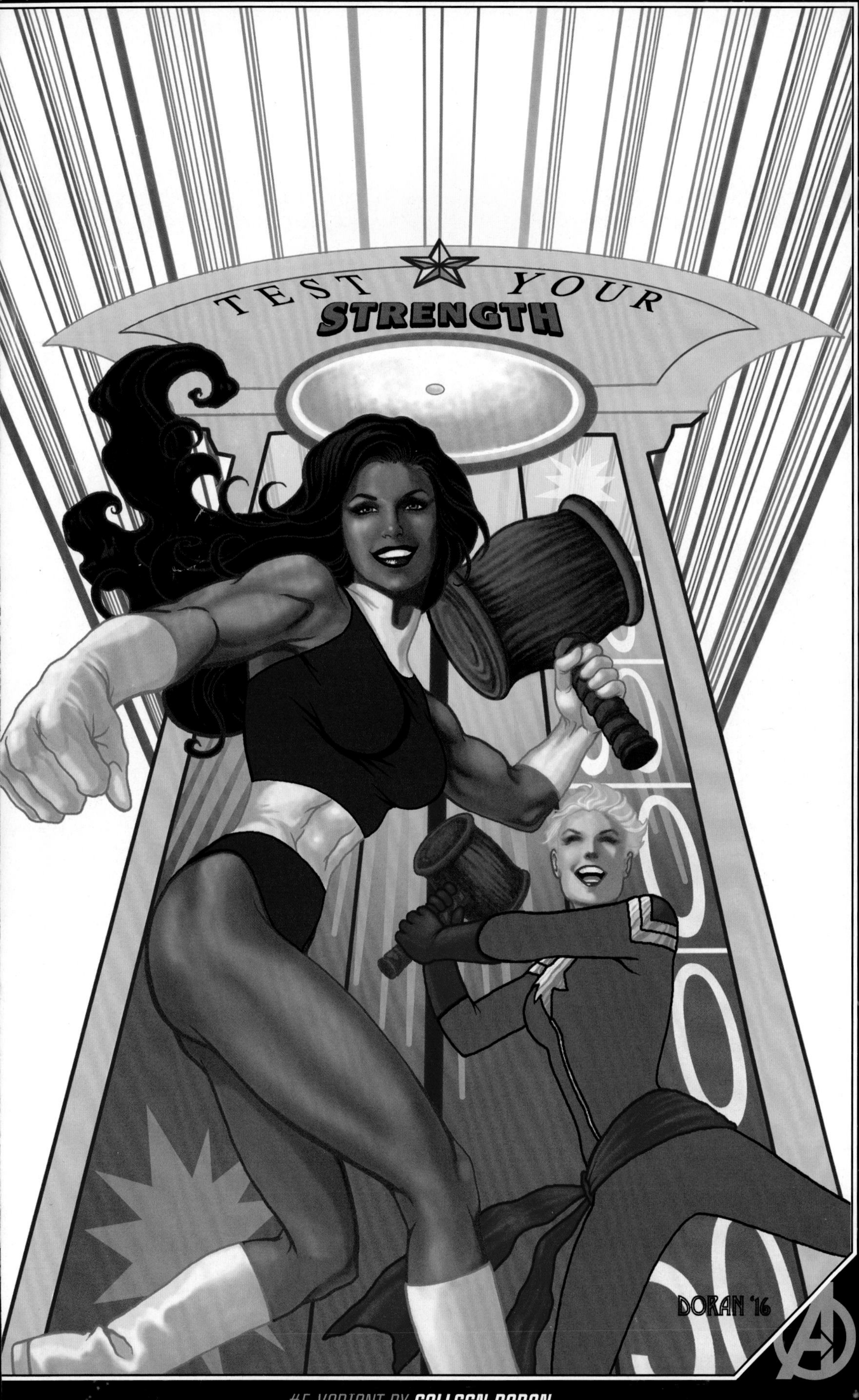
TEST YOUR
STRENGTH
DORAN '16

#5 VARIANT BY **COLLEEN DORAN**